TRUE TOLERANCE

TRUE TOLERANCE

Liberalism and the
Necessity of Judgment

J. Budziszewski

Transaction Publishers
New Brunswick (U.S.A.) and London (U.K.)

JC
571
.B764
1992
15 6949
Sept. 1992

Copyright © 1992 by Transaction Publishers,
New Brunswick, New Jersey 08903

Library of Congress Catalog Number: 91-36844
ISBN: 1-56000-026-0
Printed in the United States of America

Library of Congress Cataloging-in-Publication Data
Budziszewski, J., 1952–
    True tolerance: liberalism and the necessity of judgment
/ J. Budziszewski.
      p. cm.
    Includes bibliographical references.
    ISBN 1-56000-026-0
    1. Liberalism—Moral and ethical aspects. 2. Toleration.
3. Indifferentism (Ethics) I. Title.

JC571.B764 1992
320.5'12'01—dc20   91-36844
                                                              CIP

To Sandra
"Sole partner and sole part of all these joys:
Which were they toilsome, yet with thee were sweet."

A republic once equally poised must either preserve its virtue or lose its liberty.
—John Witherspoon, 1783

Contents

Acknowledgments

Forerunners of some of the arguments in this book were presented in the form of scholarly papers at the 1986, 1987, and 1988 meetings of the American Political Science Association. In these connections, and others, I received valuable suggestions and criticism from many people, including Frank Balog, John Francis Burke, Clarke E. Cochran, Stephen Conrad, Leon Epstein, James Fishkin, William Galston, Robert Hardgrave, Paul Kens, Wallace Mendelson, Benjamin Page, Michael Perry, Stephen Salkever, James V. Schall, SJ, and Ashley Woodiwiss. To them all, my gratitude. Special thanks to Gary Freeman, who makes his friendship indispensable by fiercely debating every proposition that I have ever maintained.

I owe a great debt to the graduate and undergraduate students who have taken my classes and seminars for the late nine years. The great majority have been ethical neutralists in outlook, though some were surprised and disconcerted to learn this. Without the experience of teaching them, I might never have realized the breadth and force of the cultural movement of which ethical neutralism is but one of the expressions. Moreover, I believe that I have learned at least as much about the forms that ethical neutralism may take by following them down their thirty-nine roads as by reading professional journals and studying the opinions of learned judges. My heart goes after them.

Final and greatest thanks are for my own Florentine girl, so called because it was from Dante that I learned the name of her teaching: she is one of the *donne ch'avete intelletto d'amore* of whom he spoke.

Prologue:
The Liberal Vocation

"I love him who does not want to have too many virtues," said Nietzsche in the last years before his madness. "One virtue is more than two, because it is more of a noose on which his catastrophe may hang."[1] We nurslings of the liberal tradition in politics[2]—that great mother of constitutionalism and liberty—were hardly the sort of lovers he had in mind. But although we do not necessarily accept Nietzsche's theories, we seem more and more to follow his advice. Our ancestors could hardly speak five connected sentences on a political topic without mentioning the virtues.[3] Our own speech, though, is increasingly forgetful of—I was about to say, "the whole idea." Rather, of every virtue but one. And from that noose hangs our own catastrophe.

That we should finally come to honor but a single virtue is understandable, if not commendable. Just as individuals have callings or vocations, so, in a sense, do traditions, and arguably the vocation of the liberal tradition has been to explore the virtue commonly known as "tolerance."[4] But vocations can be betrayed.

The usual way of betraying a vocation is through neglect. Betrayal can also be accomplished through a perverse variety of indulgence. The latter is what concerns us here. Our most gifted thinkers no longer treat tolerance as a queenly virtue to be guarded among many others equally precious, but as a shrewish virtue that excludes all the rest. For now we are told that the meaning of tolerance is *ethical neutrality*—neutrality about which things are worth the love of human beings and which traits of character are worth praising.

All too frequently, the only part of a person's conception of the things or traits worth love or praise about which we dare to breathe any judgment whatever is the part of his conception that tells how good it is to be indifferent to everyone *else's* conception of things or traits worth love or praise. If someone regards such indifference as good, we call him "tolerant," and approve. If he does not, we call him "intolerant," and disapprove. And, of course, if tolerance really is nothing but indifference about what is lovable or praiseworthy—why, then, thinking that tolerance is a virtue prohibits any public claim to the effect that anything else is a virtue.

The fatal flaw in this understanding of tolerance is not hard to find. Suppose that tolerance really were nothing but a kind of indifference. Shouldn't we at least be consistent in our difference? And if we are consistently indifferent, then we must be indifferent about tolerance itself.

Someone clever might reply, "Instead of being consistently indifferent, mightn't a fellow simply be simply indifferent to consistency?" Of course. But if this move is permitted, the scoundrel can get away with anything: tolerance or intolerance, as his mood takes him.

A more serious objection can also be made: "If we give up ethical neutrality, then we open the door to the fanatic." But notice that although we can sensibly speak this worry about giving up true tolerance, we cannot sensibly speak it about giving up ethical neutrality. For if we are consistent neutralists—consistently indifferent—we may only fear the fanatic; we may no longer disapprove him. We have disqualified ourselves from challenging his idea of the things worth loving and the right way to love them. By abandoning the high ground, we have let him take it for his own.

I do not think that I am exaggerating the condition of the liberal tradition. To date, all of our attempts to escape from what is widely confessed as a "foundations crisis" have failed for the same reason: their "bootstrap" quality. We persist in trying to derive moral knowledge from the reluctance to admit to any moral knowledge, like trying to pull ourselves up by the bootstraps.[5] No one has been so naïve as to endorse the simple mottoes about indifference of which I have been making sport. But see how close they come: philosopher John Rawls invents the Veil of Ignorance and tries to convince us that in order to figure out the principles of justice, we must pretend to forget not only who we are, but also everything we ever thought we knew about morality; philosopher Robert Nozick exploits sweeping claims about *rights* as a device for avoiding collective decisions about *goods*; legal theorist Bruce Ackerman posits as a precondition of the good life a society whose members are debarred from enacting any ideas about what the preconditions of the good life may be; social choice theorists like Kenneth Arrow and Amartya Sen endlessly elaborate the gambit of substituting procedural rules for substantive norms; and so on.[6]

What does it mean, then, when—asked at last, at long last, to make a genuine moral judgment—a judgment that does not pretend that it is not a judgment, a judgment about which dispositions of character are genuine moral virtues—we stand up—reply with sudden courage that the first, the very first, the most important of these virtues is tolerance—and then, refusing to say another word, sit down? Tolerance is a virtue indeed; but if it is the only virtue, it can hardly be anything more than good conscience in our continuing lack of convictions.

We might have known that in following Nietzsche's advice we would wind up here. Against his praise for having only one virtue, for twenty-three centuries we have had Plato's simple testimony, "Virtue is one."[7] Same words; different idea. What Plato meant is that all of the different virtues make up a whole. They depend on each other, so that any attempt to cultivate less than the entire ensemble is bound to be in some measure a chasing after wind.

Consider a lover devoid of courage. There will be something lacking in his love as well: the thing he loves needs defense against the things by which it might perish, and this he cannot give. Consider a father who values nothing but kindness. There will be something lacking in his kindness as well: utterly unable to give his children pain for any reason, he will never allow them enough responsibility to fail in any undertaking.

As a lover without courage is defective in love, a tolerator without ethical judgment is defective in tolerance. As kindness is addled in the solely kind man, tolerance is addled in the solely tolerant man. The aim of this book is to rectify the intellectual error which ratifies this defect, this addlement. I hope to show that true tolerance differs as much from neutrality as a shape differs from a shadow.

To be sure, we have labored so hard under the delusion that the essence of tolerance is ethical neutrality that, in attacking ethical neutrality, I run the risk of coming across as a foe of tolerance itself—worse yet, of having my arguments taken out of context and exploited by fanatics who (as always) are arming at every frontier. These, if we are not to yield the Continent of Judgment to those who have no judgment, are risks that must be run. I know of no insurance against that sort of disaster but to be as clear as possible.

Let that begin now, with a declaration of intent. This book is written not in condemnation of tolerance, rather in its praise—but also in an effort to defend it against its imposters while there is yet something to defend.

Notes

1. Nietzsche, *Thus Spoke Zarathustra*, Prologue, Sec. 4, at 127.
2. As I repeat later, I use the term "liberal" to designate this entire tradition. Liberals are all those, whatever their other differences, who are committed to constitutionally limited government, the principle of representation, and broad individual liberties. If I had a better term, I would use it, because to some people the term "liberal" conveys ideas I do not intend: for instance the cultural views of the nonsocialist Left, or the economic views of the nonfascist Right. The former usage is widespread in the United States, whereas the latter is widespread in England and on the Continent.
3. Among the founders of our own republic, this theme was particularly dear to the Anti-Federalists. However, the common notion that the Federalists had no concern at all with the virtue of the citizenry is far from true; rather they seem to have entertained different theories about it than their opponents. Speaking of representatives, James Madison asked "Is there no virtue among us? If there be not, we are in a wretched situation. No theoretical checks, no form of government, can render us secure. To suppose that any form of government will secure liberty or happiness without any virtue in the people is a chimerical idea. If there be sufficient virtue and intelligence in the community, it will be exercised in the selection of these men; so that we do not depend on their virtue, or put confidence in our rulers, but in the people who are to choose them." (Jonathan Elliot, ed., *The Debates of the State Conventions on the Adoption of the Federal Constitution, as Recommended by the General Convention at Philadelphia in 1787*, 2d ed. (Philadelphia, 1866), vol. 3, at 536–37; cited in Herbert J. Storing, *What the Anti-Federalists Were For*, at 72.) For Madison's ideas as to how to design electoral districts in such a way as to maximize the likelihood that the voters will be guided by their virtue rather than by baser considerations, see *Federalist* #10.
4. For early statements of the vocation, see Milton's *Areopagitica* and Locke's letters on toleration.
5. Even many of the critics of neutralism fall into this trap, for instance the "communitarians" typified by Alasdair MacIntyre (*After Virtue* and *Whose Justice? Whose Rationality?*), Michael Sandel (*Liberalism and the Limits of Justice*), and Michael Walzer (*Spheres of Justice*). Moral claims, say the communitarians, are intelligible only within specific communities or traditions; in their view there are no universalizable norms at all, not even "Thou shalt be neutral." Ironically, this merely produces a new twist on the universalizable norm, "neutrality," that I am criticizing: "Though thou canst not be neutral within a community or tradition,

thou shalt be neutral among communities and traditions." Moreover, it is clearly just one more attempt to derive moral knowledge from the reluctance to admit to any moral knowledge. In this respect it differs from ethical neutralism only as much as pulling one's self up by the bootstraps differs from pulling one's self up by the hair.

6. Rawls, *A Theory of Justice*, 136–42; Nozick, *Anarchy, State, and Utopia*, 28–33; Ackerman, *Social Justice in the Liberal State*, 4–12; Arrow, *Social Choice and Individual Values*, 2d. ed.; Sen, *Collective Choice and Social Welfare*. For a shorter example of social choice theory, see Kenneth O. May, "A Set of Independent, Necessary, and Sufficient Conditions for Simple Majority Rule."

7. This paraphrase is widely used. For the discussion of which it is based, see *Protagoras* 329–49. Also compare *Republic* 4.445c and *Laws* 12:963c–965d (which approach the idea from a different direction and to somewhat different effect), and contrast *Statesman* 306–7 (where the young Socrates apparently assents to a different view).

Part One

What Is True Tolerance?

Introduction to Part One

This book is a critique: that means an attack (though scholarly), a polemic (though theoretical), an exposé (though intellectual). However, the critique is undertaken in the name of something more positive, in fact a vision: a vision of true tolerance. So the question may arise: why not dwell on the vision, and put aside the critique? There is a simple reason for this. Like a statue of clean and noble line, true tolerance is a very simple thing. It is much too simple, in fact, to require an entire book of explanation and analysis to tell the beholder what he beholds. But the statue is set in a jungle. As jungle overgrew the city of Angkor Wat until it was lost to view, so the statue is burdened with mould and creepers until its line is cluttered, dim, and obscure.

I may rightly be accused of teaching little that is new. The vision of true tolerance is something we recollect, not something we acquire. To elicit it, one need only assemble a few reminders of what we know already.

Thus, the seeker in the jungle can quickly be told what he is looking for. That is the purpose of the beginning of the book. After that he needs a machete. That is the purpose of the rest of the book.

1

The Idea

The Idea Roughly Sketched

True tolerance is one of the virtues. Virtues are complex dispositions of character, deeply ingrained habits by which people call upon all of their passions and capacities in just those ways that aid, prompt, focus, inform, and execute their moral choices instead of clouding them, misleading them, or obstructing their execution. From time to time I will quote this formula.

I mean the formula as presupposing that there are objective goods and evils, objective rights and wrongs, sometimes harder and sometimes easier to discern. It is, I hope, broad enough to be useful to people with understandings as different as those of Aristotle, Jesus, and the prophet Micah. However, it cannot be all things to all people.

For instance, it will not be congenial to those who think of virtues *merely* as dispositions to follow known rules—a point to which I will return. Obviously, it will not be congenial to neutralists either. Less obviously, this includes those who apply their neutralism between groups, as well as those who apply it between persons: those who say "each *group's* notion of good and evil is equally valid," as well as those who say "each *individual's* notion of good and evil is equally valid." (Neutralists, by the way, prefer such words as *valid* and *viable* because they fudge the question of whether a notion is, simply, true.)

People who apply their neutralism at the level of the group are sometimes called "communitarians." Oddly, because their own neutralism passes unnoticed, they see themselves, and are seen by many intellectuals, as representing the main alternative to the distortion of the liberal tradition that goes by the name of neutralism. Partly because of this perception—and partly because some communitarians have reappropriated the language, without the living heart, of the concept of virtue—I must distinguish my position from theirs as sharply as possible.[1]

When I say something is a virtue, I do not mean "my community admires this disposition" any more than I mean merely "I admire this disposition" (although either statement may happen to be true). Rather I mean "this disposition really does aid, prompt, focus, inform, and execute the moral choices of those who possess it, instead of clouding them, misleading them, or obstructing their execution; it is an objective good, and helps them toward a right relationship with other objective goods." If someone objects, "But we must take people as they *are*," I agree. But we *are* in need of the virtues. If someone objects, "But most people admire other traits more than the virtues," again I agree; in fact, I would say that all of us admire other traits more than the virtues, much of the time or even most of the time. But this only shows the more clearly our need. And if some theoretician opines, "Morals are a branch of taste; there *are* no objective goods with which we could be brought into right relationship," I readily admit that the point cannot be proven either way. One must take it on faith. But I will add this: I have never known a theoretician who could not suffer indignation—a *moral* passion. Break into his house and see what happens. For an even faster reaction, contradict him! Scratch a subjectivist and you find a moralist every time. The principle, I think, is plain. Many people are *confused* about the distinction between good and evil, but only those *forget* it who have ceased, altogether, to be human. Human beings are so obsessed with it that they will try to derive moral imperatives even from the proposition that there is no moral knowledge. It is one of our most popular parlor games.

Here is another way of saying the same thing: Because the virtues concern objective goods and evils, if true tolerance is a virtue at all, then it is a human virtue, not a "liberal virtue." Among the virtues incumbent upon everybody, it is merely one the liberal political tradition has made a point of. In passing I should like to stress that as political theorists sometimes do, I use the term "liberal" to designate this entire tradition, not just its left wing. We are speaking of a mansion of institutions and practices the construction of which began around 1688, and which is now inhabited by Ronald Reagan no less than by Edward Kennedy.[2]

The specific virtue of true tolerance has to do with the fact that sometimes we put up with things we rightly consider mistaken, wrong, harmful, offensive, or in some other way not worth approval. This is something that may be done well or badly, for it is a complicated sort of thing. We do not put up with everything we disapprove, and we do not usually put up with any of the tolerated things at all times, in all places, in every way, or to every degree. We may also put up with something for good or bad reasons. Ethics, etiquette, and expediency all have something to say about the matter, but ethics claims the right to weigh the claims of etiquette and expediency in her own scales, and it is with her claims, therefore, that we are presently concerned. "Tolerance" is simply the name of the virtue that interprets these claims.

True tolerance is not the art of tolerating; it is the art of knowing when and how to tolerate. It is not forbearance from judgment, but the fruit of judgment. We may disapprove something for the love of some moral good—yet we may be moved to put up with it from still deeper intuitions about the same moral good or other moral goods, and on such deeper intuitions the discipline of tolerance is based.

What sorts of deeper intuitions? Examples come easily. In colonial America, Nathaniel Ward preached the use of force against heresy for the sake of saving souls, intolerance for the sake of God. For those who believe in God, there is no more ultimate loyalty; here, if anywhere, one would think intolerance justified. But Roger Williams asked *What if souls cannot be saved in that way?* and *What if persecution is not what God wants?* He argued that the sword breeds a nation of hypocrites, that the loving God does not require blood, and that scripture teaches other means of persuasion. In preaching tolerance he loved God not worse than Nathaniel Ward, but better. True tolerance, then, is a special case of what Aristotle called practical wisdom: of practical wisdom, because it is concerned with means and ends; a special case, because its most important function is the protection of ends *against* pretended means—and given that seeming paradox, it is no wonder that it has been misunderstood.

Like every virtue, true tolerance interacts with all of the other virtues, and is untrue to itself if it fails to acknowledge their importance. From time to time in this book I touch on the co-dependence of true tolerance with humility, mercy, charity, respect, and courtesy, and could have touched on its co-dependence with any.

A virtue is much more than a readiness to follow a rule; it includes, in fact, a developed ability to distinguish good rules from bad, and to choose rightly even where there are no rules or where what rules there are seem to contradict each other. Because of this, no virtue can be exhaustively described just by listing various and sundry rules to which it prompts obedience. Nevertheless, to list a few of these rules may help to form the image of true tolerance in the mind. For convenience I will call them "counsels of tolerance." Some of them are treated in greater detail later on. Still later, some of them will be formulated in an artificially precise way to adapt them to the purposes of Constitutional jurisprudence. In that context, I will call them not counsels, but "principles" of tolerance.

The truly tolerant man or woman believes that each person is entitled to defend his understanding of what is good for human beings by rational arguments, be that understanding true or false; and to attempt to persuade others that it is, in fact, true. If any person proposes that some public action be taken, he shows his respect for others by honoring their demand to know on what understanding of the good his proposal rests. In return, they show respect for him by forbearing to demean his understanding by treating it as a mere subjective taste or preference, unless he refuses to offer a rational defense for it. Their respect for him does not require them to treat his understanding as true, or even to treat it as having just as great a share of truth as other understandings. Its truth is for him to show. However, they do make it *possible* for him to show it. Consequently, in the ensuing debate all parties honor liberty of thought and discussion.

Without denying that true virtues should be cultivated and practiced by all human beings, the truly tolerant man or woman recognizes the wide variety of characters, cultures, and callings with which these virtues are consistent. He carefully distinguishes mere social conventions from the facts of ethics—mores from morality—and works to avoid confusing conformity with good character. He does not assume that each other soul necessarily knows her good best—but he is far from thinking that he infallibly knows better; for he realizes that no one else has better opportunities for learning her strengths, weaknesses, needs, and circumstances than she herself.[3]

True tolerance also requires each man or woman to walk the razor's edge in his relations with those in whom he finds something to disapprove. He must avoid connivance in the fault of these others, but at the same time he must avoid moral pride—a fault in itself second to none. Thus, as we see later in the book, the truly tolerant man or woman may avoid their society, but he may not parade the avoidance. He may warn others against them, but he may not do so out of malice. Though he knows that his aloofness may cause pain, the production of pain must not be his aim. He may deny them optional benefits if it is his office to make the decision, but he may not deny those benefits that are their due as human beings, especially those which might assist the amendment of their lives. Though he withdraws approval toward their flaws, he does not withdraw charity toward their persons. He refuses to indulge in himself the conceit that he can examine souls; he remembers his own proneness to vice and error; and at all times, he remembers that he himself is an object of tolerance to others—especially when he is most inclined to pass judgment on them.

A little-known quality of the truly tolerant man or woman is that he shows courtesy to those who through scruples arising from their own weakness have difficulty putting up with things about himself in which there is *no* moral wrong. For their sake, he will sometimes deny himself innocent things that they cannot bear, so that they will not find it necessary to exclude themselves from society. They, for their part, will try to master their weakness, so that they need not make themselves burdensome by objecting to what is innocent. This is one piece of masonry in their own endeavor toward true tolerance.

Finally: no truly tolerant man or woman will tolerate practices that tend to destroy or cripple the inward power of choice in himself or in any other. Perhaps it is not hard to see that these may include certain uses of drugs and surgery, as well as hypnosis, sensory deprivation, and torture. However, they also include the subtler destroyers, such as suffocating forms of supervision. He regards their defense—whether in the name of rearing or rehabilitation—as fatally flawed: moral agency is a precondition not only for the exercise of virtue, but for being human at all.

The Idea Elaborated

Our skeptical age naturally thinks that skepticism is somehow essential to tolerance. About this the age is not skeptical at all. But skepticism is irrelevant to true tolerance. If a skeptic finds reason for tolerance, he finds it not by reason of the things he is skeptical about, but by reason of the things he is not skeptical about. This is not hard to perceive. For a person who was skeptical about everything could not say, "Because all is in doubt, all may as well be tolerated." Rather he would have to say, "Tolerance and intolerance are equally in doubt." By contrast, if a person is skeptical only about some things, there is a chance that he will be unskeptical at just those points true tolerance requires. Consider, for instance, tolerance in discussion—not the whole of true tolerance, but an important part of it. The partial skeptic might say, "I am in doubt about what is true in general, but I am not in doubt about whether truth is good, about discursive reason as a way of finding it, nor about the kind of manners that the pursuit of that way requires. Therefore join me in discursive reasoning, and let each of us be tolerant of the attempts of the other to rebut his arguments."

The argument can be taken one step further, for as John Stuart Mill recognized, even a person who was skeptical about nothing whatsoever might value the confrontation with false opinions if, from the exercise of rebutting them, he expected to gain deeper insight into the truths he held already.[4] To be sure, he might *not* expect this. In that case he might not be tolerant. But that is not the point. The point is that although—depending on what they believe—both the partial skeptic and the thoroughgoing nonskeptic *can* be tolerant, the complete skeptic *cannot*. True tolerance, then, depends on beliefs, not doubt.

We can be more specific. True tolerance depends on having convictions—the right convictions—about what is good for human beings and about how to realize these goods. For consider. We said in the last section that true tolerance means knowing when to put up with various evils. But why would we put up with evils at all, except for the sake of goods? Intolerance never results from caring too much for the realization of human goods. Rather, one portion results from ranking goods in the wrong order—pursuing less important goods at the expense of more important goods. The rest results from ranking goods in the right order, but understanding too little about them.

The first portion is clear; to be equally clear, the second portion requires an illustration. We might foolishly think that we can train children in virtue by depriving them of all choices; that we can promote the truth by suppressing discussion of falsehoods; or that we can nourish the love of God by requiring of adults religious observances that they hate. The problem here lies not in being dedicated to virtue, truth, or God. The problem is that virtue, truth, and God require different services than these. By such means we end only with more vice, more lies, and a yet deeper exile from our Source. This is what was meant in the previous section in saying that the most important function of true tolerance is not the disregard of ends, but the protection of ends against pretended means; and it is what was meant, just above, in saying that just as a portion of intolerance results from ranking ends wrongly, another portion results from misunderstanding them.

A Coarse Distinction

I do not think it is necessary, for the elementary practice of true tolerance, that we know in advance, and agree about, every last point in the true ranking of what is good for human beings, but by now it will be obvious that we cannot go further without saying something about it. I suggest a coarse distinction between three ranks, or orders, of goods.

This distinction is obviously incomplete. There may be other orders, and there are certainly distinctions of value to be made within two of the three I suggest. Moreover, the distinction is tentative. No doubt the distinction could be improved in many ways. Sometimes, in order to elaborate an example, I have gone beyond it. For instance, Part Three illustrates general claims about expressive tolerance by discussing obscenity, and in order to discuss obscenity I have had to make claims about the goods involved in sexuality. Certainly these claims go beyond the original coarse distinction. On the whole, however, it serves the purposes of the book.

Obviously, *any* claims about good and evil, coarse or fine, can be disputed. Part of the point of expressive tolerance is to make their disputation possible. But even in saying that disputation should be possible, certain things are presupposed good—such is my argument.

The lowest order of goods is what I will call *prima facie goods*. Included are the things most often called "the good things in life," such as health, happiness in the everyday sense, good repute, bodily and mental capacities, peace, bodily beauty, companions, the physical conditions required for living, and external possessions. I call them prima facie because they are not in all cases good, and because their contraries are not in all cases bad. They derive their goodness, when they are good, and badness, when they are bad, from their relation to goods of the next higher order. To put the matter more plainly, the question "What are the good things in life?" is in some measure an error. We should ask rather, "What kinds of life are good?", for the good things are good in those lives and not otherwise. External possessions are good *as such* but not when possession becomes an end in itself. Unhappiness is evil *as such* but not when it is an inducement to reflect on an ill-spent life.

The next order is what I will call *intrinsic goods*. These are the virtues, as well as certain other goods including truth. The reason for placing these above the prima facie goods are, first, that they are not themselves prima facie, except with respect to themselves; second, that only they can make the prima facie goods actual goods. Both points need explanation. The first point: "Intrinsic goods are not themselves prima facie, except with respect to themselves." This means that the only thing that can make an intrinsic good evil, or make good a deficiency in an intrinsic good, is imperfection in itself or in another intrinsic good. Cowardliness is evil *as such* but good if it inhibits the commission of a crime. Practical wisdom is good *as such* but without humility it can be a soul's disaster. The second point: "Only intrinsic goods can make the prima facie goods actual goods." This means that without the intrinsic goods, prima facie goods are snares, whereas with them, prima facie goods are not snares but servants. External possessions, for example, are prima facie goods; but what is the actual good if a person is possessed by his external possessions, enslaved by accumulation? Aristotle remarks that such a man's mistake is as though he regarded musical instruments themselves, rather than the art of playing them, as the cause of brilliant music.[5]

The highest order in this threefold distinction is what Reinhold Niebuhr calls *unconditioned loyalty*, and Paul Tillich *ultimate concern*.[6] In every life or way of life—whether lived simply, lived with the guidance of an ethical theory, or even lived in defiance of an ethical theory—given enough time, some concern eventually emerges as paramount. Some consideration eventually is put before all others. Eventually there is something to which, or some direction in which, every knee in the personality bows. This is the person's god—be it money, power, or affection; wife, husband, or children; church, nation, or race; duty, tribal totem, or God proper.[7] As a matter of theory, one may deny that any concern deserves ultimacy. That is, one may deny that any claim deserves total surrender; one may deny that any concern could give total fulfillment even should all other claims have to be rejected in its name.[8] Thus, I say, as a matter of theory. But as a matter of practice, no one escapes giving some concern ultimacy, whether it deserves ultimacy or not.[9]

Why is this so? Because choices between incompatible urgencies are unavoidable. To preserve a bland pluralism, to prevent the rise of some one of these urgencies to supremacy, a person would have practice a truly Stoic discipline of inconsistency in one's choices, and in the end such discipline would merely reveal an ultimate concern of a different sort: for we would have to ask what urgency a man were serving in so disordering himself.

In short, one need not be conscious of one's god, or even conscious that one has a god. One might think one has no god, or that one is "looking for" or "waiting for" a god. One may even be converted from one god to another. But one will have a god—or at least, one will be on the road to one.

The ultimate social conflict is conflict over the claims of competing concerns to ultimacy. Naturally, therefore, the coherence of tolerance in the face of ultimate concern is the acid test of any theory of this alleged virtue, and, therefore, of any political society which claims to be founded on it. This includes our own.

We are now prepared to state true tolerance as a formula. Before doing so we should remember what was said before: no virtue, including the virtue of true tolerance, can be exhaustively described just by listing various and sundry rules to which it prompts obedience. But that is not what the formula intends. It is not a "decision rule," not a replacement for the virtue of true tolerance, but a statement of its point.

The formula has nothing grand about it. It is simply that *an evil must be tolerated in just those cases where its suppression would involve equal or greater hindrance to goods of the same order, or any hindrance at all to goods of higher order.*

Notes

1. I do not mean to suggest that communitarians have had no helpful ideas about virtue and other things, and I would be ungrateful not to admit that from these ideas I have been a gainer. As with the other kind of neutralist, however, what makes some of these ideas worth considering is that they do, in fact, presuppose certain objective goods—and what makes them finally stumble is that these presuppositions are not only unacknowledged, but denied.

2. See Prologue, note 2.

3. *Standard disclaimer*. Where pronouns are concerned, I generally follow prerevisionist English usage, according to which "he" is understood as inclusive unless the context clearly indicates the masculine. However, I also observe the traditional exceptions to this rule: Nature, the soul, and Wisdom (poetically personified and understood as an attribute of God) are spoken of as feminine. The reasons for my choices would take us far afield. Readers who choose differently may write differently; I ask only that they extend the same courtesy to me. In the meantime, since my language includes masculine, feminine, neuter, and inclusive pronouns, any rational being who feels excluded has only him-, her-, or itself to blame.

4. See his essay "On Liberty," chap. 2.

5. *Politics* 7.13.1332a20-30.

6. The reason for my acceptance of the term "concern" rather than "good" is that in some theories (including Tillich's), that which truly deserves ultimate concern is the ground of good rather than "a good," the ground of being rather than "a being." Whether this is the case does not concern us here.

7. Compare Niebuhr, "The Christian Church in a Secular Age," at 204–5: "Strictly speaking, there is no such thing as secularism. An explicit denial of the sacred always contains some implied affirmation of a holy sphere. Every explanation of the meaning of human existence must avail itself of some principle of explanation which cannot be explained. Every estimate of values involves some criterion of value which cannot be arrived at empirically. Consequently the avowedly secular culture of today turns out on close examination to be either a pantheistic religion which identifies existence in its totality with holiness, or a rationalistic humanism for which human reason is essentially god or a vitalistic humanism which worships some unique or particular vital force in the individual or the community as its god, that is, as the object of its unconditioned loyalty." Compare also Tillich, *Systematic Theology*, vol. 1, at 211: "'God' is the answer to the question implied in man's finitude; he is the name for that which concerns man ultimately. This does not mean that first there is a being called God and then the demand that man should be ultimately concerned with him. It means that whatever concerns a man ultimately becomes god for him, and, conversely, it means that a man can be concerned ultimately only about that which is god for him."

8. Here I closely follow the wording, though not quite the sense, of Tillich, *Dynamics of Faith*, at 1: If a concern "claims ultimacy it demands the total surrender of him who accepts this claim, and it promises total fulfillment even if all other claims have to be subjected to it or rejected in its name." Tillich seems to think of this promise and surrender as necessarily present in consciousness, a view which I reject below.

9. The situation recalls Anselm of Canterbury's ontological proof for the existence of God. Anselm thought he had proven the logical necessity of *that than which nothing greater can be conceived*. Rather he had proven only the logical necessity of the *idea* of that than which nothing greater can be conceived. In analogous fashion, I am not here claiming (though I do believe) that a particular concern deserves to be confessed as ultimate. Rather I am claiming that in any life, some concern will inevitably be *treated as though it did*. Whether or not the parallel is at all strict between what Anselm really proved and what I here claim, I leave to any professional logicians who may find the question interesting.

2

Illustrations of True Tolerance in Three Spheres of Regulation

In each the following three illustrations I will try to make clear both the applicable counsels of tolerance and their neutralist distortions. What this will show is consistent with the theory sketched above: the restrictions true tolerance places on the means of regulation presuppose goods which are to be protected, no less than the very aim of regulating presupposes goods which are to be protected. Neutralism, by contrast, wishes to avoid any suppositions about goods, and inevitably fails.

The focus on neutralist *distortions* illustrates another characteristic of this book, which I cannot stress too highly. As stated earlier, it is a self-conscious polemic; a scholarly one, to be sure, but a polemic nonetheless. Like all polemics, it gives more space to the attack on the foe than to the articulation of the alternative—more precisely, it articulates the alternative *by* attacking the foe. Rather than slowly and suspensefully developing a complicated thesis, it begins with a simple thesis, elaborating it throughout the book by piling illustration upon illustration of the errors opposed to it. The surprises lie not so much in the twists of the thesis itself as in the ramifications of failure to grasp it. As the sculptor said: "One makes the sitter's image by starting with the marble, and chiselling away everything he is *not*."

Writers must be modest in their goals, and moderate in their satisfactions. I would be well pleased to persuade readers of just two points: first, that neutrality about what is good cannot ground tolerance; second, that this in no ways shows that tolerance cannot be grounded—rather, that it *clears the way* for grounding it. If the book's more concrete proposals were deemed even suggestive of the right way

17

to ground tolerance in a vision of the good—if they encouraged optimism about the task and spurred others to try their wits—my aim would be more than achieved.

Regulation of Harm to Others

"Morality and the law" is an enormous topic. Yet one could go a long time without discovering its true breadth, were one to take the literature of the topic as a guide. To be sure, ink has been spilled in seas. Most of it, though, has been spilled for a single narrow issue that might be called the Penal Question: *What acts should be punished as crimes?*[1] As if this were not enough, debate converges to an even sharper point over the criminalization of a small number of aberrant acts such as prostitution and pandering, public drunkenness, sodomy,[2] bigamy, cruelty to animals, and the sale of drugs.

This narrowing of the topic is unfortunate. It makes us treat the following propositions as contraries when they are really quite compatible: first, that the ethical well-being of the community is a legitimate concern of public policy; second, that criminalization is a blunt and sometimes misguided instrument of that concern. Ethical neutralism acquires a delusory attraction is largely because we so often fail to think through our reasons for objecting to indiscriminate criminalization. Nevertheless, the Penal Question is important, and will be considered first.

Obviously, the counsels of tolerance that liberalism has developed do not prohibit the state from having a penal code at all. However, they do place limits, three in number, on its use:

1. *Whatever the law does not clearly prohibit should be treated as permitted.*

This first counsel of tolerance rules out vague laws, ex post facto laws, and the practice of regarding as prohibited whatever is not permitted. It reflects beliefs not only about the goodness of fairness, but also about the competence of normal adult human beings.[3]

2. *Even when there is cause to discourage certain acts, the presumption of the legislator should always be against their criminalization and in favor of other means of discouragement.*

This precept reflects the idea that the penal code should not be the primary means of socialization, but a backup device. It does not mean that nothing may be prohibited, but that an act may be listed in the criminal code only if arguments for doing so can be offered that are *strong enough to overcome* the presumption against doing so. To express such a counsel does not prejudice the legislator's decision. It only tells him where to lay the burden of proof.

3. *No argument for criminalizing an act should be entertained unless it can be framed in terms of the harm to others to which the act contributes.*

Like the second counsel of tolerance, this last counsel may be misunderstood. It does not mean that any demonstration of harm whatsoever is sufficient to warrant prohibition. What it means is that without a demonstration of harm, no argument at all is sufficient to warrant prohibition. I believe that at the deepest level at which it can be understood, the third counsel reflects an understanding about the nature of the good of responsibility. Those who believe in a personal God may regard themselves as responsible to Him even for harms they do to themselves. Still we do not regard ourselves as responsible to one another except for harms done likewise to one another.

The third counsel of tolerance is often called "the harm principle" and credited to John Stuart Mill. This is not quite right. Note that as it is expressed above, it does not even begin to tell us which things are to count as harms and which are not. Many different kinds of harm principle compete in the public argument of liberal societies; each gives a different answer to this question. The third counsel of tolerance marks only the point on which they all agree. For this reason, we might call it the *generic* harm principle. At the time Mill wrote in the nineteenth century, the generic harm principle was already widely accepted. He was the author, not of the generic harm principle, but of a particular and still influential brand of harm principle.

Indeed its currency was a fact of which he knew well how to take advantage. Consider for instance the rhetoric of his dispute with Lord Stanley over prohibition of traffic in strong liquors. Both men—not just Mill—couched their arguments in terms of harm. As Mill's own quotations make clear, Lord Stanley held that the sale of strong liquors harmed him—as a representative citizen—in four ways: (a) by endangering his security; (b) by creating a misery that he was taxed to support; (c) by tempting him to what would threaten his moral and intellectual development; and (d) by weakening and demoralizing society, that society from which he had a right to claim mutual aid and intercourse. What Mill could responsibly have argued is that although these were indeed harms, they were not the kinds of harms that could warrant prohibition. I cannot say how he might have done this, or how successfully, because he never began. Instead, he implausibly held that Lord Stanley was not speaking of harms at all. His pretense was that Lord Stanley merely demanded the right "that every other individual act in every respect exactly as he ought."[4] This obscured the issues that divide and continue to divide the different brands of harm principle from one another, and went far toward persuading later generations of liberals that the choice was between Mill's brand of harm principle and no harm principle at all.

Inspection of Mill's particular brand of harm principle shows that besides such genuine merits as it may have, and besides his own admirably crafted rhetoric, it has one other thing in its favor: the misleading promise it holds for making the practice of tolerance *easier*. This is no mean temptation, for to balance the oft-subtle risks and harms to which society might be exposed by a particular line of conduct against the corresponding risks of prohibition itself is a great burden, and one could hardly expect any brand of harm principle to be so helpful as to eliminate the need for spirited debate and sheer wisdom. But that is exactly what Mill's brand seems to do.

Mill produces the illusion of simplicity in two ways. First, he completely ignores the troublesome fact that just how much harm a particular line of conduct is likely to bring about depends on the context in which it takes place. For instance: how much harm might be caused to others by my riding a motorcycle without a helmet? That depends on such things as whether I have a family that counts on me for love, counsel, and financial support, and whether I pool my risks with others through private or social insurance. To mention a factor of a somewhat different sort, it may also depend on whether others, seeing me injured, are ethically bound to render aid.[5]

Of course, minor differences in conduct do not always produce major differences in the likelihood of harm to others. However we can state generally that the more extensive the society's network of mutual obligations, the more probable such linkages will be. Because Mill neglects this problem, he naïvely proposes applying his brand of harm principle in a rough, case-by-case fashion. Unfortunately, the most likely consequence of case-by-case application is the very opposite of what he intends: an increasingly "administered" society. For if our general statement is true, then the more restricted liberty is already by the mutual obligations in place, the greater the latitude his brand of harm principle gives us to restrict it still further.[6]

Before considering the second way in which Mill produces the illusion of simplicity, let us take thought whether there is any way to escape this consequence of the first way. Is there? Well, we might try to assume our social context away; we might make our network of mutual obligations the thing to be justified, instead of a mere background condition. We could do this by starting as Thomas Hobbes began his social contract theory: with the fantasy of an obligation-free world at the very beginning of history. However, this would not erase the problem of case-by-case application, for because the results we reach when we apply a harm principle are context-dependent, they are also *path*-dependent. That is, starting from the zero-obligation point, we may get different results if we apply our principle first to conduct A and then to conduct B, first to conduct B and then to conduct A, or, in one stroke, to the compound conduct A plus B. Therefore, we are still exposed to the likelihood of unanticipated slippage in the liberties that we think the achievement of the human good requires. The bottom line, I think, is this. Case-by-case, or "local" balancing of harms can be safe only within unbroachable limits—limits set *beforehand*, as the result of a rougher balancing of harms that is global rather than local. But for that sort of limit-setting, Mill gives us no guidance at all. We need a more general theory of tolerance.

The second way in which Mill produces the illusion of simplicity is by assuming that there is a large (and what is better, easily identifiable) class of acts which simply have *no effects on other people at all*—concerning which, debate about harms is therefore needless. Indeed, Mill seems to think that almost all individual conduct lies in this category. On the face of it, the assumption is preposterous. Mill forestalls this judgment with an explication of harm that seems to give his assumption support. We learn for instance that harm to mores that are regarded as essential to the security of human good is not harm; that seduction to evil is not harm;[7] that harm to which a person consents is not harm;[8] that the harm of giving offense is not harm;[9] that conduct by which a person destroys his abilities to fulfill his obligations to others is not harm;[10] and that the risk of harm, distributed in such a way that we do not know on whom the sword will fall, is not harm.[11]

I use the phrasing of "harms that are not harms" not for dramatic coloration, but to bring out the mystifying character of Mill's overall argument. Indeed, sometimes he does describe some of the harms I have just mentioned as genuine. In such cases he merely maintains that they are trivial, and in any case overborne by countervailing goods. Some of his arguments to this effect are persuasive; others are carried off merely by insinuation, but at least he recognizes the kind of argumentation that a commitment to any brand of harm principle requires. So far, so good. Yet in the same essay he persistently resorts to the fiction that he is mapping out "that portion of a person's life which affects only himself"—which would be a different enterprise altogether.[12] Taken seriously, the phrase means not that these are trivial harms, harms that are overborne by good, or harms that ought to be tolerated; rather that they are not harms at all. To be sure, if absolutely anything could be called harmful, commitment to a harm principle would not be a limitation at all. Yet in this rhetorical mood Mill seems to think that almost nothing should be called harmful. Here, too, argumentation would be welcome, but this is a lot to swallow without it.

Well—are these harms, or aren't they? Because Mill gives us two different versions of his own argument, we will never know his answer to the question. Unfortunately, the crude version of the argument is the one he uses when he is on the hunt, for instance when he tries to spear Lord Stanley. Naturally, then, that is the one that persists in memory—especially the memory of ethical neutralists. It is not itself neutralist; however, it can be described as a sort of prolegomenon for neutralism.

Now the last sentence makes two claims. Both of them deserve explanation.

The reason for saying that not even the cruder version of Mill's argument is itself neutralist is the particular warrant he gave for defending the liberty of allegedly self-regarding acts in the first place. Such liberty, he thought, would further goods in which society has a legitimate concern, among these the development of moral character, the advancement of truth, and the discovery of new and better ways of life.[13] Although this reasoning makes it even harden to see how Mill could ever have thought that by the acts in question an individual "affects only himself," at least his moral (that is to say, nonneutral) intention is clear. Moreover, he freely admits that even self-regarding acts may be morally *wrong*. So long as they are self-regarding, of course, he denies that they may ever rightly be punished. Yet so long as they are morally wrong, he does insist that social disapproval make itself felt in other ways—ways to which I have alluded in an earlier section, and to which I allude yet again in a later. He says, for instance, that we may argue with the perpetrator of a self-regarding moral wrong, even to the point of making ourselves obnoxious; indeed, in his view we ought to do this "much more freely" than common notions of courtesy permit. Further, we may avoid his society, and warn others against it as well. We may give him last place among those upon whom we confer those benefits to which they are not by right entitled, and we may even warn him ahead of time that this will be among the consequences of our disapproval. In fact, Mills says, we may do a great many things that will probably make his life unpleasant—so long as making his life unpleasant is not our very intention. Only malice can put such responses to his conduct in the category of "punishment."

But if even the cruder of the two versions of Mill's argument is not neutralist, in what sense may it be described as a prolegomenon to neutralism? The difficulty is that Mill's vulgarization of his own argument lends itself to a second vulgarization at the hands of his would-be heirs. This vulgarization has two parts. One has to do with what the harm principle means; the other has to do with the reasons for following it. We should look at each in turn.

1. Regarding its meaning. We being by repeating the Millian formula that individuals are not *liable to punishment at the hands of others* for self-regarding conduct. Second we blur the phrasing: individuals, we now say, are not *answerable to society* for their self-regarding conduct. This expression, of course, is equivocal. We finish by refocussing it: the harm principle comes to mean that no one may *rightly take notice* of self-regarding conduct. After all—if it is self-regarding, doesn't it "concern" the agent alone? But that is not what Mill meant.

2. Regarding the reasons for following it. We begin by saying, with Mill, that the reason we do not punish *all* moral wrongs is that not all of them harm others. At this stage, the rationale clearly recognizes that acts may be morally wrong whether or not they are self-regarding; that the only issue addressed by the harm principle itself is whether to punish; and that forbearance from punishment is itself the result of a moral judgment. But now we redraw the distinction that the rationale involves. We say that the reason we do not punish *moral* wrongs is that *none* of them harm others. By treating "harm" and "morality" to be unrelated, the new rationale makes the harm principle itself appear to express moral neutrality.

Something like this is behind the common claim that good laws rest on utilitarian, "rather than moral" grounds—as though utilitarianism itself were not a moral theory.[14] Something like this is behind the odd twist of language whereby only a few acts like sodomy and prostitution are called "morals offenses"—as though murder and armed robbery were not also immoral. And something like this is behind the new prejudice that publicly expressed ethical concern is a form of intolerance. For, of course, once we persuade ourselves that the true reason for following the harm principle is that neutrality demands it, we begin to look for the other demands of this jealous and negating god. Not only in the penal code, but everywhere else as well, we take sponge and solvent to wipe the ethical smudge from the pristine face of the law—and with that smudge, whatever flesh comes along.

Regulation of Honor

A good portion of government activity either deliberately, or incidentally, regulates honor. What I mean is that it selectively reinforces public judgments about the things deserving of esteem and disesteem. Sometimes it does so rightly, sometimes it does so wrongly. The reason for putting the point in terms of reinforcement is that government cannot make something honorable or dishonorable by *fiat*. In the regulation of honor it can only play on mores that already exist.[15]

Like the regulation of harm, the regulation of honor should be governed by certain counsels of tolerance. In this section, however, it will be convenient to reverse the order of exposition used in the last. Rather than beginning with the counsels of tolerance and then turning to their distortion by neutralism, we will begin with the neutralist view, creeping up on the counsels of tolerance by way of correcting its misunderstandings.

Briefly, the neutralist view is that the regulation of honor is wrong.

The clearest exposition of this view is found in certain works of Ronald Dworkin.[16] Dworkin's basic demand is that government treat all people with "equal concern and respect." As I hope to make clear, in saying this he has almost put his finger on a genuine counsel of tolerance. The difficulty is not with Dworkin's phraseology, but with the interpretation he gives it. He interprets the demand for equal concern and respect as requiring official neutrality "on what may be called the question of the good life." On the contrary, it could not *require* neutrality about the good life because it is nonneutral about the good life already. To demand that all be treated with equal concern and respect is to concede at least the prima facie goodness of enjoying concern and respect, and perhaps the intrinsic goodness of according concern and respect.

Nevertheless Dworkin proceeds to the mechanics of implementing his demand. In his neutralist interpretation, equal concern and respect requires two things. The first is that every political decision reflect some accommodation of the *personal* preferences of everyone—that is, preferences people have about what they themselves shall have or do. The second is that it reject any accommodation of the *external* preferences of anyone—"that is, preferences people have about what others shall have or do."

This second is what concerns us here. Dworkin considers any accommodation of external preferences inherently insulting and punitive. By depriving certain individuals of opportunities and esteem, it "invades rather than enforces the right of citizens to be treated as equals." The argument, however, seems to miss the point. Are external preferences pernicious? Sometimes, certainly. The external preference that blacks should not receive the same opportunities and advantages as whites is pernicious. But why is it pernicious? Obviously, because it is bigoted; color of skin has no moral significance, and this treats it as though it has. On the other hand, the fact that the preference is external is irrelevant to its bigotry. Not all external preferences pivot on moral irrelevancies. Those that pivot on relevant distinctions deserve consideration—not because they are preferences, but because the underlying moral judgments may be true.

Dworkin also offers an argument that the accommodation of external as well as personal preferences should be rejected because it leads to "double-counting." When the votes are totalled, some people will be beneficiaries not only of their own personal preferences, but also of the external preferences of others. But of course, this argument tacitly identifies the good with the satisfaction of preference or desire. That is precisely the kind of commitment that Dworkin is trying to avoid with his neutralist interpretation of equal concern and respect.

To illustrate the second argument, Dworkin asks us to imagine a community faced with a decision whether to build a civic swimming pool or a civic theatre when it cannot afford both. Then,

> suppose many citizens, who themselves do not swim, prefer the pool to the theatre because they approve of sports and admire athletes, or because they think that the theatre is immoral and ought to be repressed. If the altruistic preferences are counted, the result will be a form of double counting; each swimmer will have the benefit not only of his own preferences, but also of the preferences of someone else who takes pleasure in his success. If the moralistic preferences are counted, the effect will be the same: actors and audiences will suffer because their preferences are held in lower respect by citizens whose personal preferences are not themselves engaged.[17]

Thus, voters should disregard their external preferences and consider only whether they, personally, would rather swim or go to the theatre.[18]

The example derives what plausibility it has from the nature of the choice Dworkin asks us to imagine. So few people in our century really do find either theatre or swimming reprehensible that we find it hard to imagine that anyone could. For that reason, we take the imaginary beliefs of Dworkin's "altruists" and "moralists" less seriously than we should. To bring out the difficulties of his position more clearly, we might imagine the choice to lie not between a building civic swimming pool and building a civic theatre, but between building a civic swimming pool and building a civic house of prostitution. Is it plausible that "equal concern and respect" requires citizens to cast their votes as Dworkin demands? Do citizens really have an ethical duty to ignore their moral convictions, and cast their vote according to whether they, personally, would rather swim or consort with prostitutes? The absurdity lies in the very idea of regarding moral convictions as equivalent to bigotry.

In advancing his arguments against the accommodation of external preferences, Dworkin seemed to be moved primarily by antipathy to their *censorial* aspect. That is not to be taken lightly; this is what was meant by the earlier remark that he has stumbled on a genuine counsel of tolerance, but misinterpreted it. Let us consider this more closely. There would be something wrong indeed with discouraging prostitution by appointing public hectors to follow prostitutes about the streets shouting, "Unclean! Unclean! Unclean!" But Dworkin's antipathy to the distribution of esteem and disesteem is insufficiently discriminating. He is unable to tell us how the dishonor of appointing a public hector is *different* from the dishonor of refusing to subsidize.

The difference is that one case concerns the practice, while the other concerns persons. The ancient republics believed in firming the resolve of the good by disgracing the wicked. In other words they dishonored persons as well as practices. We draw the line at persons. Why? Because virtue is less important than we thought? No: because in some small way perhaps we understand it better, and at the same time are less inclined to credit ourselves with other kinds of understanding that we do not have. In particular: we can know what is disgraceful, but not who. Suppose I have committed a crime. I have behaved disgracefully; I deserve punishment. But would you punish the disgrace of my conduct by disgracing my person? To know that I deserve some sort of punishment you need only see my outward self; to know that I deserve disgrace you would need to see my inward self, which is hidden from you and probably even hidden from me. When you disgrace my person you assume the pretense that you can see hidden things. This is likely to cause grave hurts whether I accept your pretense or not.[19] If I accept it, I may come to believe that I am irredeemable. If I do not, I may come to be filled with resentment of an intensity that other forms of punishment could never incite. In the meantime, what about you? Seeing how you have disgraced me may make me even more despicable in your sight than I was before. This may confirm you in your pretense, and convince you that you are a higher being. Should these things take place to you and to me, no service had been done the cause of virtue; we had both been made worse. I suggest (without pretending that believers have always been a good advertisement for it) that the distinction between dishonor to practices and dishonor to persons originates in the Christian maxim "Hate the sin, but love the sinner." But one need not belong to the Christian faith in order to acknowledge the maxim's force, and it has been absorbed into the liberal tradition as a counsel of tolerance.[20]

There is no need to be naïve about this. Certainly, if a practice is held to public dishonor, the persons who engage in it will find themselves at a disadvantage in polite society. If we object to this, we had better abolish the government; all civil and criminal law has the same effect. But it is different from passing judgment on souls. Despite having criticized him for another reason earlier, I believe that John Stuart Mill expressed a true insight when he said that the man who suffers social injuries because of noncriminal moral faults "suffers these penalties only in so far as they are the natural, and, as it were, the spontaneous consequences of the faults themselves, not because they are purposely inflicted for the sake of punishment." The distinction Mill draws is delicate, but, as he insists, far from "merely nominal." It is one thing to avoid someone's society; it is another to "parade the avoidance." It may be our duty to warn others against him; it cannot even be our right to do so out of malice.[21] The idea is that disapproving what he does must not be connected with a withdrawal of love for his person.

I am speaking of things I do not fully understand. But someone who understood them better,[22] I think, might speak to us as follows. In fear you must tread the razor between connivance at my immorality, and the greater monstrosity of moral pride. If you avoid me because of what I do, do it because you are not good enough to be with a man as bad as me: not because you are too good. If you say in your heart that you are too good, it were better that you sought my company. If you say in your heart that you are better than me, it were better than you connived at my wrong. For that secret will make you the worse of us, unless I play at the same game.

These then are the three alternatives: connive, give in to pride, or tread the razor. There is more for trembling here than liberalism has yet perceived, but this much our norms admit: true tolerance is treading the razor.

Regulation of Relationships

We have spoken of the regulation of harm and the regulation of honor. Of all of public policy's engagements with ethical practice, the last that I will discuss is the regulation of relationships, with special attention to the marital relationship. The main objective here is to show that, contrary to many neutralist arguments, true tolerance is not necessarily violated by such regulation.

Of course, a great many kinds of relationship *are* far better left to individual conscience and informal social norms than touched in any way by law. Friendship is a good example. However, certain other kinds of relationship have special properties that jointly make their regulation proper—and it is a counsel of tolerance to regulate no relationships but those that have all three. These properties are:

1. that the common good is intimately dependent on their stability;
2. that their stability is intimately dependent on very close adherence to the relevant social norms; and
3. that either because of universal human weakness, or because of the characteristics of the society in question, these norms are too fragile to thrive without additional support from the law.

The relationships involved in marriage and family are admirably suited to the illustration of this point. If any relationships possess the three listed properties in our society, certainly these do, and that is exactly why certain ways of regulating them are both proper and consistent with true tolerance.

Often this is misunderstood. Many people have the idea that the state's interest in marriage is merely a survival from the days when governments undertook the enforcement of religious obligations. The confusion, I think, arises from the fact that the term "marriage" is used in two senses, one of which is purely civil while the other is purely religious. According to the first, the term designates entrance into a legal relationship; according to the second, it designates entrance into an ethical and possibly sacramental relationship. Of course, since the state cannot administer sacraments, having a purely civil marriage does not necessarily satisfy the religious obligations of parties undertaking an alliance.[23] Likewise, unless the legal formalities are also observed and the alliance is registered in the way the state requires, having a religious marriage does not satisfy their civil obligations. In fact, in some countries religious marriage is legally invisible. A complete civil ceremony is required by the state; whether the parties have a separate religious ceremony is up to them. Clearly, then, whatever influence religion may still have on family law, the intention of the state in marriage as such cannot be explained by a desire to enforce religious obligations. The historical origin of its involvement is in this respect irrelevant. (Of course, this does not make our state of affairs theologically *neutral*; different religions will render different judgments of it.)

More than just an opening example, marriage and family provide the focus of this entire section. However, because our economy is organized around private ownership and voluntary exchange, another obvious candidate for regulation would be the relationship of contract. Indeed, contract is sometimes viewed as the model not only for relationships of voluntary exchange, but also for the marital relationship itself. Here rests another confusion which we would do best to disturb before going on.

Just what kind of relationship is contract? Legal rules that stabilize contractual relationships may be viewed as special cases of what H.L.A. Hart calls "power-conferring rules."[24] Now most power-confirming rules confer powers upon individuals who are acting by themselves. A paradigm case is found in the rules that give legal effect to the provisions of an individual's will. These empower him to do something that would otherwise be impossible: he can decide his heirs and settle the distribution of his estate even if the manner in which he desires to do this is contrary to custom. By contrast, the set of rules that gives legal force to the provisions of contracts confers powers on *several* consenting individuals—specifically, powers to penalize each other for reneging on properly executed agreements.

Now, what kind of relationship is matrimony? It is a *status* relationship.[25] A status relationship differs from a contractual relationship in that its terms are arranged by law or custom rather than by the principals. But although individuals cannot contract the terms of a status, sometimes they can contract to enter it. This fact produces a surprising amount of confusion. Each of the following should be distinguished from the others:

Matrimony	The *status* in which husband and wife stand to one another.
Marriage	The *act* of entering into the matrimonial status.
Marriage contract	The legally binding *mutual promise* to live as husband and wife by which the act of marriage is carried out.

Marriage ceremony   The legally prescribed *ritual* in which the marriage contract is executed and solemnized, with
or without religious additions according to the
customs and consciences of the principals.

However, the English language permits the use of the term "marriage"
for all four of these things, leading people to think that the marriage
contract characterizes the *terms* of the matrimonial status rather than
the promise by which it is entered. Thus they ask the question, "Why
can't the principals arrange this contract to suit themselves as they do
every other contract?"[26] when they should be asking, "Why is matrimony a matter of status *rather than* of contract?" The reasons are
twofold. First, the parties to matrimony are not necessarily equally
able to protect their interests; for instance, divorced women are eco-
nomically vulnerable compared to men. Second, the parties to matrimony are not the only parties whose interests the matrimonial relationship affects; the children of the parties are directly affected, and all
of society is indirectly affected.[27]

In establishing relative monogamy as our marital and family norm,[28]
we are somewhat out of step with the rest of the human race. Over
most of history the norm has been polygamy. However, the mere fact
of discrepancy should not be taken to suggest that our norms lack
rational warrant. Polygamy reflects and reinforces a rigidly hierarchal
culture in which the number of one's wives in an index of prestige. It
keeps women civilly and socially inferior, and, by generating a short-
age of marriageble young females, causes hardship among young men
who do not belong to the privileged strata. The practice is not only
unjust but productive of social tension.[29] There is no need to inquire
into the ethical status of relative monogamy vis-à-vis absolute monogamy; even those of our religions and ethical theories which assert the
superiority of the latter regard divorce as a subject of true tolerance.
Probably the most insistent condemnation of divorce is found in Christianity—so uncompromising that it astonished the disciples. However,
in prohibiting divorce to his followers, even Jesus implied that it should
not be *legally* impossible.[30] The issue here is not one of law vs. ethics,
but rather of which ethical prescriptions should be supported by law and
which should not.

Although, as we have seen, the rules that stabilize contractual relationships can best be viewed as a special case of power-conferring

rules, the same cannot be said for status norms—norms like those that tell parents and children what they owe each other or set forth the mutual obligations of husbands and wives. Status norms are special cases, not of power-conferring rules, but of ordinary prescriptive rules. For like the laws that require registration for the draft and prohibit murder and theft, they do not, at first blush, empower people; they command and prohibit them. And behind the newly fashionable preference for conceiving matrimony along the lines of contract rather than along the lines of status, there is, I think, a certain proposition: that since power-conferring rules merely confer upon individuals the power to exercise their own desires, power-conferring rules are ethically neutral, whereas ordinary prescriptive rules are not.

This proposition breaks down into two parts. The first is that prescriptive rules cannot be made neutral. That is quite correct. The second is that power-conferring rules can. That is mistaken. Let's see why.

To begin with, it is clear enough that the power-conferring rules provided in current law are not neutral as they stand. It would be easy to argue that their nonneutrality arises solely from the fact that they are hedged about in various ways. They are not open-ended enhancements of individual agency; they are conditional enhancements of individual agency. For instance, in most legal codes even the power-conferring rule that gives effect to the provisions of wills does not permit a testator to leave his minor children without support. Likewise, in most legal codes even the power-conferring rule that gives effect to contracts does not permit the enforcement of meretricious contracts. But it isn't true that removing these restrictions would remove the nonneutrality. For even an open-ended enhancement of agency would be valued precisely for being an enhancement of agency. This is not ethically neutral; it is an affirmation that enhancement of agency is a good that ought to be promoted by the state.

In the second place, open-ended enhancements of agency would inevitably impose burdens on the achievement of *other* goods. Suppose we gave individuals the completely open-ended power to will their worldly goods to whomever they pleased. This would certainly enhance the agency of testators; but it would burden social stability (a consequence which could be avoided by requiring primogeniture), burden the circulation of elites (a consequence which could be avoided by *prohibiting* primogeniture), and burden the equalization of wealth (a consequence which could be avoided by requiring the division of estates among the poor). Or suppose we gave individuals the completely open-ended power to contract with others for whatever purposes they pleased. This would certainly enhance the agency of contractors; but it would burden domestic peace (a consequence which could be avoided by barring the enforcement of agreements to murder), burden personal honesty (a consequence which could be avoided by barring the enforcement of agreements based on fraud), and burden the cultural primacy of the family (a consequence which could be avoided by barring the enforcement of agreements whose purpose is meretricious). The point is not that these other goals are better than the goal of enhancing agency. Rather, ranking any goal above another is a choice among conceptions of the good; it violates neutrality.

In the third place, no conceivable power-conferring rule could be neutral even with respect to *whose* agency is enhanced. Every power-conferring rule, by conferring power upon individuals in one circumstance, withdraws it from individuals in another. We can return to our previous examples to see this. Would an open-ended testamentary power be neutral about who gains and who loses? No; it would value the agency of testators more highly than the agency of the disinherited. Would an open-ended power of contract be neutral about who gains and who loses? No; first it would esteem the agency of contractors who stood to gain from their agreements more highly than the agency of contractors who stood to gain by defaulting. Second it would esteem the agency of contracting parties in general more highly than the agency of those who suffered the external costs of their agreements.[31]

For that matter, so long as we are speaking of the enhancement of agency it is worth observing that power-conferring rules do not necessarily perform any better on this score than do ordinary prescriptive rules. Prescriptive rules merely "confer power" in a different fashion. This is clearly illustrated by the status norms that govern matrimony. Marital obligations of spousal support certainly enhance the agency of dependent wives: they enable them to direct their lives in ways they otherwise could not. In the same fashion, obligations of alimony and child support that arise from the breakup of matrimony enhance the agency of ex-wives who must now make households by themselves, not to mention their children. New attitudes to alimony and child support that do not recognize the social fact of female economic dependence have made divorce a boon for ex-husbands. As in power-conferring rules, so here: someone gains and someone loses.

The conclusion to be drawn from all of this? Power-conferring rules are no more neutral than ordinary prescriptive rules; in particular, the rules that give legal effect to contracts are no more neutral than the rules that give legal effect to status norms. Anyone who argues that reconceiving marriage along the lines of free contract would strike a blow for moral neutrality should be forced to come down to earth—to tell why his nonneutral moral judgments are more deserving of assent than those of his opponents.

This section has concentrated on the war between contract and status in our conception of marriage and family because it dominates our rhetoric. Claims Mary Ann Glendon, however, a scholar of marital and family law, "the shift that is currently taking place in the family law of the United States, far from being a shift from State regulation of status to State regulation of contracts, is a shift from regulation of the formation, effects, and dissolution of marriage to *non-regulation*. The trend is toward leaving questions such as who can marry, who can marry whom, and how people form, conduct, and terminate their life in common, to social rather than legal norms."[32] This observation could have been made with equal justice about questions of who may bear and beget children.[33]

I hope it will not be necessary to show at length that a shift from regulation to nonregulation is no more ethically neutral than a shift from regulation of status to regulation of contract. Nonpolicies are still policies. He who chooses between policies chooses between their known or foreseeable consequences. Ironically the progressive withdrawal of the state from every aspect of the regulation of matrimony and fertility has forced it to become more and more heavily involved in the economic fallout of family disintegration—through the provision of welfare services to divorced or never-wed girls and women with dependent children.

But there is an even greater irony. In at least one area of family law we are beginning to see signs, not of deregulation, but of reregulation—and under the same neutralist banner. In almost every state, the legal fiction of common-law marriage has long since been dismantled.[34] In a few states it is now being resuscitated under a new name.[35] The same species of justification is invoked for its re-invention as was once invoked for its destruction. Whereas once rang out the plaint, "What right has the state to practice moral discrimination by treating me as though I have entered a relationship I do not desire?", it now runs, "What right has the state to practice moral discrimination by denying me the protections routinely granted to those who *have* entered the relationship I do not desire?"[36] We can say this for false tolerance: it is flexible to a fault.

Notes

1. A similar point is made by Kent Greenawalt in "Some Related Limits of Law," 84: "Most assertions about spheres of behavior that should be beyond the reach of the law focus on criminal prohibition and punishment. This focus tends to obscure whether the fundamental objection is to coercion or to the use of state power."
2. *Not* "homosexuality"; "sodomy" refers to the act, rather than the disposition. Public debate obscures the fact that the morality of the one and the morality of the other are separate issues. So far as I know, no one has tried to criminalize the disposition. For instance, the Supreme Court case *Bowers v. Hardwick* (1986), which is often represented as concerning the constitutionality of state laws against homosexuality, really concerns only the constitutionality of state laws against consensual sodomy.
3. Some of these beliefs about adult competence rank as counsels of tolerance in their own right, and are included in the list of such counsels designated Appendix One.
4. Ibid., at 108–110 in *John Stuart Mill: Three Essays*.
5. The last is the so-called question of Moral Effect.
6. For rather different arguments that are nevertheless distantly related to these, see Gerald Dworkin, "Paternalism," and Peter Jones, "Toleration, Harm, and Moral Effect."
7. In "On Liberty," the skepticism of chap. 2 and the experimentalism of chap. 3 work against recognizing harm to mores or seduction to evil as real harm, although Mill wavers where there is a pecuniary interest in the corruption of others (as in ibid., 121–22). A closely related confusion concerns the problem of "bad examples," first mentioned at 98 but not addressed until 102. Mill first admits that conduct may harm others through example. He then asserts (without argument) that this is *especially* true of conduct which also harms others in a more direct fashion, and assumes still further (also without argument) that if conduct involves both direct harm to others *and* harm to others through example, just the former should be set in the scales. At this point, "especially" comes to mean "only." For yet another assumption is made silently about conduct which does *not* offer direct harm to others, but just to the agent: that its bad consequences for the agent will be clearly (and presumably promptly) evident to everyone else. This assumption allows Mill to say that in all such cases, the effect of example will be good rather than bad.
8. Mill's generous presumption in favor of consent is especially clear at ibid., 113:

although he says that in his view, polygamy is "a mere riveting of the chains of one-half of the community, and an emancipation of the other from reciprocity of obligation towards them," he maintains that the practice should be tolerated by non-Mormons because Mormon women consent too it. Yet Mill is also well-known for maintaining that chattel slavery should be suppressed even when individuals take the initiative in selling their own freedom. He does not explain how his openness to what is called the *violenti* maxim in the case of polygamy squares with his rejection of it in the case of chattel slavery. For related discussion see Donald H. Regan, "Justifications for Paternalism," and especially Michael D. Bayles, "Criminal Paternalism." The latter offers an interesting argument for the retention of the *volenti* maxim, but construes "consent" so stringently that the maxim is reduced to a surd.

9. Mill's argument against accepting offense as genuine harm is put most concisely in ibid., 102–4.

10. Mill's reluctance to view as harmful conduct by which a man destroys his abilities to fulfill his obligations to others is signalled by his dictum at ibid., 99, that only "distinct and assignable" harm may be taken into consideration. However, since he accepts the idea that obligations to society as a whole are sufficiently distinct and assignable to be taken into consideration, just why he rejects the idea of an obligation not to lay waste one's own powers is not clear.

11. Yet another dictum signifies Mill's reluctance to regard as harmful the risk of harm, distributed in such a way that we do not know on whom the sword may fall—this one at ibid., 100, where he says that we may consider only those risks of harm that are "definite."

12. The first appearance of any of the permutations of this phrase is at ibid., 17, but other versions appear throughout chaps. 1, 4, and 5. What makes this particularly odd is that at 118, Mill embraces a version of "true interest" doctrine which could easily justify violations even of his own brand of harm principle. The violations would probably be along the lines of Gerald Dworkin's suggestions in his article, "Paternalism."

13. See especially ibid., chaps. 2 and 3.

14. A bold example of this nonsense may be found in Louis Henkin, "Morals and the Constitution: The Sin of Obscenity," 402, 405, 414. According to Henkin, "due process of law" requires that all legislation have an "apparent," "rational," and "utilitarian" social purpose. He adds that laws violate due process when they are based on "unfounded" assumptions about character and its corruption. We later learn that he regards *all* assumptions about character and its corruption as unfounded; that "morals," "religions," "superstitions," and "prejudices" are indistinguishable; and that this being the case, morals can never be either apparent, rational, *or* utilitarian.

15. This point was first recognized by Rousseau, *The Social Contract* bk. 4, chap. 7. However, Rousseau did not accept the counsels of tolerance in the matter and did not believe that the "censorial" authority needed to be tempered.

16. See especially "Liberalism," at 127, and *Taking Rights Seriously*, at 234–35, on which I base my discussion. A more recent Dworkin piece, "What Liberalism Isn't" (a very sharp review of Bruce Ackerman's *Social Justice in the Liberal State*), has led some readers to think that Dworkin is no longer a neutralist. However, "What Liberalism Isn't" criticizes not neutrality per se, but only neu-

trality per Ackerman. Dworkin believes that had Ackerman pursued neutrality in his way instead of in his own, his social policy recommendations would have been more egalitarian. The problem appears to be that whereas Dworkin derives neutrality from equality, Ackerman merely derives equality from neutrality. Still later works by Dworkin do not mention the views I discuss in the text; however, nor do they repudiate them.

17. *Taking Rights Seriously*, 235.

18. In another publication Dworkin concedes that voters usually do not act this way; thus, he says, judicially-enforceable rights should be devised to guarantee neutrality despite them.

19. Notice that here, where a kind of doubt is most firmly expressed, the argument is driven not by skepticism but by conviction. What prompts true tolerance is not simply doubt that I can know the souls of others, but certainty that the pretense to such knowledge causes harm.

20. A related counsel of tolerance is to reject ways of dishonoring conduct that work *through* dishonor to persons. For instance (as David J. Danelski remarks in "The Limits of Law," 27, n. 47), there is no practical obstacle to putting a person on trial, convicting him of a crime, and then withholding penalties simply as a way to show that the conduct in question is wrong. Yet I think that a truly tolerant system of justice could not allow this, because the wrong of the conduct would be demonstrated only through a pure and deliberate humiliation of the person who committed it. This would be the procedural equivalent of putting people in stocks.

21. I have dealt with some of this already, of course. Mill's discussion is found at the beginning of the fourth chapter of "On Liberty." All of my quotations are taken from *John Stuart Mill: Three Essays*, 95, 97.

22. For example, Thomas Merton, *New Seeds of Contemplation*, 56–60. Some help can also be found in C.S. Lewis, "After Priggery, What?", found in *Present Concerns*.

23. Marriage is regarded as a sacrament among the Catholic churches, whether Roman, Anglican, or Eastern. In the churches of the Reformation as well as in Judaism, it is regarded as a "covenant between the spouses in the sight of God." In Islamic law, it is viewed as a contract. These faiths present considerable variety of opinion as to the conditions (if any) under which purely civil marriages are recognized as valid. See Paul Heinrich Neuhaus, "Christian Family Law," at 16; Ze'ev W. Falk, "Jewish Family Law," at 29; and Norman Anderson, "Islamic Family Law," at 57. The quotation in the second sentence of this note is taken from Falk.

24. H.L.A. Hart, *The Concept of Law*, 28–38.

25. Western law used to recognize a larger number of status relationships than today, but most have disappeared or been transformed, unable to withstand modernity. For instance, the tutelary relationship of master and servant, once governed by status norms, is now a relationship of employer and employee, governed by contract; meanwhile the status of "female under tutelage" has vanished altogether. This is important; in the fact that tutelary norms are no longer applied to normal adults we may discern the lineaments of yet another counsel of tolerance. However, the family is still the bosom of such status relationships as survive. These include matrimony, parenthood, and childhood. The classic discussion of the great historical shift from Status to Contract is Henry Sumner Maine, "Law

in Primitive Society," a chapter in *Ancient Law: Its Connection with the Early History of Society and its Relation to Modern Ideas*. See especially pp. 140–41 of the edition listed in the bibliography.

26. See Glendon, ibid., 665, and the sources cited there.

27. Confusions about whether marriage is a matter of contract or status are nothing new. However, greater efforts were made formerly than presently to dispel it. In the 1888 case *Maynard v. Hill*, for instance, the Supreme Court remarked that "whilst marriage is often termed by text writers and in decisions of courts a civil contract—generally to indicate that it must be founded upon the agreement of the parties, and does not require any religious ceremony for its solemnization—it is something more than a mere contract. The consent of the parties is of course essential to its existence, but when the contract to marry is executed by the marriage, a relation between the parties is created which they cannot change. Other contracts may be modified, restricted, or enlarged, or entirely released upon the consent of the parties. Not so with marriage. The relation once formed, the law steps in and holds the parties to various obligations and liabilities." *Maynard v. Hill* (1888), 210–11. The contrast between the status and contract conceptions of matrimony is brought out even more clearly by various excerpts from state court opinions, presented by the Court in *Maynard* as precedent for its own decision. From Maine (cited at 211): "[Marriage] is not, then, a contract within the meaning of the . . . Constitution. . . . It is, rather, a social relation, like that of parent and child, the obligations of which arise not from the consent of concurring minds, but are the creation of the law itself." From Rhode Island (cited at 212): "[M]arriage, in the sense in which it is dealt with by a divorce decree, is not a contract, but one of the domestic relations. . . . When formed, this relation is no more a contract than 'fatherhood' or 'sonship' is a contract." From New York (cited at 213): "The relation [of matrimony] is always regulated by government. It is more than a contract. . . . It partakes more of the character of an institution regulated and controlled by public authority, upon principles of public policy, for the benefit of the community." Finally, from Indiana (cited at 213): "Some confusion has arisen from confounding the contract to marry with the marriage relation itself. And still more is engendered by regarding husband and wife as strictly parties to a subsisting contract. . . . [I]t is not so much the result of private agreement, as of public ordination." From the tenor of neutralist writing on marriage and family law, one would think that this doctrine were obsolete. Not true at all. The Supreme Court still cites *Maynard* as its authority for the proposition that marriage is a "social relation," or status, rather than a contract, and that it is therefore subject to the regulatory power of the federal government. For instance see *Loving v. Virginia*, at 7. I should add that *Maynard* also endorses the statements of various authorities in order to explain *why* the law treats marriage as a "social relation" rather than a contract. At 211–12, for instance, marriage is described as "the first step from barbarism to incipient civilization, the purest tie of social life and the true basis of human progress"; and at 213, as "the basis of civil institutions, and thus an object of the deepest public concern." However, in view of the fact that this explanation addresses only the first of the three criteria that I stated earlier for the regulation of relationships, it must be regarded as incomplete.

28. "Relative monogamy" is an anthropological term signifying the practice of permitting more than one matrimonial partner—but not at the same time. "Absolute

monogamy" signifies the norm of having one partner for life. Another term that anthropologists use for relative monogamy is "successive polygamy"; however, to prevent confusion I will use the term "polygamy" to denote only the "simultaneous" variety of the practice.

29. René König, "Sociological Introduction," 42. In "Marriage and the State: The Withering Away of Marriage," 64–75, Mary Ann Glendon also stresses "the economic limits on the number of wives a single man can support," and observes that "the proliferation of successive polygamy may be subject to the same limitations." She adds, "The applicability of the second point to our present situation hardly needs demonstration. The states are currently wrestling with the question of whether responsibility for successive spouses belongs to their one-time marriage partners or to society at large." Noting that "countries in the climates that Montesquieu thought favored such marriages are now moving toward the abolition of simultaneous polygamy," she wryly suggests the possibility that "under conditions of modern industrialization the climates favoring polygamy are a high gross national product and a welfare state."

30. The Law contained provisions for divorce, Deuteronomy 24:1–2. Jesus said he had come to fulfill rather than destroy the Law, Matthew 5:17. Yet he emphatically forbade divorce, e.g., Matthew 19:3–9. For his explanation of the fact that the legal ideal falls short of the ethical, see verses 7–8. For the disciples' reaction, see verse 10. What to make of infidelity, the qualifying circumstance mentioned in verse 9, is contested. Some Protestants interpret the verse as authorizing full divorce when a partner has been unfaithful. Roman Catholics, and other Protestants, see it as authorizing only separation, without the option of remarriage.

31. In economics, a transaction's "external costs" are the burdens it imposes indirectly on third parties.

32. Mary Ann Glendon, "Marriage and the State: The Withering Away of Marriage," 665–66. If it is true that the state has progressively withdrawn from every aspect of marital regulation, how has this come about? Glendon's own discussion suggests part of the answer. According to Glendon, the abandonment of the older view of the family as a small society of special and state-guaranteed obligations, privileges, and liabilities has been—though not caused—at least catalyzed by the tendency of contemporary jurists to invent new fundamental rights that all citizens possess regardless of status or qualifications. For the United States, her example is the invention of a fundamental "right to marry" in the 1967 case, *Loving v. Virginia* (though the Court had already come very close to announcing such a right several decades earlier; see *Skinner v. Oklahoma* [1942], at 541). In pulling this right from the hat, the Court seems to have intended nothing more than to enliven the rhetoric of its attack on state antimiscegenation laws. No such right was necessary to overturn them; enough had already been said in the opinion to show that such statutes deprived citizens of the equal protection of the laws guaranteed by the Fourteenth Amendment. But as Glendon observes, however gratuitous the invention of the right might have been to its immediate context, its announcement had unanticipated, long-range consequences. It produced a new "atmosphere" for the "withering away" not only of state regulations concerning who can marry whites (the demise of which is welcome), but also all other matters concerned with matrimony. These include age and other restrictions on who may marry, number and choice of spouses, compulsory marriage preliminaries, and

compulsory formalities for the solemnization of marriage. Ibid., at 668–69; compare the discussion of other judicially imposed obstacles to the state's expression of an interest in the ethical well-being of the community in the next note and in the next section of the text.

33. Parallel to *Loving v. Virginia* (1967), which established the doctrine that people have a "right to marry" (see the preceding note), *Eisenstadt v. Baird* (1972) established the doctrine that people have a right to be free from state interference with the decision whether to produce children. As in *Loving*, the new right was gratuitous to the immediate context. All the Court was trying to show was that unmarried people should be allowed to prevent conception. There was no need to ask whether they should be allowed to *achieve* conception—much less to answer the question in the affirmative. Unable to resist, the Court answered it anyway, sending waves into distant and still uncharted seas. "If the right of privacy means anything," said the Court at 453, "it is the right of the *individual*, married or single, to be free from unwarranted governmental intrusion into matters so fundamentally affecting a person as the decision whether to bear or beget a child." Difficult counsel. Today we hear of young men who "make babies" with as many women as possible as a swaggering proof of manhood; of even younger women and girls who conceive out of wedlock in order to escape loneliness, parental control, or the boredom of school. In the ghettoes this is epidemic. What public policy can do to discourage these decisions isn't clear, but in the wisdom of the Court we have apparently been spared the trouble of asking. We must not "intrude" when individuals are exercising their "right" to arrange matters that "fundamentally affect" them. Society and their children will bear the burdens—and about those "fundamental effects," apparently we need not be concerned.

34. By treating cohabiting couples as though they were married, the legal fiction of common-law marriage made them subject to all of the usual obligations of marriage. This went a long way toward protecting the moral and material interests of vulnerable family members, meaning, in most cases, women and children. Of course, it could not fully satisfy those who believe that individuals planning an alliance ought to get married for religious reasons. But as we have seen, a purely civil marriage does not create a sacramental relationship either, and anyway, it is not the business of the state to administer sacraments or to enforce religious obligations. This legal fiction was simply a humane and prudent institution—one of the finest works of true tolerance.

35. I am thinking of experiments in the states like the invention of "palimony" in the 1976 California case *Marvin v. Marvin*. In this case, a woman alleged that she and a man had entered an oral agreement that she would give up her career and serve as his companion, housekeeper, and cook; that he would support her for life; and that they would combine their earnings and share equally any property that they accumulated. After six years of cohabitation, he told her to leave, refusing either to divide their property or to pay her support. She brought action against him, asking the Court, as it were, to make him keep his promises. Now division of property does take place upon the dissolution of marriage, and under the common law, cohabitation could have been construed as implying entrance into the marital status. In California, however, common-law marriage had been abolished. As an alternative, the California Supreme Court held that cohabitation *could* be construed as involving a *contract*, either express or implied. One obstacle might have been that California law barred the enforcement of meretricious contracts. But as

the Court explained (670–72, 683), a contract is not necessarily meretricious just because it is executed in the context of a meretricious relationship; after all, the woman in the case had not mentioned sex as one of the services she had agreed to provide in return for financial support and property. Another obstacle might have been that it would be very difficult to ascertain just what agreements the man and woman had made. But by treating their agreement as implied rather than express, the Court avoided this difficulty completely. Whether the man and woman had agreed to share fifty-fifty, sixty-forty, or eighty-twenty—indeed, whether they had made any express agreement at all—became irrelevant. The Court simply relied upon the principles of equity to fashion guidelines for monetary relief (682, 684). Two points are crucial: the decision to treat the agreement as implied rather than express, and the imposition of a formula without regard to the wishes of the parties. Although the case was packaged as a regulation of contract, these elements made it more like a regulation of status. As the lone dissenter observed, it laid certain highly specific obligations on their cohabitants even though they "may have rejected matrimony in order to avoid such obligations." "[T]he majority," he said, "perform a nunc pro tunc marriage, dissolve it, and distribute its property[.]" (At 686, Judge Clark, concurring in part and dissenting in part.)

36. Said the *Marvin* Court, "we recognize the well-established public policy to foster and promote the institution of marriage" but "the mores of society have indeed changed so radically in regard to cohabitation that we cannot impose a standard based on alleged moral considerations that have apparently been so widely abandoned by many." (At 683–84.)

3

Is True Tolerance Constitutional?

There would be little point in writing a critique like this if the error it attacked was an error that befuddled scholars alone; if it posed no danger to the world at large, caused no addlement in the way we live together. But this is not the case. Arguments of principle do affect real life. As we have already begun to see, this is especially clear in the empire of law.

But of all the duchies of that empire, constitutional jurisprudence has become the most influential American forum for arguments of principle. Considering the strain to which jurists must often put themselves to give their principles constitutional coloration, this is surprising; nonetheless it is a fact. And this fact is the reason why I discuss the constitutional question from time to time, in different contexts, throughout the book. By the constitutional question I mean simply, "Is true tolerance constitutional?" A general orientation to the question is provided *here* in order to prepare the reader for the more focussed discussions *there*.

To be sure, if this book's defense of true tolerance is correct, then, even if true tolerance did clash with the Constitution, it would be the Constitution, not true tolerance, that needed amendment. That is not a reason to dismiss the constitutional question, because constitutional change is not something to be undertaken lightly; one ought to be very sure the hand does not fit before altering such a rare and expensive glove. Even so, "Is true tolerance constitutional?" may seem a peculiar question from another point of view. How could true tolerance be *un*constitutional? If anything the Constitution seems pro-tolerance, because of its meticulous guarantees of rights and the restrictions on means of regulation that these rights imply.

But the premise here is faulty. As we have seen, true tolerance does not mean tolerating everything; it means tolerating what should be tolerated. To make the distinction between what should and what should not be tolerated requires some grasp of the goods that are important in fully human lives. The promotion and protection of these goods is presupposed *both* by proper regulation *and* by proper restrictions on the means of regulation. Therefore, a Constitution that prohibited regard for these goods would be just as detrimental to true tolerance as a Constitution which permitted wrong means of regard for them.

The framers and ratifiers of the U.S. Constitution seemed to grasp this. On the one hand, they dedicated both the federal and the state governments to the promotion and protection of various goods.[1] On the other hand, the framers and ratifiers further promoted and protected these goods by guarantees of rights which channelled the ways the government could pursue them—making off-limits those ways that would ultimately undermine them.

Thus the outlook of the Constitution itself is broadly consistent with true tolerance. Unfortunately, certain modes of constitutional interpretation are not. This tendency is not, as widely thought, confined to the Left; it finds itself just as much at home in the jurisprudence of the Right. Former Judge Robert Bork, for instance, a Supreme Court nominee of President Ronald Reagan whom the Senate refused to confirm because of his conservative views, states that "there is no principled way to decide that one man's gratifications are more deserving of respect than another's or that one form of gratification is more worthy than another. . . . There is no way of deciding these issues other than by reference to some system of moral or ethical values that has no objective or intrinsic validity of its own." Committing the fallacy that confessing an inability to rank-order gratifications is the same as placing them in the same rank, he says that the Constitution should be treated as though it contained an "equal gratifications clause."[2]

Part One closes with illustrations of the confusion brought about by neutralist abuse of three Constitutional concepts: equal protection of the laws, due process of law, and the right of privacy. All three abuses are commonly, and falsely, regarded by neutralists as bulwarks of tolerance. For greater ease of comparison, my examples of all three abuses have been taken from the same context: governmental interest in marital and family relationships. The examples cover both regulatory and non-regulatory ways of expressing such interest. In addition, I consider constitutional interpretation not only by the U.S. Supreme Court, but also by the Supreme Court of a state particularly given to neutralist tendencies in this realm of policy.

Abuse of the Concepts of Equal Protection of the Laws and Due Process of Law

Remember that true tolerance is not the same as tolerating everything; that making the distinction between what should and what should not be tolerated requires some grasp of the goods that are important in fully human lives; and that the promotion and protection of these goods is presupposed *both* by proper regulation *and* by proper restrictions on the means of regulation. The first general notion that has tended to erode the state's ability to promote and protect healthy marital and family norms—and thus blur the meaning of true tolerance—is a peculiar interpretation of the "equal protection of the laws" guaranteed by the Fourteenth Amendment.

Under the narrowest possible construction, the original intent of this clause was only to protect freed slaves from invidious racial classifications. Modern jurists regard it as entitling them to scrutinize classifications of all kinds, racial as well as nonracial, for analogous invidiousness. This may be within the intention of the clause; I will not investigate the matter here. However, a prominent contemporary tendency is to regard *ethically* motivated classifications with particular suspicion. This is really a very peculiar idea. Any conception whatsoever of a good to be achieved or an evil to be avoided may be called an ethical motivation. All but completely arbitrary classifications escape every conception of goods to be achieved or evils to be avoided. Therefore, none but completely arbitrary classifications should be able to escape the general suspicion of ethically motivated classifications.

In practice, however, jurists of the neutralist persuasion have deigned to notice the ethical quality only of *certain* conceptions of goods to be achieved or evils to be avoided. One such conception is that which holds that human life is best served when family relationships are contained within the civil institution of matrimony. Thus, any classification between people in the married and unmarried states is likely to be treated severely.

The tendency began in a 1973 case styled *U.S. Department of Agriculture v. Moreno*. This case concerned the constitutionality of a provision contained in the Food Stamp Act of 1964 as later amended. The provision denied participation in the food stamp program to households containing unrelated members. "In practical effect," as Justice Brennan pointed out, the statute "creates two classes of persons for food stamp purposes: one class is composed of those individuals who live in households all of whose members are related to one another, and the other class consists of those individuals who live in households containing one or more members who are unrelated to the rest."[3]

Now, in order to pass the equal-protection test as the Court has developed it over time, this classification would have had to be rationally related to the promotion of some legitimate governmental purpose. Therefore, the first question was what the purposes of the provision in question were and whether they were legitimate, while the second was whether sorting people into classes in the manner in question really did advance these purposes. As Justice Brennan found, the history of the statutory amendment that first made households of unrelated individuals ineligible for stamps was intended "to prevent so-called 'hippies' and 'hippie communes' from participating in the food stamp program." But "[t]he challenged classification clearly cannot be sustained by reference to this congressional purpose. For if the constitutional conception of 'equal protection of the laws' means anything, it must at the very least mean that a bare congressional desire to harm a politically unpopular group cannot constitute a *legitimate* governmental purpose."[4] This was not the only reason for which the participation rule was overturned, but it is the only one that concerns us here.

What is wrong with this? Justice Brennan was playing with words. In the first place, no one would doubt the injustice of denying a benefit to a group *because* it is politically unpopular. However, this is not the same as denying a benefit to a politically unpopular group; for there may be another reason for the denial. By treating these cases as the same, Justice Brennan enabled himself to practice a kind of selective blindness to the ethical considerations by which Congress may really have been moved. For there was good reason for the hippies' unpopularity; hippie communes tended to be drug-ridden, unstable, and polymorphously promiscuous. In the second place, Justice Brennan used the term "harm" tendentiously. Withholding an optional benefit and inflicting an injury are two altogether different things. By refusing participation in the food stamp program, the government was not harming so-called hippies, but only declining to subsidize their freely chosen way of life. But by conflating refusal to subsidize with injury, Justice Brennan made the subsidy mandatory.

This kind of reasoning reappears in a number of other judicial opinions in both state and federal cases. One of the most striking is the California case *Atkisson v. Kern* (1976). The case concerned a county housing authority's policy of prohibiting its low income tenants from cohabiting with unrelated persons of the opposite sex. When the authority attempted to evict a female tenant for violating her lease agreement by living as if husband and wife with an unrelated man, the woman went to law for declaratory and injunctive relief. The Supreme Court of California ruled in her favor. Not all of the reasons for the Court's decision concern us here. One does, however: The Court used *Moreno* to argue that the county housing authority's policy was based on an "irrational" classification, and therefore denied cohabiting tenants the equal protection of the laws.

If anything, the case of the county anticohabitation rule in *Atkisson* was far stronger than the case for the federal anticohabitation rule in *Moreno*. First, fostering normal family ties was prominently included among the purposes of the county housing authority. Second, the authority asserted that its thirty-one years of experience had left no doubt that besides creating problems in management and demoralizing tenants, cohabitation definitely had a bad effect on tenant families. The Court allowed this assertion to pass unchallenged, and made no attempt to argue that reducing management problems, preventing the demoralization of tenants, or fostering normal family ties were illegitimate governmental purposes.[5]

Reduced to its essentials, the Court's argument may be put as follows. It is not necessarily true that every single instance of cohabitation produces bad effects. For this reason, tenants would have been deprived of the equal protection of the laws unless the anticohabitation policy had been applied "flexibly." Instead, the county housing authority had applied it across the board. So far reasoned the Court. Then, killing another bird with the same stone, it claimed that by creating an "irrebuttable presumption" that every cohabiting person is immoral, irresponsible, and demoralizing to others, the authority had also deprived tenants of due process. Apparently, in order to slip the noose of the Fourteenth Amendment, the county housing authority would have had to study each and every instance of tenant cohabitation, distinguishing the good cases from the bad cases.

What is wrong with this? A distinction between good and bad cohabitation would have made the ethical reasons for which the authority had enacted its policy completely incoherent. Let's begin by looking at the three prongs of the allegedly irrebuttable presumption one by one: first, that cohabiting tenants are irresponsible to management; second, that they are immoral; third, that they demoralize other tenants and have a bad effect on families. Now if number one—irresponsibility to management—had been the authority's only motive for enactment, I think we would have to agree with the Court. For concreteness we may consider just one aspect of responsibility to management, the payment of rent. Surely some cohabiting tenants paid their rent on time; surely management knew perfectly well who didn't and who did; therefore, had irresponsibility to management been the authority's only problem, it could more rationally have responded by evicting just the tenants that did not. The irrebuttability of a presumption that cohabiting tenants never paid their rents on time would certainly be unfair to those who did.

But the irrebuttable-presumption argument does not touch the authority's other two reasons for prohibiting cohabitation—and either would be sufficient to justify the policy. Consider number two, "immorality." Had the housing authority concurred that some cohabitation is moral while other cohabitation is immoral, then it would obviously be unfair to presume, with no opportunity for rebuttal, that every tenant who practiced cohabitation was practicing the immoral rather than the moral kind. But this was not the housing authority's position. It did not concur that some cohabitation is moral while other cohabitation is immoral; it claimed that cohabitation *as such* is immoral. Now consider number three, "demoralization and bad effect on families." Had the housing authority concurred that some cohabitation sets a good example while other cohabitation sets a bad example, then, again, it would be unfair to presume, with no opportunity for rebuttal, that every tenant who practiced cohabitation was setting the bad rather than the good kind. But this was not the housing authority's position either.

It did not concur that some cohabitation sets a good example while other cohabitation sets a bad example; it claimed that, by virtue of its intrinsic immorality, the example of cohabitation is *always* bad. In short: the housing authority was not guilty of an irrebuttable presumption in either of the two reasons for its policy that concern us.

But we can go further. An across-the-board ban on cohabitation preserves not only due process, but also equal protection of the laws. This is because if reasons two and three do not involve any irrebuttable presumptions, then by the same token the anticohabitation rule need not be applied "flexibly." The Court's argument to the contrary is very much like saying that an absolute ban on dumping plutonium wastes into the public reservoir establishes an irrebuttable presumption that all plutonium is radioactive, and that the policy should be flexible instead because even though plutonium in general is hazardous, this or that lump of it may be perfectly harmless. The flaw, of course, is that all plutonium *is* radioactive. Likewise, the housing authority says all cohabitation is harmful to family life.

Needless to say, a housing authority may not do whatever it pleases about cohabitation. Evicting tenants merely on the rumor of cohabitation would have been a very real violation of due process; banning cohabitation among black tenants but not among whites would have been a very real deprivation of the equal protection of the laws. But nothing like either of these was the problem here. Evidently the Court was predisposed against any attempt whatsoever to use the distribution of optional benefits to encourage the containment of family relationships within the civil institution of matrimony. This is false tolerance.

Abuse of the Concept of Privacy

Fully as much as by eccentric judicial interpretations of due process and equal protection of the laws, the ability and will of the state to support marital and family status norms has been eroded by eccentric judicial interpretations of privacy. Now the idea of privacy can take two forms. One of them is innocent. In fact, the protection of privacy in this sense is a counsel of true tolerance. The other idea, unfortunately, does a great deal of damage. To get started, we must briefly explain both.

Privacy number one, which may be called true privacy, concerns what others may know about my affairs and do with my things. This is what ordinary speakers mean by privacy. It is what we mean when we say that our privacy is infringed by people peering in our windows or opening our mail. Guaranteeing a right of privacy in this sense furthers a number of important goods including the intimacy of personal relationships. Clearly, then, a right to true privacy would not bar the state from being concerned with the well-being of the family; on the contrary, a right to true privacy may even *express* such concern with the well-being of the family. Justice Harlan seemed to recognize this in the 1960 case, *Poe v. Ullman*. Though accepting the notion of a privacy right, he could yet observe that

> [s]ociety is not limited in its objects only to the physical well-being of the community, but has traditionally concerned itself with the moral soundness of its people as well. Indeed to attempt to draw a line between public behavior and that which is purely consensual or solitary would be to withdraw from community concern a range of subjects with which every society in civilized times has found it necessary to deal.

He includes in this "range" of subjects "[t]he laws regarding marriage which provide both when the sexual powers may be used and the legal and societal context in which children are born and brought up," laws which, he says, "form a pattern so deeply pressed into the substance of our social life that any constitutional doctrine in this area must build upon that basis."[6]

By contrast, privacy number two, which might be called false privacy, concerns not what others may know about my affairs or do with my things, but what I myself may do and whether others may discourage me in any way from doing it. Probably because jurists fail to distinguish false privacy itself from true, false privacy is often defended in the name of the same goods which true privacy nurtures. Thus, its neutralist bearing can be overlooked. Hailed, for instance, in the name of the "noble purpose" of the marital alliance—as Justice Douglas hailed it[7]—its effect on family law is more in the nature of a slow-acting poison.

From seemingly unobjectionable beginnings in *Griswold v. Connecticut* (1965), the false concept of privacy has little by little eaten away the state's involvement with marital and family status norms.

Griswold did no more than overturn an ill-advised law that criminalized the use of contraceptives by married people.[8] In *Eisenstadt v. Baird* (1972), the doctrine swelled to take in both not only contraception but also conception, and not only inside but also out of wedlock. In *Roe v. Wade* (1973), it swelled still further to take in abortion.

Coincidentally, the state case *Atkisson v. Kern*, used in the previous section to illustrate the abuse of the concepts of due process and equal protection of the laws, can also be used to illustrate the abuse of the concept of privacy. This case is particularly interesting because it shows how a right to false privacy eventually establishes a sphere, or, as the Supreme Court says, a "zone," in which everything is not only permitted, but encouraged.

Atkisson's argument about privacy was simple. *Eisenstadt* had already established that the privacy right covers the right of unmarried people to bear children. The *Atkisson* Court reasoned that if it covers the right to bear them, it must include their right to raise them. Now if cohabiting couples are denied the privilege of public housing, often one parent will have to separate from the children. Therefore, to deny cohabiting couples the privilege of public housing is to violate their right of privacy.[9]

What is wrong with this? The major premise, the minor premise, and the conclusion of this deduction are all flawed. As to the major, we don't need to legitimize conception out of wedlock in order to give the care of children to their parents. Whether they should have been conceived under those circumstances is now moot, and in most cases to be cared for by their parents is clearly in their best interests. As to the minor, in order to give the care of children to their parents, we don't have to subsidize parental cohabitation. Cohabitating couples can restore their eligibility for the privilege of public housing simply by getting married. As to the conclusion: Marriage of the parents is in the best interests of the children as well as the parents themselves. It formalizes parental obligations, obligations to the children and to each other, not only while the marriage lasts, but also in the event of its dissolution.

Overlooking all of this, *Atkisson* declares that in the name of privacy, unmarried cohabitation must be not only tolerated, but financed. Needless to say further, the fetishism of false privacy does not contribute to the understanding of true tolerance. Ending this fetishism, along with the other Constitutional fallacies we have discussed, is much to be desired.

Notes

1. The general goods to which the federal government was dedicated were summarized in the Preamble. In turn, the states were left with most of the power of "domestic police," understood in the common law as the power to issue suitable regulations for the "welfare" of the public—traditionally elaborated as its "safety," "health," and "morals." *The Federalist* simply presupposed, rather than asserting, the assignment of the power of domestic police to the states. In the first paragraph of *Federalist* #17, for example, Hamilton argues that the new national government will have little motive to invade the powers of state governments because "the mere domestic police of a State appears to me to hold out slender allurements to ambition." "Commerce, finance, negotiation, and war," he adds, "seem to comprehend all the objects which have charms for minds governed by that passion."

2. Robert Bork, "Neutral Principles and Some First Amendment Problems," especially 256. This article involves a certain confusion in the meaning of the term, "neutrality." Herbert Wechsler, in "Toward Neutral Principles of Constitutional Law," had argued persuasively that the reasons given for any judicial decision should be general enough to transcend the outcome of the particular case. He was at some pains afterward to make clear that what he called a "neutral" principle was not an *ethically* neutral principle, but simply a principle with this kind of generality. Judge Bork, by contrast, considers ethical neutralism a logical extension of Wechslerian "neutralism."

3. *U.S. Department of Agriculture v. Moreno* (1973), at 529.

4. Ibid., at 534.

5. *Atkisson*, at 93.

6. *Poe v. Ullman* (1960), at 545–46.

7. *Griswold* at 486.

8. Even here the reasoning was poor. Justice Douglas, author of the plurality opinion, used the Ninth Amendment to suggest that the Constitution contains unenumerated rights, then tried to identify some of them by calling attention to certain clauses of the First, Third, Fourth, and Fifth Amendments. These provide that citizens may peaceably assemble, that soldiers may not be quartered in private houses in peacetime without the consent of the owners, that unreasonable searches and seizures may not be conducted, and that no one may be compelled to give testimony against himself. He claimed (1) that all four provisions protect privacy; (2) that the Constitution therefore affords a *general* protection of privacy; and (3) that this protection, being general, *encompasses* the use of contraceptives by married people. Even the first claim is specious. As the wording of the First Amendment shows, the framers connected peaceable assembly not with privacy, but with a very public political act—petitioning the government for the redress of grievances. The most certain reason for the self-incrimination clause in the Fifth Amendment seems to have been to prevent the government from eliciting confessions by means of torture; neither has this anything to do with privacy. The prohibitions involving

searches and seizures and the quartering of soldiers without permission clearly do have something to do with privacy. But in the first place, neither is absolute—one allows a wartime exception, the other a "reasonable" cause exception. In the second place neither is general—each protects citizens only against certain *kinds* of intrusions on their homes, bodies, records, and property. And in the third, the privacy protected by these prohibitions concerns what others may know about our affairs or do with our things. Justice Douglas, by contrast, is talking about what we may do. If privacy really did mean being allowed to do whatever I please, then a Constitution that made it a right would be a startling thing indeed.

A privacy right is indeed firmly established in the common law of torts, and that, on my view of the Ninth Amendment, is certainly grist for the constitutional mill (see Appendix Two). However, such an approach cannot support an argument like that of Justice Douglas. The standard analysis of the tort for invasion of privacy is found in William L. Prosser, "Privacy." Prosser demonstrates that it is really an amalgam of four different torts: (1) intrusion upon a person's seclusion or solitude, or into his private affairs; (2) public disclosure of embarrassing private facts about him; (3) publicity which places him in a false light; and (4) appropriation, for another's advantage, of his name or likeness. Of course, if we construe the ideas behind these torts as material for Constitutional rights, we are speaking of guarantees against the government, rather than against other individuals. This shift of context requires certain adjustments. The Ninth Amendment might well give individuals protections against government that are closely analogous to the protections against individuals involved in torts 3 and 4. In the adaptation of the idea behind tort 2, however, numerous exceptions would have to be made, for instance to allow civil and criminal trials to be matters of public record. The idea behind tort 1—"intrusion"—is the only one that might suit Justice Douglas's argument. However, the Third and Fourth Amendments have partly pre-empted this field, because they presuppose the constitutionality of certain governmental intrusions in the very act of prohibiting others; for instance, the possibility of legitimate search and seizure is presupposed by the Fourth Amendment's list of criteria for the issuance of warrants.

9. *Atkisson*, at 98.

Part Two

The Heads of the Hydra

Introduction to Part Two

Old bestiaries used to tell of a fabulous creature called the Hydra. The Hydra was exceptionally difficult to kill; not only did it have thirty-nine dragonish heads, but whenever one head was cut off, several new ones sprouted immediately from the stump. The only way to prevent this was to sear the stump with fire. Some political doctrines are like that. Cutting off their heads merely redoubles their life. One must cut and sear, cut and sear, until they stop moving.

Ethical neutralism affords a paradigm case of this phenomenon. Knight after knight has tried his blade: thus Brian Barry remarks that anyone in political argument "must take his stand on the proposition that some ways of life, some types of character are more admirable than others"; Ronald Beiner insists that "the possibility of circumventing the theory of the good is bogus"; Gerald E. Frug says that governmental value choices can be "disguised," but never eliminated; Joseph M. Boyle suggests that any ground on which conflicts between moral perspectives can be arbitrated "will in fact be *some* moral perspective and the illusion that it is neutral will have the effect of disregarding the moral views of some citizens"; Michael Perry calls neutrality "an impossible goal"; John Horton observes about a single common neutralist shibboleth that "what liberalism represents as the neutral requirement of preventing harm to others will be perceived by those with different conceptions of what is harmful as the enforcement of a morality they do not share"; and Gilbert Harman says simply that "you can't get something from nothing."[1] Each knight has struck only to find the creature coiling up again with more heads than it had before. There is as much life in the Hydra Neutralism as ever.

The thirty-nine heads of the Hydra are the galaxy of seemingly good reasons distinguished thinkers have given us for being neutral. It belongs to true tolerance that these reasons be taken seriously. One by one they must be tried by the sword of reason. Would that there were fewer! This is a long and tiring task.

The reason these heads must be attacked by heat as well as by sword is that the cultural force of ethical neutralism exceeds the force of its arguments. By many things it makes its way. The most understandable is that the sheer number of good reasons for neutralism has a sort of hypnotic effect. Glowing in their dozens, the eyes of the Hydra entrance us; we don't stop to think whether any of these good reasons are themselves neutral, or, for that matter, whether neutrality is possible at all. Once weakened—so works the human mind—we become susceptible to less creditable appeals. One allurement is that neutralism clears the conscience of an age whose convictions are in decay. Another is that it gives us something to say when we have nothing to say. A third is that neutralism puts opponents on the defensive by defining opposition itself as "bias." A fourth depends on a property of neutralism that I have not yet demonstrated, but demonstrate later in this part: its logical inconsistency. This logical inconsistency is just too convenient to do without. Consistent doctrines offer little enough resistance to manipulation. But when doctrines lack consistency altogether, they can be bent into more shapes than modelling clay. So it is that there are neutralists of the Left, neutralists of the Right, Marxist neutralists, and even anarchist neutralists: for example John Rawls and Bruce Ackerman, Robert Nozick and Michael Oakeshott, Jürgen Habermas, and Robert Paul Wolff, respectively. Each acts as if his neutralism is responsible for his position. A maxim in logic called the Law of Duns Scotus explains this: From a contradiction, anything can be proven. Manipulation, I should add, does not require guile; just a certain ability to overlook the obvious, with which political theorists, as a class, are in all ages too richly endowed.

This part of the book is devoted to battling the Hydra. In the first section we take up all thirty-nine of its heads, those "good reasons" for being neutral. The goal of the section is a bit more complicated than sheer refutation. I do, of course, show that they do not justify neutrality. However, another purpose is to find out why some of them are so tempting, and what, if anything, can be learned from them. More than a few of them offer real insights. They may not be roads to neutrality, but they are roads to somewhere.

The second section begins with the admission that there may be more "good reasons" for being neutral than I have been able to catalogue. However, it goes on to render this point moot by showing that ethical neutrality is logically impossible. This may be viewed as a vindication of the intuition that choice, by its nature, is never neutral.

Note

1. Barry, *The Liberal Theory of Justice*, at 126; Beiner, "What's the Matter with Liberalism?", at 43; Frug, "Why Neutrality?", at 1591; Boyle, "A Catholic Perspective on Morality and the Law," at 233–34; Perry, "A Critique of the 'Liberal' Political-Philosophical Project," at 231–32; Horton, "Toleration, Morality, and Harm," at 132; and Harman, "Liberalism Without Foundations?", at 402. See also the articles listed in the bibliography under George P. Fletcher, William Galston (1982), Joseph Raz, and the contributors to Brian Barry (1983).

4

Arguments for Ethical Neutrality

The simplest refutation of ethical neutralism would seem to be asking the question, "Why be neutral?"—in the knowledge that every possible answer will somehow involve some view of the scheme of things, some conception of what is good for human beings, and thereby violate neutrality. One neutralist, Charles E. Larmore, has at least recognized the problem. However, his attempt to develop genuinely neutral arguments for neutrality illustrates the fruitlessness of this approach. Though Larmore inexplicably claims success, in the end even he adopts as a criterion the "least restriction" of neutrality rather than neutrality per se. Moreover, the standards by which he steers in minimizing restrictions are themselves nonneutral. First, "One could admit beliefs that are the least central to anyone's idea of the good life"; second, "One could admit beliefs that the least number of people do not hold." The first, bizarrely, presupposes the goodness of acting only on premises that literally no one cares much about. The second presupposes the goodness of deferring to the majority.[1] Thus both presuppose goods; neither is neutral.

A bolder attempt to parry the "Why be neutral?" gambit is due to the political theorist Bruce Ackerman. Let us see whether it works.

The Many-Roads Argument

Ackerman asks us to imagine "that there was one, and only one" view of the world that made neutralism look sensible. He frankly admits that in this case, the effort to put neutralism into practice would be "pretty much an empty gesture" because neutrality would be violated by the argument in its own favor. But now he states that if there is *more* than one path to neutralism, more than one argument that might serve as its warrant, the situation changes. A multiplicity of paths, he says, brings about "a perfect parallelism" between "the role of political conversation within" the neutralist regime, and "the role of philosophical conversation in defense" of the neutralism regime. To illustrate his claim, he surveys "four of the main highways" to neutralism: (1) "realism about the corrosiveness of power"; (2) "recognition of doubt as a necessary step to moral knowledge"; (3) "respect for the autonomy of persons"; and (4) "skepticism concerning the reality of transcendental meaning." He tries to show that any of these highways might be travelled toward ethical neutralism, and "doubtless there are other paths as well."[2]

Does Ackerman's parry succeed in turning back the claim that neutrality is violated by argumentation in its own favor? The answer to this question is "No." Ackerman considers it sufficient to show that arguments for neutrality can be generated by more than one world view or conception of the good. Actually, it would be necessary to show that a warrant for neutrality arose from *every* world view of conception of the good. Otherwise, his claim amounts to saying that those views and conceptions that support neutrality are better or truer than those that do not; and that is certainly not neutral.[3] To put his dilemma in a formula, it isn't enough for Ackerman to show that some roads lead to Rome, that many roads lead to Rome, that most roads lead to Rome, or that our favorite roads lead to Rome. It isn't Rome unless all roads lead there. This brings us to the clinch. Not all roads lead there; therefore it isn't Rome.

But if it isn't Rome, Rome isn't really where any of these roads were leading. We are left with a perplexing problem. Where do they lead? In circles? Onto other roads? Into the abyss? Some of them might even lead to true tolerance. We had better trace them out.

As soon as we begin to do this, we realize that Ackerman was right to suggest that his four highways were not the only roads that people have attempted to travel to neutralism. Indeed, several of the four are really crisscrossing networks of paths that look like solid lines only when we remove our eyeglasses and hold the roadmap at arm's length. "Respect for the autonomy of persons," for instance, is a notoriously ambiguous idea. On closer examination it seems to split into three or four, some of which might equally well have been included under some other super-heading.

Because a finer-grained treatment is necessary, we will try to do without such super-headings. Instead of main highways, I have tried to list converging and diverging footpaths, leaving readers to group and regroup them as they please. Naturally, some of the paths on the list have come from the professional literature of political theory. However, because we are dealing with a broad cultural movement rather than a squabble in the academy, others have been taken from conversation with students, colleagues, and friends, from letters and editorials in newspapers, from the texts and subtexts of televised situation comedies, and from other places too tedious to recount. There seem to be (at least) thirty-nine of them: thirty-nine arguments for ethical neutralism, or, equivalently, against the proposition that any views of what is good for human beings should figure in public policy.

In what follows, each is taken seriously. However, because they are so numerous I list them in the same form in which we usually encounter them—in the form of slogans. To spare some of the tedium, the presentation moves swiftly, though some of the slogans are obviously weightier than others, and to these I usually reply at greater length.[4] Here, then, are the thirty-nine neutralist slogans, the thirty-nine heads of the Hydra.

1. DESPAIRING. Nothing can be done about the ethical standards of the community.[5]
2. UTOPIAN. Something can be done, but not without the total renovation of man and society.
3. CONTEMPTUOUS. Nothing can be done without trusting the state, which is a stupid beast.[6]
4. COMPLACENT. If something is good, it doesn't need a public revelation—the good will always drive out the bad.[7]
5. JURISTIC. To put the force of law behind something as vague as the prohibition of vice subjects people to intolerable uncertainties about the legality of their actions.
6. APPRECIATIVE. More than one way of life is good.[8]
7. SKEPTICAL. No one can know what is really good for human beings.[9]
8. NIHILISTIC. There is no moral truth to be found.[10]
9. KNOWLEDGEABLE. Only I know what's best for me. Certainly the state knows no better.

10. Autodidactic. I don't always know what's best for me, but I'm my own best teacher.[11]

11. Cartesian. Doubt is a necessary step in the individual's pursuit of moral truth.[12]

12. Disestablishmentarian. Government may not pass laws on principles in which citizens are entitled to disbelieve.[13]

13. Shifting Sands. Mores are now changing rapidly.[14]

14. Distant. Lawmakers cannot ascertain the moral judgments of the people.[15]

15. Melting. Legal concern with morality freezes mores as they happen to exist at the moment, whether they are right or wrong.[16]

16. Egalitarian. For lawmakers to concern themselves with ethical matters is inconsistent with having equal concern and respect for all. (Vulgarly: I'm as good as you.)[17]

17. Forbearing. Personal preferences are legitimate grounds for public policy; external preferences are not.[18]

18. Forgetful. In dealing with people who hold different conceptions of the good than ours, the only fair thing is to act as though we can't remember just what our own conceptions of the good are.[19]

19. Nautical. The political community is a raft, not a ship. The object is to stay afloat, not to get somewhere.[20]

20. Privatizing. Since law aims only at the *common* good, it may not touch self-regarding acts.[21]

21. Domestic. A public concern with the ethical well-being of the community would encroach on the educational prerogatives of the family. (Alternatively: of the Church, etc.)

22. Slippery Slope. Allowing ethical motives to enter public policy will inevitably lead to tyranny.[22]

23. Offensive. If an act could be prohibited just because someone took offense to it, nothing would be permitted.[23]

24. Pacifist. Imposing moral standards on a pluralistic community would rupture the peace.

25. Pious. Judging others is a sin.

26. Analytical. Crime and sin are different.[24]

27. Protective. We are not competent to pry into the depths of others' souls.[25]

28. Indulgent. That an act is corrupt is not a sufficient warrant for its regulation; to be regulated, it must corrupt or exploit others.[26]

29. Compassionate. To punish acts that arise from compelling desires is cruel and excessive.[27]

30. Expressivist. People need to be themselves.[28]

31. Developmentalist. People need to *become* themselves.[29]

32. Choosey. People need to develop the capacity for choice.[30]

33. Libertine. Because I have free will, no one may do anything to me without my consent.

34. LIBERTARIAN. Because I have *natural rights*, no one may do anything to me without my consent.[31]
35. CONSCIENTIOUS. People should never be forced to act against their convictions.
36. PARADOXICAL. Good things, by their nature, cannot be imposed. Attempting to impose them deprives them of the character of being good.[32]
37. BALANCING. A good that is imposed may still be good, but because imposition destroys other goods—for instance, liberty—the net change is always for the worse.[33]
38. INDIGNANT. Telling me what to do denies my dignity by making me a means to your ends.[34]
39. AUTOCRATIC. Individuals must be self-legislating; otherwise they are slaves.[35]

An Objection

Unlike Ackerman, most neutralists do *not* think that any road to neutrality will do, and I am likely to be criticized for "failing to take the classical idea of liberal neutrality seriously." One correspondent complains, for instance, that "many of these [39 slogans] are logical entailments of one another," and that by giving an independent rebuttal of each, I "make the idea of ethical neutrality appear more confused than is in fact the case," failing to show that I "really understand" why neutrality has been understood to be such an important principle, "the foundation of liberal politics, law, and policy."

"The missing appreciation of the ideal of ethical neutrality," says my correspondent, "might be phrased something like this":

> Liberal politics is founded on the Cartesian notion that no one is entitled to enforce an idea of the good on another, without irrefutable rational justification. Failing this, the individual is assumed to be the only immanent source of value. Furthermore, the individual is understood to be a moral agent, and to reach full humanity only when the choice of right and wrong is possible. From this is follows that a liberal polity must be neutral among ideas of the good. This implies that to be non-arbitrary, such a polity must rest its policies on known, general, and impartial principles.

I daresay that another theorist might have phrased his sense of my "missing appreciation" in a different way than this. However, this one will do as well as another; the way in which a response can be constructed to this one will show how a response could be constructed to any.

My correspondent's first claim—which is tacit—is that no one can develop an irrefutable rational justification for any idea of the good. This is true, but does not lead where he thinks it does; I would refer him to the discussion of the Skeptical slogan.

Second comes one of the "entailments" he speaks of: that *because* no one can know what is really good, the individual must be the "only immanent source of value." Now this may mean three things. (1) It may mean that individuals are the sole source of what is really good. But this is not a logical consequence of his premise; it is a non sequitur. It may even involve a contradiction, because it is hard to see how individuals could be recognized as the sole source of what is good if we cannot know what good is. (2) The notion that the individual is the "only immanent source of value" may mean merely that because no one's judgments about good and evil can be irrefutably known to be better than those of the individual in question, the individual's judgments cannot be second-guessed. But if no one's judgments about good and evil can be irrefutably known to be better than his, then by the same token no one's can be irrefutably known to be worse. Thus nothing useful follows. As to the general idea that "Only I know what's best for me," I would refer the correspondent to the discussion of the Knowledgeable slogan. (3) Finally, the phrase may intend the Kantian idea that individuals are ends in themselves rather than means to others' ends. If so, then like 1, it simply does not follow from what has gone before. But if it is taken simply as a new premise, then I would refer the correspondent to the discussion of the Indignant slogan.

Now we have another new premise. For "furthermore," the correspondent says, the individual is "understood to be a moral agent, and to reach full humanity only when the choice of right and wrong is possible." I agree that the capacity for choice is good. But in the first place it is again hard to see how the correspondent can maintain this while clinging to his earlier skepticism about the knowability of the good; and in the second place, the goodness of the capacity for choice in no way entails that the state should be neutral about the conceptions of good among which the choice is made. Here I would refer the correspondent to the discussion of the Choosey slogan.

Finally the correspondent says that a polity must rest its policies on known, general, and impartial principles. With this I have no quarrel. But it is a red herring. The only issue is in what way the notions of generality and impartiality are to be interpreted; and I have already given my reasons why they should not, indeed, *cannot* consistently, be interpreted in terms of ethical neutrality. If more were wanted, I would interrogate the correspondent as to what *he* meant by generality and impartiality; depending on the reply, I might refer him to the discussion of either the Disestablishmentarian, the Egalitarian, the Forbearing, or the Forgetful slogan.

We seen, then, that the "missing appreciation" of ethical neutrality that my correspondent has tried to express is vague, weakly reasoned, and unconvincing. More important, though, we see that it is merely a way of arranging a subset of the thirty-nine slogans. For this reason, the most efficient way, first to *clarify* it, and then to *rebut* it, is to deal with each of these slogans as we encounter it.

Efficiency does not always make for pleasant reading. Except for those few who still enjoy scholastic disputations like those of the middle ages, twentieth-century readers will not gladly submit to a thirty-nine-times-extended exercise in objection and refutation. For most I suggest selecting merely a subset of slogans and replies to read, those which are linked together in the particular neutralist apologetic they find most plausible.

The Many Roads Themselves

Now let me keep my promise by briefly examining each slogan. Some are shown to make no good points. Others are shown to make good points, even very good points, that simply do not offer warrants for neutralism. Considerations of great variety are raised in very rapid succession. A number of different kinds and orders of goods are thought of, but especially the goods of character, because these are the one neutralists most frequently say ought not be thought of.[36] The way to keep one's sense of direction in this hail of arguments is to recall the description of true tolerance given in Part One, and see how many of these hailstones are really bricks from that edifice. Let us begin.

1. Against the Despairing Slogan: "Nothing can be done about the ethical standards of the community." The conviction that action is useless may stop *you* from acting; unless I share it, why should it stop *me*? For without trying to do something, how am I to find out whether you are right? Perhaps you think that trying to do anything at all will only make matters worse. In that case, you ought to try a different slogan. For you said that action can do nothing. But if action can make matters worse, perhaps it can also make matters better. At any rate, there is nothing neutral about forbearing to act for fear of bringing about an evil; it presupposes a notion of evil, and (by contrast) of good. The trick is to know when to forbear, and when not to forbear. That is part of true tolerance.

2. Against the Utopian Slogan: "Something can be done, but not without the total renovation of man and society." The objection to the counsels of despair applies here as well—it applies, that is, unless your *real* fear is that a small reform now would derail the ultimate reform that you think our descendants will bring about in the future. We had better examine that. Such a fear is reasonable only if either (a) in order to have virtuous revolutionaries, we must keep them as corrupt as we can until the final moment, or (b) these revolutionaries can found a virtuous society even if they persist in their corruption. Neither assumption is even remotely plausible. To this first argument I would add a second. Everything that is in our power to change is merely a contributing cause rather than the ultimate cause of human wickedness, and reforms that begins from the opposite assumption—the assumption that the ultimate causes of human wickedness really can be rooted out by human action—always end up merely reinforcing its contributing causes. But you don't have to agree with that. The first argument will suffice.

3. Against the Contemptuous Slogan: "Nothing can be done without trusting the state, which is a stupid beast." Often enough, politics *is* both stupid and bestial. But what does it mean to put the well-being of the community on the political agenda? Well-being includes good character. Moreover we wish to encourage good character not only among the ruled, but also among the rulers. Just as some of our institutions were intended in part to make citizens virtuous, so others—for example, representation—were intended in part make rulers virtuous.[37] Maybe they don't. If so, that is an argument for reforming them. There is nothing neutral about that. To find an institution wanting is not to throw out the criteria by which we judge it in the first place. But are you untouched by these arguments? Do you think that the state can *never* be far enough removed from stupidity and bestiality to take an interest in good character? Very well; but then why do you think that the state may be permitted to take an interest in anything at all? Your only consistent position would be anarchism. But that is no barrier to the stupid and the bestial either.

4. *Against the Complacent Slogan: "If something is good, it doesn't need a public revelation—the good will always drive out the bad."* Whether the good drives out the bad, or the bad drives out the good, depends largely on the character of the institutions under which they carry on their competition. This is true whether we are talking about good and bad literature, good and bad scholarship, good and bad money, or any of a great many other things—including, of course, the thing that concerns us at the moment: good and bad ways of life. Is it so foolish, then, to give some thought to the way in which these institutions work?

5. *Against the Juristic Slogan: "To put the force of law behind something as vague as the prohibition of vice subjects people to intolerable uncertainties about the legality of their actions."* Yes, of course, laws with vague objects expose the citizens to manifold and unpredictable miscarriages of justice. But this would be a reasonable objection to the state's concern with the ethical well-being of the community only if both of the following assumptions held: (a) that the only possible expression of such a concern were the criminal prohibition of acts contrary to virtue, and (b) that the only possible mode of such prohibition were a decree that "Everything contrary to virtue is subject to punishment, whether it is listed in the criminal code or not." Both of these assumptions are false; just how wildly false should have been clear in the discussion of the Penal Question in Part One. Could it be that the real reason for the Juristic Slogan is a suspicion that the concept of vice is vague *in itself*—that however we try, we *cannot* specify in just what it consists? If so, then the one who is attracted to the Juristic Slogan should try the Skeptical Slogan instead.

6. *Against the Appreciative Slogan: "More than one way of life is good."* Of course more than one way of life is good! From that it does not follow that no way of life is bad. "But doesn't the diversity of good lives refute the principle of virtue, and confirm the truth of relativ-

ism?" That question is well-asked, and I will repay question for question. You tell me: Does the diversity of good melodies refute the principle of harmony, and confirm the pleasure of noise? On the contrary, the precondition of all diversity in melody is the principle of harmony itself, for all noise is at bottom alike. Wonderful to relate, for us it is the same as for melodies. Only by taking our first tottering steps toward the standard that is the same for us all do we begin to glimpse how wildly different we really are, for what a profusion of works we were made. Do not reproach me with Stravinsky. If a symphony may include discordant passages, that is because it is not a melody, but a story about melodies. Just as a story in words may tell of both good and evil, a story in tones may tell of both harmony and discord. Our pleasure is not in the discord, nor yet in the evil, but in the story.

7. Against the Skeptical Slogan: "No one can know what is really good for human beings." The speaker is usually skeptical especially about the goods of character. But it is by no means clear why truths about these goods are different from truths about any other kind of good or evil; why, for instance, one should be skeptical about the notion that gratitude is good (which might arise from mere socialization), but not about the notion that being burned by fire is painful (which might arise from mere hallucination). What human good is the skeptic trying to preserve by refusing to act on assumptions about what is good for us? In other words, if you really think that no one can know what is good for human beings, how can you be so sure that anything the state does is *bad*? And if you *can't* be sure, then how can you object when the state takes an interest in something that it calls, rightly or wrongly, "the ethical well-being of the community"? If you do object, perhaps you aren't a skeptic after all, in which case you ought to try another slogan. Or perhaps you ought to try a different kind of skepticism. Ancient skeptics subscribed to such a different kind. They did not claim that we cannot know anything at all, but only that our knowledge lacks absolute certainty. For the conduct of life, they proposed acting on whatever principles seemed on rational reflection *most likely* to be true; for often, arguments may be persuasive even though they fall short of being probative.[38] Skepticism of this kind certainly does not bar the state from taking an interest in what seems, to our best judgment, to be the ethical well-being of the community.

So much as to neutralism. But as to the greater theme of this book: we have already seen in a number of places that skepticism is not a support for true tolerance. Though skeptics can be tolerant, their tolerance never flows from what they are skeptical about, but from what they are not skeptical about.

8. *Against the Nihilistic Slogan: "There is no moral truth to be found."* Here the situation is still more clear-cut. Because the nihilist does not believe in moral truth, he cannot possibly raise a moral objection to anything that the state may do. It makes no difference that the moral basis of this particular objection happens to be a conviction that acting on a bogus truth is wrong. Either there is no moral truth, in which case nothing can be wrong; or else something can be wrong, in which case there is moral truth after all.

9. *Against the Knowledgeable Slogan: "Only I know what's best for me. Certainly the state knows no better."* The fact that the individual is in a unique position to know his own strengths, weaknesses, needs, and circumstances deserves weighty consideration in the design of public policy. However, we should not flatter ourselves. No one is so poor as to lack a richly stocked storehouse of self-deceptions, often transparent to everybody but himself. The alcoholic who insists that he is indifferent to the bottle is merely a conspicuous example of the kind of dishonesty with self we all practice inconspicuously. Moreover, even when we do know what is best for us, we do not always pursue it. This is due only in part to pride and weakness of will. Defects in our institutions can actually make our best courses impossible to follow. Then again, without closing off any course completely, they may yet offer all-but-irresistible temptations to ignore the long-range consequences of wrong or foolish choices. The need for circumspection is clear; but to say that none of these circumstances *ever* calls for ethically motivated institutional reform seems merely obstinate.

10. *Against the Autodidactic Slogan: "I don't always know what's best for me, but I'm my own best teacher."* So you are your own best teacher. Very well, but how do you learn? All by yourself, by trial and error? But that method may be misleading. The short-range consequences of our actions may give not the least clue to their long-range consequences; whether they give any clue depends on the character of

the institutions within which our experiments are undertaken. Moreover, while trial and error may teach us the *personal* consequences of some choices, it is much less likely to teach us their invisible effects on those around us. For both reasons it hardly seems good to cut ourselves off from the experiences of others, both contemporary and ancestral. Or do you learn from others after all? But in that case, even if you *are* your own "best" teacher, the *other* teachers must provide a whopping large part of your curriculum. The institutions and circumstances in which we live and move are already, for better or worse, providing an education—an education that is mostly unplanned and unconscious. There is no way to prevent them from doing so. We would be very naïve not to try to shape our circumstances and institutions in just such fashion that they are least apt to miseducate us.

11. Against the Cartesian Slogan: "Doubt is a necessary step in the individual's pursuit of moral truth." Whoever spoke of suppressing doubt? Because the airing of opposing judgments is necessary to the formation of both good judgment and good policy, the citizens of a tolerant republic are permitted to doubt whatever they please. There is no reason to take away this permission just because one of the objects of policy and judgment is the ethical well-being of the community.

12. Against the Disestablishmentarian Slogan: "Government may not pass laws on principles in which citizens are entitled to disbelieve." True tolerance is, it so happens, disestablishmentarian, but this slogan distorts that ism. The slogan comes from the English jurist Patrick Devlin. Lord Devlin suspects that ethical dogmas have their sole warrant in religious dogmas. Citizens are no longer legally obligated to believe in religious dogmas; therefore, he reasons, they cannot be obligated to believe in ethical dogmas.[39] But to repeat: the citizens of a liberal republic are permitted to doubt whatever they please. They may doubt religious dogmas, of course. They may also doubt the principles of ethics. They may doubt whether there is a right of social self-preservation (as Lord Devlin maintains that there is[40]). They may for that matter doubt whether the state is entitled to try to keep them from killing each other, or whether the earth is really round. If the government may not pass laws on principles in which the citizens are entitled to disbelieve, then it may not pass laws on any principles whatsoever—which is to say that it may not pass laws. So the fact that the intention of a law is, or is not, to promote the ethical well-being of the community is quite irrelevant; we had better simply dismantle the government. Then again, doubt as to the wisdom of anarchy is also permitted. Better, then, to dismantle the slogan.

13. *Against the Shifting Sands Slogan: "Mores are now changing rapidly."* The target of this slogan is "moralism"—the view that the state should enforce whatever mores happen to prevail in the community.[41] But this book does not defend moralism; indeed, moralism is just another wing of neutralism. Moralist Patrick Devlin is quite frank about this. His own neutralist credentials were established in the discussion of the preceding slogan. But for some reason Lord Devlin considers it perfectly neutral to assert that societies have a right to survival. This is what prompts his moralism. The survival of a society *as it is understood by its members* requires the preservation of its mores, says he; thus, for him, it makes no more sense to say that we may not punish deviations from community mores than it would to say that we may not punish treason. Now the point of the Shifting Sands Slogan is that in cases where mores are in rapid change, it simply isn't clear what mores the moralist state is supposed to be enforcing. Quite so! But since moralism is a branch of neutralism, this is merely a "hit" by one branch of neutralism against another. As such, it does not concern us.

To distinguish the position of this book from moralism, let me fix meanings for the contrasting terms "mores" and "morals."[42] "Mores" is a common name for custom. "Morality," as the term is used in this book, means patterns of choice, whether customary or not, that express or support true goods in suitable ways. Moralism expects the state to take an interest in mores, and forbids it to take an interest in morality. True tolerance expects the state to take an interest in both— but a primary interest in morality, and at most a derivative and qualified interest in mores.

Why even a derivative and qualified interest in mores? Because mores sometimes have moral content. The great advantage of good mores is that they stabilize social expectations in such a way as to encourage the acquisition of those personal habits of conduct that are the seedbed of virtue. To the extent that mores do have moral content, indeed the state may take an interest in them. But let us not lose everything in a rosy haze. The problem is that *not all* mores have moral content. Some might stabilize social expectations in just such a way as to encourage the acquisition of vice instead of virtue. Therefore (to bring these reflections back to the Shifting Sands Slogan), if mores are shifting, this may from a moral point of view be either good or bad; it may be something that the state should encourage, or something that it should discourage. Generally speaking, such a shift should be encouraged just when two conditions are satisfied. First, the shift from the old mores to the new must bring with it a gain in true moral content. But second—on the chance that the old mores had some true moral content too—this moral gain must be sufficient to offset the moral *loss* occasioned by the temporary confusion of expectations and disruption of habits.[43]

14. Against the Distant Slogan: "Lawmakers cannot ascertain the moral judgments of the people." In the first place, it is probably no more difficult to ascertain the moral judgments of the people than it is to ascertain their judgments as to anything else—for instance, their prudential judgments as to whether the deployment of antiballistic missiles would be more likely to deter or to encourage nuclear attack by other nations. Odds are, in fact, that moral judgments are easier than other kinds of judgments to ascertain, because here we often have mores as an index.

I could stop here—but it is very important to be clear about the reasons for which we are interested in the moral judgments of the people anyway. We may be interested in them because, though wrong, they accidentally serve to constrain the government in the execution of certain bad policies, or in the execution of good policies in certain bad ways; then again, we may be interested in them because of the possibility that they are right. Other things being equal, the possibility that a moral judgment of the people is right ought to be taken *most* seriously when it does not appear to be self-serving and is of very long standing.

I am sure that the reason for the first of these two conditions is clear. As to the second, venerability is no light matter; the considerations that ought to weigh in judgment may very well exceed the knowledge or experience of any one generation or several generations. The reason for saying this is to reemphasize that the state should never be interested in mores for their own sake; rather that it should have a derivative and qualified interest in them for the sake of morality.

15. Against the Melting Slogan: "Legal concern with morality freezes mores as they happen to exist at the moment, whether they are right or not." This slogan would be true only if we erased the distinction between morality and mores that was made several paragraphs earlier. Nothing more need be said.

16. Against the Egalitarian Slogan: "For lawmakers to concern themselves with ethical matters is inconsistent with having equal concern and respect for all." This slogan is inspired by Ronald Dworkin, with those arguments I have already dealt in Part One. Several points, though, may be added here. As H.L.A. Hart reminds us, Dworkin himself admits that his equal-concern-and-respect rule can be given another interpretation besides the neutralist.[44] According to this second interpretation, treating persons with equal concern and respect *requires* rather than prohibiting reference to a conception of what is good for human beings. It does this because it means simply *treating each person as a good human being would wish to be treated.* Dworkin himself, of course, prefers the first, the neutralist, interpretation. His objection to Hart's second interpretation seems to be that its outlook is punitive; he reads it as though it meant merely *punishing the person when he lapses into fault*—that is all he can imagine that the good person would want.

Now as we saw in Part One's discussion of the Penal Question, true tolerance, too, objects to narrowing the public moral focus to the content of the criminal code. But there is no need to take Hart's second interpretation as doing this. Punitive readings can be averted by rephrasing it as a requirement to treat each person *as a desire to achieve* his moral good would lead him to wish, subject to all other counsels of tolerance.[45] Because he desires to achieve his moral good, he naturally desires all appropriate helps to that goal.

All of this, of course, is merely refinement of what is said above: we can look after the ethical well-being of the community and still regard each person with equal concern and respect.

17. Against the Forbearing Slogan: "Personal preferences are legitimate grounds for public policy; external preferences are not." The point this slogan misses is that in ethical choice, we have no business with the public's "preferences" at all; the matter with which we must deal is their *judgments.* A judgment is a resolution of a truth claim on the basis of argument. Divorced from judgment, a preference is merely a wish or want.

There is only one case in which preferences deserve consideration for their own sake. This is when judgment deems the alternatives of equal moral value. In just this case, Dworkin may be right to think that only personal and not external preferences are legitimate grounds for public policy. However, personal and external preferences are *equally* illegitimate when the alternatives are unequally ethical.

18. Against the Forgetful Slogan: "In dealing with people who hold different conceptions of the good than ours, the only fair thing is to act as though we can't remember just what our own conceptions of the good are." This slogan represents the degeneration of an originally good idea. John Rawls notes that justice is impartial. Yet he sees that when we try to draw up principles that capture our sense of justice, we face overwhelming temptations to tinker with their provisions in order to achieve personal advantages. The fact that these temptations are often unconscious only makes them more difficult to defeat. There would be only one way, he says, to empty them of their power. Each of us[46] would have to pass behind a "veil of ignorance" that temporarily erased his memory of everything that differentiated him from other human beings. Of course, we can't really do that; however, nothing keeps us from imagining it. How *would* we agree to distribute the things in which individuals ordinarily seek personal advantages, if we continued to care about our respective lots in life but no longer remembered what they were? Whatever answer we would give this question, says Rawls, ought to bind us in the real world, where we do remember what our respective lots are.

One difficulty of this approach lies in deciding which of our memories the veil of ignorance should erase. Obviously, we should forget our names, to what families and social classes we belong, and how much we have in our bank accounts. What else? But the answer to this question has already been given: each of us is to forget whatever differentiates him from other human beings. Very well, then, says Rawls: forget your wants, your tastes, your personalities, and your convictions, both ethical and religious. Forget that you have ever thought you tasted the love of a woman, the love of a parent, the love of a friend, the love of a child, or the love of God. All of these are personal idiosyncrasies that may keep you from acting impartially toward those who do not happen to share them.

Contrary to common conception, this is not the step that commits Rawls to attempt ethical neutrality. For their emptied memories are not the only sources of information that he permits parties behind the veil of ignorance to possess. If they were, the parties' deliberations about the principles of justice would grind to a halt. Though each is *deprived* of the knowledge of what differentiates him from other human beings, each is *supplied* with the knowledge of what he and all the others have in common. For instance, Rawls has us make each fellow forget whether he is a buyer or a seller, but teach him what buyers and sellers are, along with the principles of economics. Obviously this strategy poses certain problems. Just what the principles of economics are is a matter of controversy, the outcome of which will certainly affect the deliberations of the parties. But because we can't simply teach them nothing, Rawls tries hard not to flinch. We teach them the *true* principles of economics, he says, and as his argument proceeds he makes many assumptions as to what these principles are.

Now this may work very well, so long as we are consistent. We will have to make each fellow forget what he likes to eat, but teach him the true principles of nutrition and palatability; make him forget his social class, but teach him the true principles of sociology; make him forget his wants, but teach him the true principles of the human good; make him forget his religion, but teach him the true principles of his relation with God; and so on. Without explanation, Rawls draws the line at sociology—and *that* is the step that commits him to attempt ethical neutrality. Of course, this step is completely arbitrary.

Moreover, it doesn't work. For if Rawls were really neutral about the nature of the human good, the deliberations behind the veil of ignorance would grind no less quickly to a halt than were he neutral about the principles of economics. Consequently, he teaches the parties behind the veil of ignorance a theory of the human good after all—one which defines as "rational" that plan of life which maximizes an individual's net balance of satisfactions over the course of his entire life.[47] Although he tries to preserve the appearance of neutrality even here, calling this merely a "thin" theory of the good, it is not thin at all. In fact it is a full-blown version of hedonism, differing from classical hedonism only in minor technical assumptions that do not concern us here.[48]

In conclusion: (a) when rendered consistent, the rationale of "justice as fairness' that is offered for the Forgetful Slogan does not evade, but actually generates a demand for a full-blown theory of the human good; and (b) without recognizing it, those who offer this rationale depend on such a theory already.

19. Against the Nautical Slogan: "The political community is a raft, not a ship. The object is to stay afloat, not to get somewhere." What does it mean for the political community to "stay afloat"? Does it mean to enjoy social peace? To preserve its independence from would-be conquerors? To maintain a certain minimum standard of material consumption? To keep pace in world markets? To guarantee its mores against change? Choose whichever you like, or another: obviously you *are* making a claim about what is good for human beings—the more so because in saying that "staying afloat" is the *only* legitimate object, you are making it your ultimate concern: you are saying that the good you have chosen is worth any price in other goods, human or divine.

And what is meant in saying that political community has no need to "get somewhere"? Many cultures, characters, and callings are consistent with virtue; we may sail to whichever we please, but we had better not simply drift or we may run aground on a cay where they fly the skull and crossbones. If, on the other hand, all it means to say that the political community has no need to "get somewhere" is that one opposes utopianism (as one well may, considering the Platonic origins of the metaphor of the "ship"), so be it; but as seen already, that does not commit us to ethical neutralism.

20. Against the Privatizing Slogan: "Since law aims only at the COMMON *good, it may not touch self-regarding acts."* The problem here is not with the slogan, but with its abuse. If the slogan flatters the hopes of neutralists at all, it does so only by exploiting the ambiguity of the expression, "may not touch." What does it mean to say that the law "may not touch" self-regarding acts? If it means that the law may not have any effects on the environment in which people choose to commit or forbear from such acts (and in which their habits of choice are developed), that is simply impossible. If it means that the law may have such effects, but not intentionally, it is unreasonable—for since the effects will ensue willy-nilly, may we not give thought to their direction? But if we take the slogan to mean that the law may neither *command nor prohibit* acts of the self-regarding kind, then I think that its counsel is wise—wise, moreover, for the very reason it gives: that such acts would affect only the good of the individuals committing them, and not the common good.

Accepting this does not commit us to the proposition that there really are such things as self-regarding acts, however. Even if there are, we saw in Part One that their apparent number is probably greatly inflated by the Millian rules for counting them—rules that refuse to acknowledge the effectuality of any of the kinds of "effects" that neutralists don't like to think about. However, we may at least say this: that the more trivial seem the effects of an act on individuals other than the agent (bearing in mind that not even the gauging of triviality is ethically neutral), the greater the burden of justification that the state ought to have to overcome in order to command or prohibit the act.

That was the main point. I should like to add, though, that the classical analysis of self-regarding acts is instructive. While the classical philosophers do assume that they exist, they make an interesting distinction. Their argument runs like this. Every virtue has the property that *some* of the acts that express it promote the common good. But every virtue also has the property that some of the other acts that express it do not. Consequently, if only those acts may be commanded that promote the common good, then *some* acts of *every* kind of virtue may be commanded, but not *all* acts of *any* kind of virtue may be commanded.[49] Following this train of reasoning, it would never occur to a classical philosopher to claim that the "harm principle" is ethically neutral. Rather, one selfsame argument justifies *both* the harm principle, *and* the law's interest in the virtue of the citizens!

21. Against the Domestic Slogan: "A public concern with the ethical well-being of the community would encroach on the educational prerogatives of the family." A public concern with the ethical well-being of the community is not an *alternative* to recognizing the educational

prerogatives of the family; rather, recognition of the educational prerogatives of the family is *part of* the ethical concern of a liberal
regime. There are good reasons for this. The most important is that
except for rare cases—as when a father is sexually abusing his daughter—
the family will see to the nurture and primary ethical instruction of the
child better than anyone else could. René König, a sociologist, observes of orphanages that

> [c]are is commonly taken to give such institutions a homelike character; neverthe-
> less, it seems to be clear that the younger children in particular thrive less in these
> homes, even when they are better organized in every respect (hygienically, med-
> ically, psychologically, pedagogically) than in an average family.[50]

Even aside from family failures, there are two good reasons why
recognition of the educational prerogatives of the family should not be
public policy's only expression of ethical concern. The first reason is
that besides the family's ethical instruction, the young experience a
competing socialization in television, in advertisement, in the mass
youth culture of centralized high schools, in entertainment, and (as we
say) on the streets. Can the family compete without help from the
schools, and without restraints on the forms that the competing socialization may take? There is every reason to think that the competing
socialization is already becoming more powerful than the family's
teaching.

The second reason why recognizing the educational prerogatives of
the family cannot be public policy's only expression of ethical concern
is that adults, too, continue to be socialized into certain patterns of
conduct and traits of character. They are influenced by the presence or
absence of a full employment policy, by the particulars of labor law, by
the eligibility requirements for public assistance, by the overall design
of family law, and by a host of other things that are in the public
domain. And, of course, what he can learn about his parents' world is
part of the socialization of the child as well. The conclusion of all this
has already been stated. It is that public policy's other expressions of
ethical concern can complement its recognition of the educational
prerogatives of the family, rather than competing with it.

*22. Against the Slippery Slope Slogan: "Allowing ethical motives to
enter public policy will inevitably lead by tyranny."* Actually, two

different kinds of tyranny must be considered in assessing this slogan. The first, totalitarianism, is an affair of regimented bureaucrats with visions of utopia and a lot of help from the secret police. Right after the next steel mill, they expect to produce the Man of the Future, and to that end put every social institution that they do not simply pulverize under the most minute and intrusive supervision that their resources in technology and personnel allow. Obviously, totalitarian social policy is just brimming with moral motives. One can understand why ethical neutralism may seem a good defensive strategy. But what will such a strategy really achieve? I have already intimated (and later demonstrate) that there cannot be such a thing as an ethically neutral social policy; then again, there *can* be such a thing as official hostility to whatever is *admitted or recognized* to be ethical in motive. Unfortunately, the consequences of such hostility are not hard to anticipate: demoralization and ethical decay of the citizenry.

More's the pity, that merely sets the stage for the other kind of tyranny, the more old-fashioned kind, whose aim is merely to gratify the various lusts of the ruler. For the more disorderly and vice-ridden the citizens have become, the more apt they will be to welcome his accession to power. And even this is not the end of the story. The collapse of the republic also opens the skylight of opportunity for totalitarian revolution from above. That is why Lenin, who was no slouch, looked forward to the degeneration of the bourgeois democracies.

What can we conclude from this? Totalitarianism, whether of the Left or Right, represents a flawed conception of what is good for human beings, and a political style that is seemingly adapted to achieving it. Liberalism represents a different conception, and this different conception entails a different style. Unless we thought that the liberal conception of the good contained a greater share of truth than the totalitarian, it is hard to see why we would oppose totalitarianism in the first place. Shouldn't our *mode* of opposition reflect the *reasons* for our opposition? We do our cause no service when, shocked by illiberal proposals for the ethical regimentation of the citizenry, we cry out in dismay and indignation, "God save us from the abomination of ethics!" Rather we should argue that the wrong moral goals are being promoted—or (if that is not the problem), that the right goals are being promoted, but by means that will end in their destruction. Nor should we think that it is enough to voice a protest. Armed with a liberal understanding of the ethical well-being of the community, we should always be prepared to ask our adversaries, "Why not *these* goals, why not *these* means, instead?"

23. *Against the Offensive Slogan: "If an act could be prohibited just because someone took offense to it, nothing would be permitted."* The proposition expressed by this slogan is true. But saying that the state has a legitimate interest in the ethical well-being of the community is different from saying that the state should make war against everything that offends, for as explained above, mores and morality do not always coincide. Three cases should be distinguished. 1. If something that ought to offend does offend, the mores which call it offensive deserve encouragement. Hence the ministers of justice are entirely right to echo the public revulsion for infanticide, which would still be wrong even if the public did not think it so. 2. If something offends that ought not to offend, the mores which call it offensive should be discouraged. Hence municipal authorities should do all that they can to discredit the anger of whites who heap scorn and abuse upon blacks attempting to settle down in previously all-white neighborhoods. 3. There are also such things as acts that are morally wrong when they offend in certain ways, but morally innocent otherwise. Public nudity is a good example. In itself, it is morally innocent. Disapproval of nudity in tropical cultures where it is the norm would be grossly misguided. Yet in a culture like our own, in which public nudity is not the norm, the spectacle of a young man or woman walking downtown without any clothing would arouse lust and provoke disorder. Though public nudity is not intrinsically blameworthy, these circumstances would make it blameworthy, the more so if lust and chaos were what were intended.

We need a name for the subject of this third case. Let us call "decent" the acts that are right, when they are right, *just because* they are also in conformity with mores. Now a problem arises. For, as ethical wrongs, violations of the standards of decency should not be ignored. Yet change in standards of decency is not wrong; therefore, apparently, the law should not resist such change. Obviously, penalizing violations of the standards of decency does resist such change. So should such violations be penalized, or not? The solution to this conundrum, I suggest, is that although change in standards of decency is not wrong in itself, it becomes wrong if it is rapid. The reason is that not all segments of the community shift at the same time. Discrepant rates of change produce a situation in which acts to which some people give no thought whatsoever produce unbearable temptations for others who cannot avoid witnessing them except by staying at home with the shutters drawn. For instance, a man who objects to skimpy clothing might, in principle, recognize that the motives of a woman who is wearing it are entirely pure. His objection may arise from concern, not for her moral good, but for his. To call the man lecherous is not only uncharitable, but misses the point. He knows that he is. That is why he objects to her display: he does not *want* to be inflamed, and wishes that someone would take thought for his effort. The point is charmingly made by a conversation between two characters in one of the thousand classics we no longer read, Bunyan's allegory *The Pilgrim's Progress*, published in 1678:

> Now Mr. Feeble-mind [original meaning: faint-heart], when they were going out of the door, made as if he intended to linger. The which, when Mr. Great-heart espied, he said, "Come, Mr. Feeble-mind, pray, do you go along with us. I will be your conductor, and you shall fare as the rest."
>
> *Feeble-mind.* "Alas, I want [need] a suitable companion. You are all lusty and strong, but I, as you see, am weak. I choose, therefore, rather to come behind, lest, by reason of my many infirmities, I should be both a burthen to myself and to you. I am, as I said, a man of weak and feeble mind, and shall be offended and made weak at that which others can bear. I shall like no laughing, I shall like no gay attire, I shall like no unprofitable questions. Nay, I am so weak a man as to be offended with that which others have a [moral] liberty to do . . ."
>
> *Great-heart.* "But, brother," said Mr. Great-heart, . . . [y]ou must needs go along with us. We will wait for you, we will lend you our help, we will deny ourselves some things . . . for your sake. . . . We will be made all things to you rather than you shall be left behind."[51]

True tolerance, we see, cuts both ways: Feeble-mind endeavors to tolerate those who enjoy conduct which he knows to be innocent but which his feelings cannot bear, and Great-heart endeavors to tolerate Feeble-mind's weakness, denying himself many innocent things so that Feeble-mind will not be left behind. In this mutuality, we are witnessing the co-dependence of the great virtue of tolerance and the great virtue of courtesy. Such mutuality can be encouraged if the law tolerates marginal, but only marginal deviations from contemporary standards of decency. A policy like this permits changes in the content of these standards, but holds such changes to a reasonable pace. I note without elaboration that it requires firm resistance to the technique of shock that earns so much money in advertising, fashion, and entertainment.

24. Against the Pacifist Slogan: "Imposing moral standards on a pluralistic community would rupture the peace." Whether "imposing moral standards" on a pluralistic community would rupture the peace would depend on what we were trying to "impose," by what means, and upon whom, wouldn't it? Besides, social peace is itself a moral concern—and it ought not be the ultimate concern. Most of us, for example, would agree that the ending of *de jure* segregation of whites and blacks was worth a certain price in social peace. Most of us would say the same thing about resistance to tyranny. For peace is like liberty: it is good because it nourishes and preserves higher goods; and therefore it is good only to the extent that it preserves these higher goods. The advisability of various ethically motivated public measures must simply be weighed case by case, with social peace receiving due consideration along with other moral concerns.

25. Against the Pious Slogan: "Judging others is a sin." This slogan is Christian in origin, for which reason some readers may wish to skip to the next. No one would repeat it except from theological motives, and I will make no pretense that it is possible to give a theologically neutral reply. In fact, I accept the theological proposition that the slogan expresses. However, it has absolutely no bearing on whether the Christian can acknowledge that the state has a legitimate concern with the ethical well-being of the community. To "judge," in Christian theology, is to commit a bundle of terrible sins (to which "religious" people are unfortunately more strongly tempted than are others): to dare the fancy that one can "earn" God's favor, to indulge the conceit that one can know other souls as He knows them,[52] and to arrogate to oneself the office of measuring the depth of others' sin. Virtue itself can become an idol. Jesus was gentle and merciful to the prostitutes, tax-collectors, and thieves who followed after him, but had harsh words for the teachers of the Law—the good men of their day, secure in the fastidious scruples. Yet he said that he had not come to abolish the Law. It expresses—though in a way to which self-righteousness blinds us—the inexorability of love. We cannot know who is deepest in sin, but we can know something of what sin is, and that the inexorable love of God cannot abide its continuation. He permits us eternal exile from this love—if so we choose—but according to the Christian teaching, if we want *Him* we must give that love its way. That is why the complete form of the slogan under discussion is not "Do not judge," but rather, "Hate the sin, but love the sinner." This is not a prescription for the intolerance that all too often tries to cut a niche for itself in love. But neither is it a prescription for ethical neutrality.

26. *Against the Analytical Slogan: "Crime and sin are different."* To be sure they are; and in a truly tolerant regime, no particular sect has a privileged position under the laws.[53] But if citizens may strike positions in ethical policy on whatever basis they find persuasive, may they not do so on the basis of their religions? Yes; but even in most theocracies, not all divine obligations are considered civilly enforceable, and not all civil obligations are considered deductions from divine law. Against whom, then, is this admirable slogan directed?

27. *Against the Protective Slogan: "We are not competent to pry into the depths of others' souls."* Right again. And this is why, although the state may *encourage* citizens to take certain attitudes in the depths of their hearts, only overt acts should be made the objects of command or prohibition. That is a counsel of tolerance. Note well: although the slogan expresses skepticism about our knowledge of souls, skepticism *as such* is not what produces the conclusion just stated. Obviously the speaker thinks he knows *something* about souls: enough to be sure that ignorant tampering can harm them. And that knowledge is not ethically neutral. It presupposes a conception of harm.

28. *Against the Indulgent Slogan: "That an act is corrupt is not a sufficient reason for its regulation; to be regulated, it must corrupt or exploit others."* This slogan was inspired by the publication of the Wolfendon Report in England during the mid nineteen-fifties.[54] Let us be clear from the outset that the slogan is not neutral. One prong involves "corruption," the other "exploitation." Obviously both terms designate moral concepts.

The slogan's failure to achieve the neutrality to which it seems to aspire is not its only incoherency. As to its first prong, even adults who give full and mutual consent to their mutual acts of immorality are "corrupting" each other, because each in the other contributes to habits which are inimical to virtue. So to draw the line at corruption is to draw no line at all.

The "exploitation" prong is much more interesting. Just how does it cut? Some of the sponsors of the slogan would say, for instance, that pimps are exploiters but prostitutes and their clients are not.[55] Whether this is right is hard to tell. Presumably exploitation means getting someone to go along with something—something that hurts him with respect to some good—either by preying on his weakness of character, or by confronting him with the prospect of a seemingly greater hurt should he refuse. One might say: "If this is what exploitation is, surely the objection to it must lie in the fact that the person is hurt, not in the particular means by which he was lured into consenting." But if the allurement is itself destructive of some good, maybe not. To make sense of the concept of exploitation, one would first have to develop an account of the good that an individual's power of giving and withholding consent is supposed to help him achieve;[56] then pair it with an account of the psychology of temptation; and finally use this to *distinguish* between circumstances in which people are competent to use their power of giving and withholding consent for their own good, and circumstances in which they are not. The result—which is beyond the scope of this book—might greatly illuminate true tolerance.

29. Against the Compassionate Slogan: "To punish acts that arise from compelling desires is cruel and excessive." Of course, the object of this reply is not to attack compassion itself, but only to attack the slogan. Now that slogan may be interpreted in two different ways.

According to the first interpretation, the compulsiveness of the desire from which an act arises is a reason to exempt it from prohibition. This may mean, for instance, that no murders could be prohibited but those committed in cold blood; by contrast, murders of passion and murders arising from mental disorders would have to be permitted. Or it may mean that we *would* be allowed to entertain proposals for prohibiting passionate and deranged murders, but that we would have to back them up with stronger arguments than for the prohibition of cold-blooded murders. To express these possibilities is sufficient to refute them, so let us proceed to the second interpretation.

The second tells us that the compulsiveness of the desire from which an act arises has nothing to do with whether it ought to be prohibited, but *does* deserve consideration at the time of sentencing. What kind of consideration? One possible reply is that acts arising from compelling desires should not be sentenced at all. This, however, makes nonsense of the previous decision not to exempt such acts from prohibition, so we must consider other possible replies. The other possibilities are (1) that the compulsiveness of the desire from which an act arises is a reason for imposing a lighter sentence than would otherwise be imposed, and (2) that the compulsiveness of the desire from which an act arises is a reason for imposing a *different kind* of sentence than would otherwise be imposed. Reply 1 is clear enough; reply 2 might mean, for instance, that convicted murderers who happen to be insane would be sentenced to spending time in a mental hospital rather than spending time in prison. This does make sense. But—does it lend support to ethical neutralism? No. For it is not a suspension of moral judgments— rather it rests on them: on judgments about culpability and mercy.

That was the main point. But it is worth adding that this slogan provides a good example of the arbitrariness of most arguments about law and ethics. One is very likely to hear the slogan proposed as an argument against criminalizing sexual acts that involve sadism, masochism, cacophagy, and so forth. Yet one never hears it proposed as an argument against criminalizing heartfelt murder. Even an ethical neutralist, one suspects, would be shocked to hear a judge say, "Young fellah, I know you beat, raped, and killed that old lady in a real mean way, but you wanted to do it so durn bad that I think I'll let you off." The fact is that the compulsiveness of desire has no bearing on the criminalization of any act whatsoever—sexual, homicidal, or what have you. Which acts should be criminalized and which should not must be settled by appeal to other criteria. Moreover we should avoid confusing the question of whether to criminalize an act with the question of whether to discourage the act by other means.

30. Against the Expressivist Slogan: "People need to be themselves." Taken in one sense, this slogan is harmless enough. Clearly, every Frank does need to know (1) that there is a continuing agent in the world with that name; (2) that it has a certain history; (3) that this history interlocks with the histories of other continuing agents that are nonetheless distinct from it; (4) that it is accountable to those others for what it does; and (5) that it is he. But from this it hardly follows that everything about Frank is all right.

31. Against the Developmentalist Slogan: "People need to become themselves." If this means that Frank needs to grow into a life that suits his unfolding gifts and responds to his calling, how could there by any objection? The astonishing diversity of human gifts and callings needs no further emphasis here; and no one is in a better position to learn what his own are, if only he will make the attempt. But without also developing the excellences of character, he is apt to gain little good by that knowledge. For in that case, it is more likely that he will misuse those gifts, or pervert that calling. This insight is hardly neutral.

Objection: "Not my gifts and calling only, but my excellences too are different from yours." To be sure, the temperament of a police officer requires certain excellences that the temperament of a teacher does not—and conversely. But we are speaking here of the more general excellences requisite to being a good human being—those denominated human virtues. One who is in doubt about these should consult the replies to the skeptical and nihilistic slogans.

32. Against the Choosey Slogan: "People need to develop the capacity for choice." My only objection here is that the slogan employs the term "capacity" in an ambiguous manner. More clearly expressed, the idea behind this slogan seems to be that people need to develop the deeply ingrained habits by which they will call upon *all* of their capacities and passions in just those ways that aid, prompt, focus, inform, and execute their moral choices instead of clouding them, misleading them, or obstructing their execution. But as explained in the first part of this book, that is precisely the definition of the virtues. Thus the slogan hardly prohibits the state from taking an interest in the moral well-being of the community.

33. Against the Libertine Slogan: "Because I have free will, no one may do anything to me without my consent." "Free will" — one of the several senses of the term, "autonomy"—signifies freedom from causal determination, not freedom from moral obligation. The idea that the free will thesis is meant to buttress is that others may hold me responsible for what I do, not that they may do nothing without my say-so.

This may be made more clear by explaining how the free will thesis functions.

We begin with the idea that to hold a person responsible for unavoidable acts is an injustice. But when is an act "unavoidable"? C.L. Stevenson suggests that an act is unavoidable just if it would have taken place no matter what the agent had chosen.[57] This way of looking at things certainly makes sense of the judgment that when I force your finger against the trigger, your firing the gun is unavoidable; however, it doesn't go far enough. For choice is also an act. Can *that* act ever be unavoidable? Perhaps your finger could be "forced" against the trigger by your genes and socialization. The free will thesis is simply that in normal human beings, *this is never the case*; that perhaps not all of the influences, but at least the decisive influences on the will originate in some way with itself.

I need not consider here whether the free will thesis is coherent or correct. Suffice it to say that if it is accepted at all—as it certainly is by the speaker of this slogan—then free will is the name of a condition, not of a moral imperative. The mere fact that whenever I am not under external constraint, I can be held responsible for what I do, tells nothing about what other people may properly do to me.

A possible objection: "This 'mere' fact is just a bit *too* mere. From the thesis that I have free will, *plus* the thesis that free will is something good to have, *plus* the thesis that whatever is good to have should be preserved,[58] a prohibition of whatever is destructive to my free will *can* be derived." Granted! But nothing in these three theses justifies the *universal* ban on intervention that the slogan expresses. In fact, taken together they actually justify certain interventions. For they imply, for example, not only that no one may inject me with will-destroying drugs, but also that I may be kept from injecting them into myself. (The harm principle might forbid this, but that is another story.) And needless to say, by virtue of the second thesis—that free will is something good to have—neither these prohibitions nor these interventions would be ethically neutral.

34. Against the Libertarian Slogan: "Because I have NATURAL RIGHTS, no one may do anything to me without my consent." Of course, this slogan is always understood to mean that no one may do anything to me without my consent, except to enforce his *own* natural rights. The question, really, is what kind of things these natural rights are; until we know that, we cannot know whether they imply such a strong prohibition.[59] By the most general definition, a natural right is a claim against others that they must honor in order for me to achieve my natural good. Already it looks as if even should the slogan be true it could not possibly be ethically neutral. But someone might protest that I am moving my proof too quickly, so let us slow down.

Where do I get this business about a natural right being a claim that must be honored in order for me to achieve my natural good? For the usual definition is rather different. It comes from social contract theory, and holds that a natural right is a claim that would necessarily be honored in the "state of nature"—that is, in the condition in which it is natural for human beings to live. Now what do we mean by calling a condition "natural"? Do we mean that we have always been in it? But then it settles nothing, because we are in it now, and here we are, arguing about what claims we ought to honor. Do we mean that we began in it? Notwithstanding the dramatic devices that people who speak of the state of nature like to employ, whether we did begin in it (for that matter, whether we have ever been in it) seems irrelevant to use to which we might wish to put the idea in the here-and-now. What, then? If the idea of a "natural" condition is to have any use at all, we should define it as a condition in which we have *everything that the complete development of human beings requires*—though not necessarily everything that we would like. I do not think that this is what Thomas Hobbes had in mind when he spoke of the state of nature, but that is the worse for Hobbes. It does seem to be what John Locke had in mind when he did.

Hobbes and Locke aside, what this shows is that *coherent* claims about natural rights can always be traced back to some conception of the human good. And that takes us back to the more general definition of natural rights with which I began.[60] For instance, debate about John Locke's theory should begin with whether his characterization of the conditions for the complete development of human beings was correct—in particular, whether he was right to think that human character could properly develop under circumstances in which there was no government, but in which individuals acknowledged all and only the claims that he called natural rights and natural duties. So: The claim is vindicated that even if the Libertarian Slogan were to turn out true, it would not be ethically neutral.

But by the way—*is* it true? It may be, but I suggest that there is, so far, no particular reason to think so. Locke's own analysis of the conditions required for the complete development of human beings was neither complete, nor in all respects persuasive. Moreover, most theorists who posit natural rights today do so in an attempt to evade discussing these requirements.[61] Rights and duties do, of course, constitute a very general language for talking about how the community should be ordered. Perhaps any way of ordering the community whatsoever could be expressed in terms of suitably fashioned rights and duties. But this will give no satisfaction to libertarian sloganeers, who have something like Locke's rights in mind, but who do not wish to speak of duties at all.

35. Against the Conscientious Slogan: "People should never be forced to act against their convictions." Some readers will find this slogan simply ridiculous. I discuss it only under the duty laid upon me by having heard it so often. Imagine a fellow who has conscientiously reached the conclusion that the world would be a better place if only several dozen people were removed from it by his own hand. After his eighth murder, the police surround him and cry, "Drop the gun or we'll shoot!" Taken literally, the slogan enjoins the police to disperse and let the poor man go about his homicidal business. Someone might object that murder is different from other acts; that conscientious conviction cannot justify murder, but that it can justify (for instance) bigamy. That may be so, but if it is, the reasons for heeding conscientious convictions in some cases but not in others must rest on other grounds than conscientiousness itself. One must already have decided one of the following: that the good that a law is intended to serve is not a true good; that it is, but that there is some defect in the way in which the law serves it; or that the law serves the good flawlessly, but at the same time subverts other goods of equal or even higher order. These, obviously, are ethical judgments.

36. Against the Paradoxical Slogan: "Good things, by their nature, cannot be imposed. Attempting to impose them deprives them of the character of being good." This is true in some senses, and of some goods; but it is not true in other senses, or of other goods. These qualifiers are crucial. (1) The slogan is true of virtue, because virtue involves choice not incidentally, but essentially. If we could somehow "program" people to live exactly as they ought—if through drugs, surgery, genetic engineering, sensory deprivation, torture, or some other means we could turn them into beings that thought, felt, and acted in every respect exactly as perfect virtue would prompt, but without choice, and hence without the possibility of acting otherwise — they would become merely very "correct" animals. Of the specific goods that appertain to being human, they would be utterly deprived. By God's mercy, we do not yet have the power to inflict this loss upon ourselves, but not for want of reaching; and although we do not yet have the power to empty people of the power to choose, we have long had the power to warp and disable it. Attempts to inculcate good character in children or adults through harsh and frequent punishment, deprivation of solitude, and the cultivation of dependence produce a variety of effects, including cravenness, poverty of imagination, help-lessness, self-pity, bleakness, a tendency to manipulate, and a strange union of resentment and obsequiousness; they produce all these, but they do not produce virtue. (2) On the other hand, the slogan is *not* true if taken to mean that *all* means of ethical education destroy the goods of character. If choice is the soul of virtue, then the soul of good moral education is training in choice itself — not in the sense that we want people to acquire all-purpose conceptual ingredients with which they can whip up their own unique versions of what counts as right and what counts as wrong; we cannot be "value-free," and should not try to be. Rather, in the sense that we want them to develop the qualities of character that will help them to recognize wrong, and embrace right, with as little external guidance as possible, knowingly and freely.[62] To "impose" virtue is to destroy it; but one may nourish it without im-posing it. (3) So far the only human good that this reply has considered has been virtue. But to the goods that are, so to speak, "beneath" virtue, the slogan seems to have no application whatsoever. For in-stance, health is good for my body whether it does my character any good or not. I do not say that health should be "imposed" on me, but it would be just as good—*for my body*—if it were. If it ought not be, the reason escapes the Paradoxical Slogan, because it involves some other good than health itself.[63] (4) Moreover, we should keep in mind that the acts of each person affect the good of others. It may or may not do a man's character any good to force him to face, say, his respon-sibility to pay child support for the children of a previous marriage. I think that it does, but be that as it may. The point I should like to make is that it does *them* a lot of good, and that is nothing to sneeze at. (5) Finally, an objection: "By 'imposing' the responsibility to pay child support, are we crippling the man's power of choice, are we wiping out his chances of developing the genuine virtue of freely undertaken responsibility?" The answer, I think, is clearly "No." We are speaking of such incentives, under the laws of the various states,[64] as being spared the garnishment of wages or a night in the local jail. Between drugs, surgery, genetic manipulation, sensory deprivation, or torture, on the one hand, and garnishment or brief confinement on the other, there is a qualitative difference. We ought to be able to discriminate between threatening a conventional punishment, and destroying the will.

37. Against the Balancing Slogan: "A good that is imposed may still be good, but because imposition destroys other goods—for instance, liberty—the net change is always for the worse." Even as stated, this slogan is anything but ethically neutral. Moreover it is incorrect. One cannot know whether the net change will be for the better or for the worse until one considers the circumstances of the exchange. We may add that loose talk about "liberty" does not help much; liberty is truly a good, but only a prima facie good. We want liberty *because* it helps us to achieve our purposes, *because* it helps us to learn what our purposes should be, *because* it gives us a field of exercise for qualities of character that we have developed or that we want to develop, and so forth. Not all forms of liberty support all these goods on all occasions.

38. Against the Indignant Slogan: "Telling me what to do denies my dignity by making me a means to your ends." This slogan is another expression (this time neo-Kantian) of the same confusion between a moral judgment as to how you should act, and a mere preference about the matter, which was explained in the discussion of the For-bearing Slogan (though the speaker there was a kind of utilitarian).[65] Except by way of this mistake, there is no way to portray your holding me to an objective moral standard as a way of making me a means to your own ends. For if the alleged moral standard really is objective, it transcends the ends you happen to have; what it tells us both is the ends we ought to have.

And there is really no way for the neo-Kantian to escape such standards, however hard he may try. Suppose that you and I make a business agreement, and I propose to formalize it in a contract that both of us would sign. Which of the following is the correct description of my proposal? (1) I am trying to make you a means to my end of carrying out the deal without being cheated. (2) I am trying to *keep* you from making *me* a means to *your* own end of cheating. Given nothing but the concepts of an "end" and of a "means," both descriptions are equally plausible. Why, then, do we unhesitatingly accept the second description and reject the first? Clearly, because we are using not only the concepts of an "end" and of a "means," but also an independent moral standard to tell us which is which.

39. Against the Autocratic Slogan: "Individuals must be self-legislating; otherwise they are slaves." This idea, even more purely than the last, comes originally from Kant.[66] To explain it, and to explain what it does or does not have to do with neutralism, requires an expedition through difficult country, all the more difficult because we must travel quickly.

First, what did Kant mean by "self-legislation"? Certainly not what neutralists mean by it. He meant that I should act only on those maxims that I could will to be universal laws. The reasoning for this conclusion seems to have had four parts. (1) Every genuine obligation is universally binding. (2) Once made impartial—that is, divested of purely personal elements—the content of every will is both identical to every other, and morally trustworthy. (3) Therefore, asking myself in an impartial mode *what I can will* to be universally binding is a reliable method for discovering what really *is* universally binding. (4) Acting on such discoveries is a liberation from "slavery" in that it frees me from bondage to my impulses, and from every authority but reason: freedom is obedience to known rational duty.

The difficulty comes in putting Kant's method for discovering the shape of duty into practice. An example will make this clear. Kant said that no one should break a promise for personal advantage. The reason is that no one could will the maxim "Anyone may break his promise for personal advantage" to be a universal law. But why not? Evidently because it would destroy the good of trust, and that would involve a contradiction—for no one could will the destruction of such a good as that. Now this is crucial. What it shows is that application of the Kantian method for discovering the shape of universally binding obligation *entails* a universally valid conception of the good.

Unfortunately, Kant did not think that it did, and this is where neutralism comes back in. He said that when the will gives heed to a conception of the good, it does not act freely. This would be true only if the conception in questions were *not* universally valid. Therefore, it is just one more way, along with the others that we have considered, of confusing true moral judgments (which *are* universally valid) with mere preferences or impulses (which are not).

If we follow Kant in this confusion—as most neo-Kantians do— then we certainly won't want to give any conception of the good a privileged role in the discovery of duty. But how can we *avoid* giving it such a role? If we try to get rid of conceptions of the good altogether, the will cannot possibly have any idea what it *can* will any longer. So we can't do that. The alternative, these neo-Kantians think, is to allow people to have conceptions of the good after all, but to put each of these conceptions on the same footing.

Of course, the result of this is that each person may come up with his own set of maxims; what I can will to be a universal law given *my* conception of the good is probably *different* from what you can will to be a universal law given yours. That produces a problem. The universal application of laws that contradict each other, all at the same time, is obviously impossible. What is to be done about this? One can't very well go on calling himself a neo-Kantian if he drops the requirement of universality altogether. So instead, he reverses it. That is, he regards us as universally obliged *not* to propound universal laws (except the one propounded in this sentence).

Doing this reverses everything else, too. What used to be called free obedience to universally binding obligations is now called "slavery" because it requires adhesion to a universally binding conception of the good, and what used to be called slavery because it kept us in bondage to our impulses is now called "self-legislation." That is how amoralism masks itself as ethical philosophy. And all for nothing! For neutralist are not *really* evenhanded among all conceptions of the good after all; rather, they say in Kant's name that what Kant called slavery is precisely what is good for human beings.

Notes

1. *Patterns of Moral Complexity*, chap. 3; quotations are from 68.

2. These quotations are from *Social Justice in the Liberal State*, at 369, but the discussion of the highways themselves begins earlier, at 361. I have omitted some of Ackerman's italics.

3. Oddly, Ackerman not only *admits* that not all roads lead to Rome, but makes a point of stating that each of the "four main highways" that he describes can be travelled away from Rome as well as toward it, e.g., that those who deny the existence of transcendental meaning might just as easily choose nonneutrality as neutrality. This he seems to regard as an additional proof that argumentation for neutrality does not violate neutrality. (Ibid., at 361). All it really shows is that his highways are not highways after all. A premise which is equally consistent with either of two other premises, themselves inconsistent with each other, cannot plausibly be called a "highway" to one of them.

4. Citations are offered for the slogans most carefully argued in the professional literature. For those that tend to be tossed off as self-evident truths, citations seem unnecessary; this includes especially those heard in classroom teaching, in conversations with colleagues, at professional meetings, and so forth.

5. This slogan might have support in certain versions of the Reformed theology of "utter depravity." For another related idea, see Holmes' "bad man" theory of the law, expressed in "The Path of the Law," *Collected Legal Papers*. Contrast Montesquieu, *The Spirit of the Laws*, bk. 6, chap. 17.

6. Ackerman thinks that the state, if not already stupid and bestial, will soon become so if allowed to take an interest in the ethical well-being of the community. See *Social Justice in the Liberal State*, 361–65.

7. The writers of *The New York Times*, for instance, shocked by the spectacle of on-stage sexual performance, optimistically concluded an editorial entitled "Beyond the (Garbage) Pale" with the thought that "the insensate pursuit of the urge to shock, carried from one excess to a more abysmal one, is bound to achieve its own antidote in total boredom. When there is no lower depth to descend to, ennui will erase the problem." For discussion, see the items listed in the bibliography under Berns (1971), Bickel, Cohen, Kaufmann, and McWilliams. My phrasing for the Complacent Slogan was suggested by a disclaimer in McWilliams, at 38.

8. Something like this is behind much of the praise for cultural pluralism; however, cultural pluralism can be supported for other reasons as well.

9. Different versions of skepticism are illustrated by Louis Henkin (1963), cited in chapter 2, note 14, and former Judge Robert H. Bork, cited in chapter 3, note 2. Because skepticism and nihilism are sometimes difficult to distinguish, see also note 11, following.

10. We don't have to go to Nietzsche to find an example of ethical nihilism; something like it is found in Holmes' essays "Ideals and Doubts" and "Natural Law," both of which are found in his *Collected Legal Papers*. The latter is particularly interesting, in that Holmes seems to derive his utter doubt in ethical truth from his utter faith in the truth of a pantheistic view of the universe. Another version of ethical nihilism is treated respectfully by Ackerman in *Social Justice in the Liberal State*, 368–69: "There is no moral meaning hidden in the bowels of the universe." However, he conflates this with simple skepticism: "But can we *know* anything about the good?"

11. Perhaps the best source for this notion is John Stuart Mill, *On Liberty*, chap. 3.

12. See, for instance, Ackerman, *Social Justice in the Liberal State*, at 365–67 (one of the passages discussed earlier) as well as 162 (in the context of the education of children).

13. This idea is implicit in Lord Patrick Devlin's more specific remarks about morality and Christianity, in "Morals and the Criminal Law," *The Enforcement of Morals*, 5.

14. The first of John Hart Ely's two reasons for rejecting the idea that society's "widely shared values" should "give content to the Constitution's open-ended provisions" is a categorical statement that "in fact there is no consensus to be discovered" (*Democracy and Distrust*, 63). Ruth Gavison uses the shifting sands idea to develop a new variation on Plato's Noble Lie: one of the many uses of the constitutional doctrine of a right to privacy, she says, is that judges may use it to protect behavior when social consensus against it has disintegrated but legislatures still refuse to legalize it ("Privacy and the Limits of Law," 452–53). Still another twist is found in Wilson Carey McWilliams' untitled response to Walter Berns' "Pornography v. Democracy: The Case for Censorship." McWilliams says at 34–35 that while the censorship of pornography might be a good idea, it becomes "an inappropriate remedy" once mores prohibiting it have already fallen apart; at that point it is, "too late." Finally, see my discussion of the use of the Shifting Sands slogan in *Marvin v. Marvin*, a case decided by the California Supreme Court in 1976, in chapter 2, note 36 (for background, note 35).

15. Ely, in *Democracy and Distrust*, 64, states that even if social consensus does exist, it is not "reliably discoverable." He is expressing doubt only about judicial attempts at discovery, but the same doubt is often expressed about legislative attempts.

16. This slogan originates in the debate sparked by Devlin's *The Enforcement of Morals*. See the bibliographic entries under H.L.A. Hart (1059, 1963, and 1967), Eugene V. Rostow, and Richard Wollheim. Devlin's own theory was strongly influenced by James Fitzjames Stephen's *Liberty, Equality, Fraternity*.

17. This idea has been discussed earlier in the book in connection with Ronald Dworkin, "Liberalism" and *Taking Rights Seriously*; for critique, see H.L.A. Hart, "Between Utility and Rights," esp. 91–97. The bracketed form of the slogan figures prominently in Ackerman, *Social Justice in the Liberal State*.

18. Ronald Dworkin again—and again, discussed previously. For a closely related idea, see how David A.J. Richards uses the term "personal tastes" in "Unnatural Acts and the Constitutional Right to Privacy: A Moral Theory," 1324.

19. This idea is formalized in John Rawls' device of the "original position," which helps him to flesh out the idea of "justice as fairness." See *A Theory of Justice*, secs. 4, 20–30.

20. The most elegant version of this slogan is found in Michael Oakeshott, "Political Education," in *Rationalism in Politics and Other Essays*. At 127: "In political activity . . . men sail a boundless and bottomless sea; there is neither harbour nor shelter nor floor for anchorage, neither starting-place nor appointed destination. The enterprise is to keep afloat on an even keel; the sea is both friend and enemy; and the seamanship consists in using the resources of a traditional manner of behaviour in order to make a friend of every hostile occasion." His allusion is to the Platonic analogy between the City and a ship, although Plato puts the analogy to very different uses (see *Republic*, 6.488a–89c).

21. See the discussion in Part One of Mill's brand of the "harm principle."

22. In the popular mind this slogan is probably most firmly associated with the public rhetoric of the American Civil Liberties Union.
23. Like the Melting Slogan, this slogan originates in the debate touched off by Lord Devlin. See note 16 above.
24. For discussion and references, see A.R. Louch, "Sin and Crimes."
25. Perhaps this is what Marshall Cohen has in mind where, at 41 in his untitled response to Berns, "Pornography v. Democracy: The Case for Censorship," he calls the regulation of obscenity "an attempt at thought control."
26. "Fornication," said Mill in *On Liberty*, "must be tolerated, and so must gambling; but should a person be free to be a pimp, or to keep a gambling house? The case is one of those which lie on the exact boundary between two principles; and it is not at once apparent to which of the two it properly belongs." The quotation may be found in *John Stuart Mill: Three Essays*, 121.
27. Louch, in "Sin and Crimes," comments on the prevalence of this view. Yet in "Justifications for Paternalism," Donald H. Regan argues that the compulsiveness of an act is a warrant for intervention, not a bar to it.
28. The increasing sway of this slogan is reflected in First Amendment jurisprudence by a tendency to say less and less about freedom of "speech," but more and more about freedom of "expression." For discussion, see Joel Schwartz, "Freud and Free Speech."
29. This is closely related to the Autodidactic Slogan, and is best exemplified by the same text: Mill, *On Liberty*, chap. 3.
30. In "Defending Liberalism," William Galston shows how this idea is involved in some of the most well-known versions of ethical neutralism. But see the distinction between the capacity to choose and the capacity to exercise choice in Douglas Husak, "Paternalism and Autonomy."
31. Robert Nozick embraces a version of this idea, but connects it with the idea expressed in the Indignant Slogan. See *Anarchy, State, and Utopia*, 28–30.
32. Ackerman, *Social Justice in the Liberal State*, presents this idea at 367–68. For critique, see Galston, "Defending Liberalism," sec. 2.
33. One example of this idea may be found in Michael D. Bayles' argument that sanctions for self-regarding acts cannot be justified by benevolence, because the sanctions are themselves harms ("Criminal Paternalism," 183–84). Of course, this argument is also an instance of the idea behind the Indulgent Slogan.
34. Nozick, *Anarchy, State, and Utopia*, at 30–31: "Side constraints upon action reflect the underlying Kantian principle that individuals are ends and not merely means; they may not be sacrificed or used for the achieving of other ends without their consent." Later on the same page, Nozick seems to reverse himself, admitting that it is literally impossible so to constrain acts toward any person that "he is not to be used for any end except as he chooses"; but at 33, he cuts the Gordian knot by adding that "political philosophy is concerned only with *certain* ways that persons may not use others; primarily, physically aggressing against them." The addition, of course, brings Nozick much closer to Mill than to Kant. For an argument against the Indignant Slogan from a jurist who approaches ethical neutralism from another direction, see Oliver Wendell Holmes, "Ideals and Doubts." Against Kant's maxim, says Holmes, "I rebel at once. If we want conscripts, we march them up to the front with bayonets in their rear to die for a cause in which perhaps they do not believe. The enemy we treat not even as a means but as an

obstacle to be abolished, if so it may be. I feel no pangs of conscience over either step, and naturally am slow to accept a theory that seems to be contradicted by practices that I approve." This quotation is found in *Collected Legal Papers*, at 304.

35. The most radical interpretation of this idea is found in Robert Paul Wolff, *In Defense of Anarchism*. For critique, see Husak, "Paternalism and Autonomy," 36–38.

36. To be sure, there seems something paradoxical in being less sure that intrinsic goods are goods than that merely prima facie goods are goods. The solution of the paradox is that if one does not believe that intrinsic goods are goods, he has no means of recognizing that the goodness of prima facie goods is only prima facie. In his view, their goodness *is* intrinsic.

37. To make representation work in favor of virtue and talent rather than against them, the Federalists established two desiderata. The first was that electoral districts should be large. This, they thought, would increase the likelihood that in any given district, someone with enough virtue and talent for the job could be found, and at the same time make it difficult for an unscrupulous candidate to tempt the possibly feeble virtue of the electorate through bribery and other wicked arts. (See *Federalist* No. 10, paras. 15–19, as well as the second sentence in para. 21.) The second demand was that terms of office should be relatively long. In many of the states, elections were held annually. The Federalists argued that this carried accountability to a fault. It neither gave the electorate enough time to take the measure of those whom it had elected, nor gave those whom it had elected enough time to fortify their virtue and talent (such as they had) with experience. (*Federalist* Nos. 52 and 53, as well as No. 62, esp. para 10.) To be sure, James Madison did not dwell much on the subject of virtue; these passages represent a few of the occasions on which he remembered himself.

38. This may be fruitfully compared with the Augustinian maxim that to understand anything, one must first believe something. Augustine, *On Free Choice of the Will*, sec. 6.

39. This is the fundamental premise of his argument in *The Enforcement of Morals*.

40. See the discussion of the following slogan.

41. Compare "communitarianism."

42. H.L.A. Hart had much the same thing in mind when he distinguished "positive morality" from "critical morality," although the presence of the same noun in both of his terms may still leave some confusion. The distinction is fundamental to his argument in *Law, Liberty, and Morality*.

43. For parallel observations see Aristotle, *Politics* 2.1268b–69a, and Thomas Aquinas, *Treatise on Law* (a portion of the *Summa Theologica*), q. 97, art. 2. I have discussed this in "Liberal Conservatism, Conservative Conservatism, and the Politics of Virtues," an essay in *The Nearest Coast of Darkness*.

44. Hart, "Between Utility and Rights," at 91–97.

45. In fact, at one point Dworkin uses an almost identical formula himself, but fails to notice the significant difference between it and the other. He sets the two formulae cheek-by-jowl in "Liberalism," at 127: "The second theory argues . . . that the content of equal treatment cannot be independent of some theory about the good for man or the good life, because treating a person as an equal means treating him the way the good or truly wise person would wish to be treated. Good

government consists in fostering or at least recognizing good lives; treatment as an equal consists in treating each person as if he were desirous of leading the life that is in fact good, at least so far as this is possible."

46. Actually he assumes that only representative individuals do this, but the results are the same.

47. *A Theory of Justice*, at 416. Surprisingly, this fundamental commitment is often overlooked.

48. I compare Rawlsian with classical hedonism in *The Resurrection of Nature: Political Theory and the Human Character*, at 57.

49. For this line of argument, see Thomas Aquinas, *Treatise on Law*, q. 96, art. 2. Aristotle probably means the same thing in *Nicomachean Ethics* 5.112b, where he explains one of the senses of justice as complete virtue, "not in an unqualified sense, but in relation to our fellow men." The quotation is taken from page 114 of the edition listed in the bibliography.

50. König, "Sociological Introduction [to the family]," 42–43.

51. Bunyan, *The Pilgrim's Progress*, 263.

52. See the discussion of the Protective Slogan.

53. Full defense of this point must await Part Five. Religious tolerance does present complexities that do not arise in other fields of tolerance. This is because one's ultimate concern claims superiority to the claims of any possible political regime. Nevertheless, Part Five will demonstrate that religious tolerance and religious conviction do not necessarily exclude each other, and may even depend on each other.

54. The same report coined the oxymoron which is now current on both sides of the Atlantic, "private morality."

55. Compare Lord Devlin's arguments in "Morals and the Criminal Law," *The Enforcement of Morals*, 11–13.

56. See the discussion of the Paradoxical Slogan.

57. The view of "unavoidability" that I attribute to Stevenson is an inference from his analysis of "avoidability," found (among other places) in his influential works *Ethics and Language* and *Facts and Values*. According to Stevenson, A's action was avoidable if, and only if, had A made a certain choice which in fact he did not make, his action would not have taken place. However, whereas I use the idea as a prelude to the free will thesis, Stevenson tries to use it to escape the need for the free will thesis. He does not see any need for the next step I take in the text.

58. This third thesis might better be called an "understanding" since it seems to express an analytic truth.

59. The amount of confusion prevailing on this topic is stupefying. Robert Nozick, for instance, vacillates between two distinct notions of rights in *Anarchy, State, and Utopia*. According to one, they are claims that cannot be violated. According to the other, they are violable by anyone who pays adequate compensation. While Nozick's critique of Rawls is driven by the former, his own theory is driven by the latter.

60. Compare A.R. Louch, "Sin and Crimes," at 84: "The libertarian has the bad habit of abdicating morality to his opponent. . . . No doubt the libertarian is right in rejecting the pressures of moral zealots on the law; but this is not because he has himself eschewed a moral view of the law."

61. For instance, whereas Locke thought that it really was natural for human beings to live in anarchy, Nozick (who makes much of the Lockean account) merely begs the question by treating "anarchy" and "state of nature" as synonyms.
62. See the discussion of education and nurture in Part Three.
63. See the discussion of the next slogan.
64. Unfortunately, the states also differ widely in the diligence with which they apply these incentives.
65. One who had accepted Ronald Dworkin's critique and agreed to stop "double counting."
66. The best single source for Kant's theory is his *Groundwork of the Metaphysics of Morals*.

5

An Exploded View of Neutrality

Choice, by its nature, is never neutral. To opponents of neutralism, this is common sense. Unfortunately neutralists and their opponents have little sense in common. What seems obvious to the latter seems merely a sign of misunderstanding to the former. The difficulty, I think, is that the term "neutrality" has so many different meanings. A neutralist can usually accuse his opponent of speaking in excessively vague terms; and should his opponent become more exact, the neutralist can often say in perfect truth, "Oh, but by neutrality I mean something different than that." Even critics of neutrality in one sense often turn out to be its defenders in another sense for which they may not use the same word. A conclusive proof that neutrality is impossible would have to be completely general, while somehow, at the same time, avoiding vagueness.

To present such a proof is the purpose of this section. Because the proof depends on classification, it resembles an "exploded view" of a crankshaft, household appliance, or electronic children's toy such as those used by assemblers and repairmen. Everyone has seen diagrams of this kind. Of course, because an exploded view shows all of the parts that are normally hidden, it never (despite its fidelity) looks much like the object it is meant to depict. This argument has much the same quality. For because it picks the term "neutrality" into thirteen very technically worded meanings, it deprives us of the immediate appeal of saying that "Choice, by its nature, is never neutral." In return for that loss, we gain the power to communicate with those for whom the sagacity of this saying isn't "immediate" in the first place—and obviously it isn't immediate for *any* of the neutralists in law, government, or the academy.

An exploded view keeps us from talking past each other. With it, one can point to each meaning of neutrality in turn and say, "I mean *this*." And in the end, the privilege of uttering the saying about choice is recovered, except that now it stands as a conclusion instead of a supposedly self-evident premise.

The "parts list" on which the exploded view is based originates with this book. However, the helpfulness of picking the term "neutrality" into these thirteen component senses was suggested to me by the plethora of coarser distinctions already current in the literature of the subject: for instance between "causal" and "intentional" neutrality, "positive" and "negative" neutrality, and "substantive" and "procedural" neutrality.[1] Unfortunately the arguments based on those coarser distinctions have been inconclusive. That is why the distinctions offered here are much more finely grained: to prevent any kind of ethical neutrality whatsoever from slipping through the net.

The Senses of the Term

The term "neutrality" is used in some ways that do not concern us. For instance, when Herbert A. Wechsler proposed "neutral" principles of Constitutional law, he meant only that the reasons given for any judicial decision should be general enough to transcend the outcome of the particular case.[2] Although this is sometimes confused with ethical neutrality,[3] Wechsler himself realized that it has nothing to do with it. Indeed it seems thoroughly unobjectionable. In what follows, when we use the term "neutrality" we mean only ethical neutrality.

Broadly speaking, neutrality may be regarded as a property of a *policy*, as a property of a *debate* over policy, as a property of *rules for the final choice* of policy, or as some combination of these properties. Each of these senses may be further divided and subdivided. Still more senses may be constructed from permutations and combinations of old senses, although I do not catalogue these. Because I want to make this demonstration as convenient for the reader as possible, I begin with an outline, then discuss each of its lowest-level entries. For convenience, I italicize the heading of each lowest-level entry. In addition, I use the term "iff" to mean "if and only if," just as it is used in mathematics and logic.

I. Neutrality of Policy

  A. Neutrality of Anticipated Impact

    1. *Abstract.* A policy is called "neutral" iff its anticipated effects are equally desirable, no matter the conception of the good by which this desirability is evaluated.

    2. *Individualistic.* A policy is called "neutral" iff its anticipated application to a person is unaffected by the particular conception of the good that the person holds.

  B. Neutrality of Language

    1. As to Content

      a. *Egalitarian.* A policy is called "neutral" iff the language in which it is expressed conveys equal esteem for every conception of the good.

      b. *Prohibitive.* A policy is called "neutral" iff the language in which it is expressed does not convey esteem for *any* conception of the good.

    2. *As to Structure.* A policy is called "neutral" iff the language in which it is expressed does not include any terms or classifications the application of which would require an understanding of any conception of the good.

II. Neutrality of Debate

  A. *Blind.* Debate is called "neutral" iff policymakers refuse to give any consideration to whether the anticipated effects of policies under consideration are desirable (as evaluated by any conception of the good whatsoever).

  B. *Recursive.* Debate is called "neutral" iff it is limited to *policies* that are also neutral, in one of the senses listed under division I.

III. Neutrality of Rules for Final Choice

  A. As to Policymakers

    1. Nonrandom

a. *View-regarding*. Final choice of policy is called "neutral" iff the weight assigned a policymaker's vote does not depend on the conception of the good that he holds.

b. *Fitness-regarding*. Final choice of policy is called "neutral" iff the weight assigned to a policymaker's vote does not depend on his fitness to make decisions (by whatever conception of the good this fitness may be evaluated.)

c. *Conduct-regarding*. Final choice of policy is called "neutral" iff only those are allowed to vote whose conduct during *debate* is also neutral, in one of the senses listed under Division II.

2. *Random*. Final choice of policy is called "neutral" iff the choice among alternatives is made as in a lottery, rather than by voting. The alternatives themselves may nevertheless be given either equal or unequal weights, just as they may be in voting procedures.[4]

B. As to Alternatives

1. *Blind*. Final choice of policy is called "neutral" iff the weight assigned to an alternative in the choice procedure (whatever kind of choice procedure this is) does not depend on whether the anticipated effects of its implementation are desirable (by whatever conception of the good this desirability may be evaluated).

2. *Recursive*. Final choice of policy is called "neutral" iff only those *policies* may be enacted that are also neutral, in one of the senses listed under Division I.

As I mentioned before, the outline yields exactly thirteen senses of the term, "neutrality," having nothing in common except an effort to get rid of the influence of all conceptions of the good. These thirteen senses are the outline's thirteen lowest-level entries—I.A.1, I.A.2, I.B.1.a, I.B.1.b, I.B.2, II.A, II.B, III.A.1.a, III.A.1.b, III.A.1.c, III.A.2, III.B.1, and finally, III.B.2. If we convert the outline into a tree diagram, they are the thirteen tips of its branches. The higher-level

FIGURE 5.1

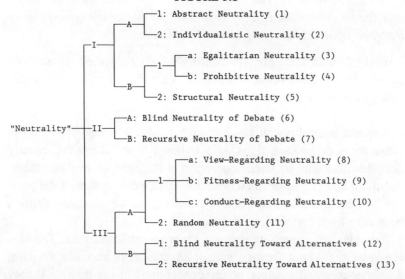

entries in the outline are needed only to show the logical relations among all of these senses of "neutrality," and by so doing, to assure the reader that they are mutually exclusive and exhaust the possibilities. However, because the task has now been accomplished, we may restrict our attention to the thirteen themselves. Since no further reference to the outline is necessary, I henceforth refer to the thirteen by the abbreviated names and parenthetical numerals shown in the diagram above, instead of by their cumbersome outline designations. These names sometimes resemble the names of neutralist slogans discussed in the previous section, but they are not meant to recall them.

For the convenience of the discussion, at each step I discuss several of the thirteen senses of neutrality at a time. The argument depends on two different kinds of logical moves—sometimes one, sometimes the other. In each, something is shown about the state of affairs contemplated by a given sense of the term "neutrality." One kind of move is to show that the state of affairs could not be brought about at all. The other is to show that whether or not it were brought about, it would not succeed in doing what it is supposed to do—in somehow suspending the relevance of conceptions of the good. Either of these logical moves justifies saying that neutrality in the sense in question is impossible.

Sense 1: Abstract Neutrality. "*A policy is called 'neutral' iff its anticipated effects are equally desirable, no matter the conception of the good by which this desirability is evaluated.*"

Sense 2: Individualistic Neutrality. "*A policy is called 'neutral' iff its anticipated application to a person is unaffected by the particular conception of the good that the person holds.*"

Abstract neutrality can be dealt with easily. It is unachievable because there is no such thing as a policy whose effects are equally desirable no matter by what conception of the good we evaluate them. Anything that can be deemed desirable by one conception of the good can also be deemed undesirable by another. So we eliminate abstract neutrality from further consideration.

Individualistic neutrality presents a more complicated case. The idea is that we should not deny individuals advantages or impose upon them disadvantages just because of the conceptions of the good that they happen to hold. Certainly nothing prevents us from following such a rule; but it presents other difficulties. Let us warm up by considering whether following it would be desirable.

At first it seems that it would be. For instance, certainly it would be wrong to deny welfare payments to poor people whose views about the good agree with the opposition party, while granting them to poor people whose views about the good agree with the party in power. On the other hand, certainly it would be *right* to deny elementary school teaching appointments to individuals who profess the goodness of sexual relations with children, while granting them to otherwise qualified people who profess no such belief. The question (to take a leaf from constitutional jurisprudence) should be whether the pattern of penalties and rewards bears a rational relationship to a legitimate governmental purpose; and whenever we speak of legitimate purposes, we must have recourse to conceptions of the good. So individualistic neutrality is not desirable.

But even supposing that it were desirable, would it *deserve* to be called a form of neutrality—would it really "neutralize" conceptions of the good? For even were it proper after all to ignore people's conceptions of the good in order to decide whether to confer advantages or disadvantages upon them, the fact is that conceptions of the good come back like homing pigeons when we try to decide *what counts* as an advantage or a disadvantage. There are two possibilities here. If we are to judge which effects of a policy count as advantages and which as disadvantages *according to the conceptions of the good held by the affected individuals*, this is as much as to reinstate the requirement of abstract neutrality—which we have already found to be impossible. On the other hand, if we are to judge which effects of a policy count as advantages and which as disadvantages *according to the conceptions of the good held by its makers*—for instance, as though policymakers were to regard health as good, enact a health policy, and then decree that its applicability to any individual would be unaffected by whether the individual himself cared about being healthy—well, this is certainly something we can do, but what is "neutral" about it?

Sense 3: Egalitarian Neutrality. "A policy is called 'neutral' iff the language in which it is expressed conveys equal esteem for every conception of the good."

Sense 4: Prohibitive Neutrality. "A policy is called 'neutral' iff the language in which it is expressed does not convey esteem for any conception of the good."

Neutrality as to content—whether egalitarian or prohibitive—is easy to deal with. In every social status quo, particular conceptions of the good are held in esteem while others are held in disesteem. The attitude of a content neutralist recalls Pontius Pilate: he wants to wash his hands of the matter, to say "I shall neither influence nor be influenced by the prevailing distribution of esteem." One hand-washing strategy is to express equal esteem for every conception of the good; the other is to express no esteem at all for any.

Now there are two difficulties with this. The first is that the very intention of neither influencing nor being influenced by the prevailing distribution of esteem needs justification, but it can be justified only by recourse to particular conceptions of the good. One might, for instance, argue that one should not be influenced *by* the prevailing distribution because it esteems what ought not be esteemed and fails to esteem what ought to be esteemed, and that one should not *influence* the prevailing distribution because however wrong it may be, the good of social cohesion is achieved by customary understandings and not by pure reason. I do not endorse these particular arguments, nor claim that no other arguments could be offered in their place. I only assert that some such arguments are necessary, and that all such arguments must rely on conceptions of the good.

The second difficulty is that it is impossible to *keep* the language of public policy from having an influence on the prevailing distribution of esteem and disesteem. Government is a socializing agent. To the extent that people are impressed with its wisdom they will model their judgments after its own. To the extent that they hold it in contempt their judgments will be shaped by reaction. Let the language of its policies express equal esteem for every conception of the good; this will have the appearance of a judgment that every conception of the good is equally estimable. Let the language of its policies express no esteem for any conception of the good; this will have the appearance of a judgment that every conception of the good is equally inestimable. In either case, the message is that one's conception of the good is a matter of indifference, and this message cannot help but alter the status quo.

Altering the status quo is defensible only if the status quo *ought* to be altered. But just as no argument *against* the alteration of the status quo can be made without recourse to particular conceptions of the good, so no argument *for* its alteration can be made without recourse to particular conceptions of the good. We see then that there is nothing neutral about either egalitarian or prohibitive "neutrality."

Sense 5: Structural Neutrality. "A policy is called 'neutral' iff the language in which it is expressed does not include any terms or classifications the application of which would require an understanding of any conception of good."

Structural neutrality is merely a matter of form. It has no interest for the ethical neutralist unless this form is connected with substance: unless it *abolishes the influence* of conceptions of the good in matters of policy. Thus to show that structural neutrality were really neutral, we would have to show that it promoted neutrality of policy in one of the other, substantive senses of the term. These other senses are neutrality of anticipated effects (sense 1, abstract neutrality, and sense 2, individualistic neutrality), and neutrality of content (sense 3, egalitarian neutrality, and sense 4, prohibitive neutrality).

However, structural neutrality *couldn't possibly* promote neutrality in any of these other four senses, because, as we have already shown, each of them is incoherent in itself; either because the state of affairs that it describes is impossible, or because the state of affairs that it describes is possible but does not do what it is supposed to do—does not suspend the relevance of conceptions of the good after all. Structural "neutrality" enters the same logical drain that they do, and for the same reasons.

Sense 6: Blind Neutrality of Debate. "Debate is called 'neutral' iff policymakers refuse to give any consideration to whether the anticipated effects of policies under consideration are desirable (as evaluated by any conception of the good whatsoever)."

Sense 7: Recursive Neutrality of Debate. "Debate is called 'neutral' iff it is limited to POLICIES *that are also neutral, in one of the senses listed under Division I."*

Recursive neutrality of debate can be banished right away, because the senses of neutrality to which it "recurs"—senses 1 through 5—have been sent away already. Blind neutrality of debate presents a different case.

On the face of it, it is gibberish. For to prohibit policymakers from considering whether the anticipated effects of their policies are desirable is to take away the only reason for which we set them to making policies in the first place. Some ethical neutralists, however, would reject this line of reasoning. They would say that whether the anticipated effects of a policy are desirable is beside the point; that what ought to concern us is whether the policy is *right*. In opposition to "teleologists" who maintain that the rightness of right actions has to do with their relationship with what is good for us, they maintain the "deontological" thesis that whatever the rightness of right actions has to do with, it has nothing to do with their relationship with what is good for us. And although this comports oddly with the alleged opposition of neutralists to "moralism"—well, it does have a nice reek of honest moral sweat about it. It suggests disinterestedness.

But all the sweating is for nothing. The fact is that the distinction between so-called teleologists and so-called deontologists is artificial and misleading. The terms "right" and "good" depend on each other in much the same way as the terms "space" and "dimension"; no clear sense can be given to either one without the other. This is the place to repeat the "Why?" gambit mentioned much earlier in this second part of the book. Whenever anyone professes that something is right, ask "Why?" To the reply, ask "Why?" again. Eventually (unless the professor scurvily takes refuge in an infinite regression), the answer will involve a conception of what is good for human beings.

Assumptions about the good lurk around every neutralist corner. Even disinterestedness must be, in some sense, a good—a good of character—or promoting it would be unintelligible.[5]

Sense 8: View-Regarding Neutrality. "Final choice of policy is called 'neutral' iff the weight assigned a policymaker's vote does not depend on the conception of the good that he holds."

Sense 9: Fitness-Regarding Neutrality. "Final choice of policy is called 'neutral' iff the weight assigned a policymaker's vote does not depend on his fitness to make decisions (by whatever conception of the good this fitness may be evaluated)."

Sense 10: Conduct-Regarding Neutrality. "Final choice of policy is called 'neutral' iff only those are allowed to vote whose conduct during debate is also neutral, in one of the senses listed under Division II."

Sense 11: Random Neutrality. "Final choice of policy is called 'neutral' iff the choice among alternatives is made as in a lottery, rather than by voting. The alternatives themselves may nevertheless be given either equal or unequal weights, just as they may be in voting procedures."

After debate is over, we come down at last to the final choice of policy. How can we make our final choice procedure neutral? Two strategies for doing this have to do with how we treat the policymakers. The nonrandom strategy is to call for a vote, but make sure that the rules about who votes and how much their votes count are uninfluenced by conceptions of the good. View-regarding, fitness-regarding, and conduct-regarding neutrality—senses 8, 9, 10—come under this rubric. The random strategy is to recognize that voting procedures cannot be neutralized, and throw the final outcome to chance instead. This corresponds to sense 11.

All three nonrandom senses can be mowed down with a single stroke of the scythe. For it is hardly "neutral" to prefer the opinions of one group of policymakers over the opinions of another merely because the first group contains more votes.[6] What reasons could we have for doing so? Perhaps we have a high regard for domestic tranquillity—we would rather count ballots than bullets. But that reflects a conception of the good. Perhaps we view majority rule as a hedge against tyranny. But that reflects a conception of the good, too. Perhaps we think that alternatives ought to be chosen on their merits, and that majorities are less likely to err than minorities. But *that* is a frank repudiation of the neutralist idea. Need we accept one of these three reasons for adopting a nonrandom final choice procedure? Not at all; others can be offered. The point is that none will come any nearer to exorcising those devilish conceptions of the good.

The plot thickens. For if nonrandom procedures for final choice cannot really be neutral, should we award the palm to random procedures instead? No again. First let us consider lotteries in which each policy alternative has an equal chance of being drawn. As even neutralists are quick to recognize, treating policy alternatives as unequally choiceworthy just because *some* conceptions of the good say that they are is a violation of neutrality. But by the same token, treating policy alternatives as *equally* choiceworthy when *not all* conceptions of the good say that they are is also a violation of neutrality. Equal-chance lotteries do just this. So—though they may sometimes be good ideas— they flunk the test of neutrality too.[7]

Could we "neutralize" the policy lottery by relaxing the requirement of equal chances? No. Either these chances would be assigned under the explicit guidance of a particular conception of the good (better policy alternatives getting better chances), or they would not. Should they be assigned according to a conception of the good, the violation of neutrality would be clear to the even meanest intellect. But should they be assigned in any other fashion, we would have almost the same problem as with equal-chance lotteries: the distribution of chances could be considered neutral only if it were endorsable by every conceivable conception of the good, which is clearly impossible.

We have just been speaking of equal and unequal treatment of policy alternatives. Parallel arguments can be drawn about equal and unequal treatment of policy*makers*, supplementing the arguments against view-regarding and fitness-regarding neutrality offered just earlier. I should not want this to be misunderstood. From the mere fact that neither equal nor unequal treatment is neutral, nothing follows about whether equality has merit. We need only bear in mind that, like any other ideal, equality is affirmed by some conceptions of the good and repudiated by others. One must simply be sure of the conception of the good to which one is committed.

Sense 12: Blind Neutrality Toward Alternatives. "Final choice of policy is called 'neutral' iff the weight assigned to an alternative in the choice procedure (whatever kind of choice procedure this is) does not depend on whether the anticipated effects of its implementation are desirable (by whatever conception of the good this desirability may be evaluated)."

Sense 13: Recursive Neutrality Toward Alternatives. "Final choice of policy is called 'neutral' iff only those POLICIES *may be enacted that are also neutral, in one of the senses listed under Division I."*

Recursive neutrality toward alternatives can be eliminated for the same reason as recursive neutrality of debate (sense 7): the senses of neutrality to which it "recurs" (senses 1 through 5) have already been knocked out of the running.

I might now be expected to say that blind neutrality toward alternatives can be eliminated for the same reason as blind neutrality of debate (sense 6); however, the parallel this time does not hold. Another parallel does hold: between blind neutrality of alternatives, and random neutrality (sense 11). We saw above that no matter how we assign chances to the policy alternatives in a lottery, conceptions of the good still come in the back door. In exactly the same fashion, conceptions of the good come in the back door no matter how we assign weights to the alternatives in a voting procedure. We may assign equal or unequal weights, and either way, we may or may not be doing the right thing. However, we should not delude ourselves that the thing we are doing is neutral.

Conclusion

We have now finished examining all thirteen senses of ethical neutrality. One may be excused for feeling as though he had just been shown in a geometry marathon that circles can never be squares — whether they are drawn with chalk, paint, crayons, or any other medium; made of felt, paper, plastic, or any other material; represented in any idiom; or whipped up out of pure thought. At least the marathon is over. Yet it could begin all over again unless I add a final word.

For someone might object that the thirteen senses of neutrality do not exhaust the possibilities after all: that because each of them concerns either policy, debate over policy, or final choice of policy, my arguments apply only to governmental activism. "You've shown that activist regimes can never achieve neutrality," my opponent might say; "but what about laissez-faire? And what about anarchy?" The objection is invalid because it depends on an artificially narrow sense of the term "policy." Let's see how this is true.

To begin with laissez-faire: (1) I have not hurled the accusation of nonneutrality against "nominal" policies that concern the what of social life while excusing "adverbial" policies that concern the how;[8] (2) I have not accused "first-order" policies that say what is to be done while excusing "metapolicies" that say what kinds of policies are to be allowed; and (3) I have not accused policymaking by commission, while excusing policymaking by omission.[9] Thus laissez-faire is a policy in my sense too, and the arguments I have offered cover it already. The same is true of anarchy. For as just stated, the arguments apply to metapolicies as well as to first-order policies, and to policymaking by omission as well as to policymaking by commission. Anarchy, of course, is no more than a metapolicy of universal omission. It is a policy of having no policies.[10]

To be sure, all of the distinctions made above — between nominal and adverbial policies and so forth — concern matters of great consequence. There are choices to be made here; it makes a difference whether we live under an activist or under a laissez-faire regime, under anarchy or under archy. But where anything makes a difference, there is no neutrality. The only way to make the choice is to weigh the goods involved or affected.

How often one hears this line: "Perhaps *perfect* neutrality is impossible after all, but shouldn't we get as close to it as we can?"[11] Let us distinguish between possible and impossible varieties of idealism. In neutrality, we are not speaking of what we can think, but never bring about, like a perfect circle; we are speaking of what we *cannot consistently think*, like a square circle. There is no "partial" neutrality for the same reason that there is no "partially" square circle.

Ethical neutralism is the doctrine and social movement that seeks after this chimæra. Though it can never effect the square circles it desires, it certainly does have effects. It has these effects by refusing to call things by their right names and misunderstanding its own premises. No doubt there is some curious conception of the good according to which such perverse effects are desirable. Just what conception that might be would be worth learning, if only to help us understand the age.

Notes

1. See, for instance, Albert Weale, "Toleration, Individual Differences and Respect for Persons," and Charles E. Larmore, *Patterns of Moral Complexity*, chap. 3.
2. Herbert Wechsler, "Toward Neutral Principles of Constitutional Law."
3. See for instance Robert Bork, "Neutral Principles and Some First Amendment Problems."
4. The introduction of randomness into the procedure for final choice might also have been classified as a way of treating policy alternatives rather than as a way of treating policymakers. This is reflected in the character of the rebuttals that I offer later in the text.
5. William A. Galston has persuasively argued that the most prominent of recent neutralists even depend on the *same* theory of the good: as he puts it, a "triadic" theory which assumes "the worth of human existence, the worth of human purposiveness and the achievement of purposes, and the worth of rationality as the chief constraint on social principles and social actions." He makes particular reference to John Rawls, Ronald Dworkin, Robert Nozick, and Bruce Ackerman. See "Defending Liberalism," at 625.
6. This, notwithstanding the contrary views of Ackerman, *Social Justice in the Liberal State*, chap 9; Dworkin, "Liberalism"; and Robert Bork, "Neutral Principles and Some First Amendment Problems." All three pieces involve a disguised or modified utilitarianism, a belief that equality is somehow more neutral than the alternative, or both. See, for instance, Bork's discussion of what he half-jokingly calls an "Equal Gratifications Clause," at 10. I return to the question of whether equality guarantees neutrality in the text.
7. I want to stress that I am not suggesting that equal-chance policy lotteries are never appropriate. One arguably appropriate circumstance is when social peace is so imperilled that we all agree to treat policy alternatives as equally choiceworthy even though no one thinks that they really are. We all know that little boys

quarreling over baseball team captaincies sometimes agree to draw straws. The Compromise of 1850 "settled" the issue of slavery in the new territories by establishing a similar lottery: that is, the deadlocked groups in the U.S. Congress agreed to take their chances as to what the territories themselves would decide. But while this sort of reasoning might make a case for equal-chance policy lotteries, it does not make a case for calling them neutral; what drives it is a conception of the good according to which social peace trumps all other concerns.

Another argument for an equal-chance lottery, this one for the selection of officials rather than policies, was made in the ancient Greek democracies. The cities were riven by class war. Election of magistrates was regarded as an oligarchic device; by contrast, selection by lot gave "the many" the edge they desired. See Aristotle, *Politics*, 4.1294b, and Montesquieu, *The Spirit of the Laws*, bk. 2, chap. 2. Of course, this argument depends on a conception of the good no less clearly than did the previous one. Any other argument would do the same.

8. This distinction is especially crucial to the thinking of Michael Oakeshott; for which, see *On Human Conduct*.

9. The idea that omission is more neutral than commission is the root fallacy of James Buchanan and Gordon Tullock, *The Calculus of Consent*. For discussion, see Douglas Rae, "The Limits of Consensual Decision."

10. Conviction of the neutrality of the metapolicy of universal omission is best reflected in Robert Paul Wolff, *In Defense of Anarchism*.

11. For instance see again Charles E. Larmore, *Patterns of Moral Complexity*, chap. 3. This aspect of his argument is also discussed in the text accompanying note 1, following chapter 4.

Mezzalogue:
Special Cases of True Tolerance

Every exercise of moral concern must be tempered by true tolerance. This leads the neutralist to think that morality and tolerance are opposites, or at the very least that the virtue of tolerance promotes a different end than all of the other virtues. On the contrary: all of the proper ends of human life are threads in the same tapestry. So long as we live, to set aside the loom is neither necessary nor possible. The point is to guide the movements of the shuttle by a deeper study of the design. This is the point of true tolerance: not an abandonment of the moral goal, but its better pursuit; the protection of ends against means.

Already we have seen quite a few instances of this. Sometimes they violate our first, immature intuitions. Consider the uses of honor. The ancient republics believed in firming the resolve of the good by disgracing the wicked. Yet we have seen that dishonoring persons makes both the censor and his target worse. Thus we draw the line at practices.

This is what I mean by saying that the vindication of true tolerance is not against the moral good, but for the moral good. Of course, some of our intuitions may take some time to catch up with our understanding. The infant in us whimpers in disappointment over the loss of its bottle; it would rather suck on simpler ideas. We will have to speak to it. But we must not say, "You are getting older now, and grown-up people do not eat." We should say, "You are getting older now, and grown-up people eat solid food." The former is the neutralist response. The latter is the wisdom of tolerance.

In this book I treat three spheres as special cases: education and nurture, expression, and religion. The reason for giving them so much attention is that each is especially counterintuitive. In each, the line of conduct that seems at first most conducive to our moral good may actually work grave harm to it. For this reason, true tolerance in each is much more than usually frustrating to immature judgment. The impassioned cry for milk provokes an equally furious call for starvation; between the competing clamors of authoritarians and neutralists, true tolerance can hardly be heard.

Few authoritarians will be in the audience for this book. Thus in each special case, though I explain the errors of authoritarianism I do not dwell on them. My hope is partly to reach those who see these errors well enough, but think that neutralism flies the only other banner on the field; partly to reach those who do see other banners, but not the one I defend; and partly to add a blade to the blades of those who followed the banner of true tolerance before us.

Part Three

The Special Case of Tolerance in Education and Nurture

Introduction to Part Three

Tolerance in education and nurture can be discussed more briefly than either of the other two special cases covered in this book. That is largely because a compendium of the characteristic features of educational neutralism is ready to hand in a book by Bruce Ackerman. This opus is by far the most impressive and explicit attempt by anyone to render the neutralist outlook coherent. Its treatments of various areas of policy are bold in conception, imaginative in argument, and daring in scope; in criticizing, I attack the neutralist theory of education at its highest rather than its lowest point. The problem is simply that it is wrong.[1]

There are, of course, drawbacks to selecting Ackerman for purposes of illustration, just as there would be had someone else been chosen. For instance, another way to say that his discussions are bold in conception, imaginative in argument, and daring in scope is to say that they are *radical*. But most neutralists are not radical; most prefer to take their neutralism with cream and sugar. Therefore, someone might suggest that I am using Ackerman merely as a straw man. Am I? I do not think so. The objection to the idea of "partial" neutrality is, at bottom, the same as the objection to the idea of "complete" neutrality. Moderate neutralism cannot be coherent unless radical neutralism is also coherent.

Another objection might be that while Ackerman uses the term "neutrality" in one sense, other neutralists use it in different senses. Actually this is not entirely true. At various points he uses the term in a number of the thirteen senses diagrammed in chapter 5. But suppose he did use it in only one sense. Bear in mind that the impossibility of neutrality in *each* of the thirteen senses has already been shown. From one point of view, then, we are covering ground that has been covered once already. In this section we are simply covering part of it on foot instead of on motorcycle, to get a better idea just how the neutralist error tends to ramify. From this point of view, the radicalism of Ackerman's which I mentioned in the last paragraph is a clear advantage. It causes him to make the neutralist error in *many more ways*, all of them imaginative and (though not in the manner he intends) instructive. Studying them sharpens the profile of true tolerance negatively — not as when an artist daubs more and more charcoal on a sheet of paper, but as when he applies an eraser to a sheet that is already black with it: "Not this! Not this!"

I begin this part of the book, however, not with neutralism itself, but with a contrast between the authoritarian and liberal approaches to education and nurture. There are two reasons for this. The first is that authoritarianism provides a glaring backdrop against which the liberal counsels of tolerance stand out as sharply as possible. The second is that in Ackerman's work, the contrast between liberalism and authoritarianism is skewed by two mistakes, like an image cast upon an uneven screen. One of these mistakes is his definition of liberalism as nothing more than neutral discourse; the other is his view that whatever isn't neutralist belongs to the authoritarian frame of mind. Because the same mistakes are rampant in contemporary politics and political theory, our first order of business is to see the contrast as it really is. Not until the chapter after that do we turn to neutralism proper.[2]

Notes

1. There is also another, less important reason for examining Ackerman's educational proposals in depth. He maintains that the proof of his pudding is in the eating; that if even after studying the general features of his theory one is unconvinced that neutrality is possible, one need only examine the detailed proposals he makes in each area of policy. To my knowledge no one has taken him up on the offer. Fairness seems to require that someone do so.
2. For other perspectives on neutralism, authoritarianism, and education, see the bibliographical entries under R.F. Atkinson, Charles Bailey, David C. Bricker, Richard H. Gatchel, John Kleinig, W. Moore, Mary Warnock, and John Wilson.

6

Liberal Education
Contrasted with Authoritarian

Most of the authoritarians with whom one might come into contact in a liberal society are half-hearted. Their authoritarianism is tempered and moderated by various principles that are really liberal. This makes it harder to see what the difference between liberalism and authoritarianism really is. To avoid this problem, what I present is not this or that version of moderated authoritarianism, but an Ideal Type of authoritarianism after the fashion of Max Weber.

The aim of the authoritarian program for rearing and educating the young is to brand certain moral precepts on the personality of the growing being. On authoritarian assumptions, this is no easy task. Human beings are regarded not as naturally good, nor even as naturally good but fallen; rather they are regarded as naturally depraved.[1] From this it follows that no one can be trusted to make moral decisions for himself. The child's first lesson must be unquestioning obedience to those in authority. In the view of the authoritarian, unless this lesson is learned well no other lesson will be possible at all.

Who wields authority? When the child is young, his parents wield it. Later it is wielded by teachers; finally, by rulers. Over all is God. The authoritarian may not believe in God himself, but he is determined that rulers and subjects themselves shall believe. He also knows that not just any conception of God will achieve the desired effect: each person must believe that God would just as soon roast him in hell as look at him.

To be sure, a form of authority is recognized in liberalism as well, otherwise politics would have to be abandoned. But the authoritarian's authority has a character all to itself. Between the child and the adult it recognizes no real moral distinction. The best an authoritarian can hope is not that the growing child will come to love good for its own sake, but that he will internalize the sanctions for wickedness. For leather is not the only stuff from which a lash can be made. It is not even the strongest. The lash of guilt is stronger. If it is not stronger at first, it can be made so.

No reason is ever given for a moral precept, nor is any to be asked. How could it? In the authoritarian outlook, the faculty of reason is not merely flawed, but a very flaw. Asking for reasons is stalling. Appealing to reasons is malingering. Offering reasons is coddling. Following reasons is pride; one ought to have followed the precepts. Obviously, reflection is an evil, not only because it tempts one to disobedience but also because it wastes his time and distracts him from his duties. The authoritarian admits that on occasion it may be a necessary evil: young children must reflect on the swiftness and certainty with which misdeeds will be discovered and punished; so, sometimes, must children that are grown. But insofar as the human clay allows, the very power of moral choice is to be extinguished.

Ideally, the grown child will always do what is required without the least awareness that he might have done differently. Because traces of awareness may remain, the grown child is expected to practice a certain kind of self-discipline. He will be able to drown his fears with the still greater fear of God and the rulers. He will be able to repress his greed, his anger, his resentment, even his despair. All in all, he will be able to hold down whatever may lie within him that would stand in the way of his duties. When all the ravings of the human heart have been subdued, the authoritarian program is complete.

Why actual authoritarians deviate from their Ideal Type is obscure; scarcely a premise may be dislodged without causing the authoritarian tower of justifications to wobble. But though this tower may rock at times, it inspires a certain awe. Its height and power, its commanding presence, arise from its confident view of human nature and destiny. The liberal alternative is hardly worth considering unless it can breath this rare air and do battle in the same high places.

The difficulty is that the moral psychology of liberal political theory is deeply ambivalent.

In some versions it honors the same ideals as the "liberal arts":

aptitude for disciplined rational reflection; critical appreciation of one's own culture; keen perception of what it is to be a human being, with all of its graces and liabilities; readiness to delight in whatever is good while opposing whatever is evil. It has a deep though often unacknowledged debt to the Jewish and Christian tradition that human beings were created in God's image—created, incidentally, for his ends and not for those of one another, and therefore, as Locke and Jefferson reasoned, endowed with certain rights.[2] It also draws deeply from the well of classical moral psychology, especially from Aristotle.[3] It does not necessarily go so far as to accept the Socratic maxim that the unexamined life is not worth living—that may merely express skepticism as to whether anything besides examination has worth. Like John Stuart Mill, it does agree that examination has deep worth, and that whatever else has worth can usually gain from examination.

But other liberal theories follow authoritarians like Hobbes in regarding man as a seething, heaving cauldron of appetites and aversions. They undermine the critical and reflective ideals, and make the authoritarian educational program look almost good.[4] I am not speaking only of contractarians, the First Wave of theorists in the liberal tradition. The same sulphurous atmosphere can be whiffed at times around utilitarians, who constitute the Second Wave, and even around neutralists. "The essence of life is force," says the utilitarian James Fitzjames Stephen. One hundred and seven years later, the neutralist Bruce Ackerman agrees that "so long as we live, there can be no escape from the struggle for power"; "only death," says he, "can purchase immunity from hostile claims to the power I seek to exercise."[5] The only decisive difference here is that Stephen sees more clearly than Ackerman what his doctrine implies. Ackerman thinks that good intentions can confine the deadly war of claims and counterclaims within the orbit of discussion. "Discussion," Stephen insists, "is at most an appeal to the motives by which a strong man is likely to be actuated in using his strength." Thus "although compulsion and persuasion go hand in hand, the lion's share of the results is obtained by compulsion."[6]

So we find ourselves with two psychologies: the classical psychology that undergirds liberal education, and the pessimistic psychology borrowed from authoritarianism. We cannot have it both ways. Singleness of vision demands a choice: that we export the classical psychology to the rest of liberal theory—or that we use the pessimistic psychology to destroy it. This book is an emblem of the former choice. That we are congenitally afflicted, in each of our faculties, with a deadly and ugly flaw I take for granted; but also that the material marred by this flaw is good. Were it not so—were our depravity truly utter—we could not even conceive of good, let alone lament our own condition. So let us get on with it.

Now the authoritarian educational program shaped its prescription for character according to certain ideals. That, however, was not what made it authoritarian. The liberal program does the same. The issue is just what these ideals are. Sweeping differences between them entail equally sweeping differences in the methods chosen for advancing them.

One place to begin explaining this would be to compare the liberal and authoritarian lists of admirable traits. This sheds a certain amount of light; docility and compliance do make conveniently sharp contrasts with independence and good judgment. But the approach does not take us as far as one might expect. In the first place, entirely too many qualities of character would no doubt be found on both lists: temperance and courage, for instance. In the second place, what we really want to know is *why* any given quality is written on or stricken from the list.

We can get further, therefore, by comparing the understandings of virtue that give rise to the two lists in the first place. The critical point is that the authoritarian construes each virtue as a *capacity*—in particular, a capacity for repressing an unruly passion in order to follow rules unswervingly. By contrast, the liberal does not regard any passions as intrinsically bad; neither does he regard any capacity (repressive or otherwise) as intrinsically good. He construes each virtue as a disposition concerned with choice;[7] as a deeply ingrained habit of calling upon his passions and capacities in just those ways that aid, prompt, focus, inform and execute his moral choices, instead of clouding them, misleading them, or obstructing their execution. I daresay all of this prating on "choice" would grate on the ears of our authoritarian.

We can get a sharper view of the liberal program of education by coming in for a closeup of the single virtue sometimes called practical wisdom. The liberal educator does not think this virtue the only one.

However, he does characteristically see it as very closely involved with the exercise of all the other virtues as well. To see this, consider courage. According to the standard account, its exercise requires enough fear to avoid being rash and enough daring to avoid being pusillanimous.[8] At first blush this has nothing to do with practical wisdom. But what is it to be rash? What is it to be pusillanimous? Conduct that would be rash under certain circumstances might well be pusillanimous under others. Courage, therefore, needs more then a fixed quantum of fear and a fixed quantum of daring. To pierce the needle's eye, it needs an insight that helps bring forth just the amounts of fear and daring that each situation demands. The elements of this insight are three. Courage needs first an understanding of the things that are worth defending. It needs second an understanding of the prices their defenses are worth, as well as of the circumstances in which all such reckoning is straw. And third, it needs an alert horror for the ways of defending these things that end by devouring their hearts. These counsels do not arise from fear and daring themselves. They are in the realm of practical wisdom. Courage, to be courage, needs knowledge of things that transcend it.

This brings us to a quandary. Take as granted that one of the qualities in which we wish to nurture and educate the young is practical wisdom. That does not tell us much. For just what kind of rearing could this be? Practical wisdom is more than a bag of precepts that we could hand out like candy. There are, of course, some precepts that are never wrong. On the other hand, not even the longest list of precepts could address every situation. Practical wisdom goes beyond the very precepts it follows. It is a kind of attunement—a way of *relating* our various passions and vulnerabilities to our various capacities: capacities like sympathy, imagination, and the power of disciplined thought. It is not so much good memory for true precepts as a fitness for recognizing them, and a readiness for judgment where no known precepts apply. If our aim is helping the young to achieve this fitness, authoritarian education would be worse than inept: it would be a catastrophe. It would destroy the very powers we hold precious, crippling choice instead of making it wise, annihilating judgment instead of making it pure and strong. Not because we don't *believe* any moral truth, but because we honor it too much to neglect its needs, we strive as liberal educators to call to life and growth the infant capacities on which practical wisdom will one day have to call. Not because we don't *know* any moral truth, but because we hope that our young will one day surpass us in its knowledge, we demand as liberal educators that they study more than our own ideals. We expect them to learn about the significant alternatives from which these ideals have drawn; even about those against which they are, in part, reactions.

There is more to say about liberal education, but most of it is brought out more fully in the following discussion of educational neutralism. However, two problems linger and must be aired before we go on. One of them concerns the "objectivity" of liberal education. The other concerns its bearing toward God.

Liberal education deserves to be called objective. It deserves this for two related reasons. One I have already given: that liberal educators present not only the ideals of their own tradition, but also the ideals of significant alternatives. The other is that liberal educators do everything they can to encourage the young to reject irrational prejudgment, in favor of disciplined and thoughtful after-judgment. Now obviously, our ideals are expressed in the very act of deciding which alternatives are "significant"—not to mention our manner and motive for presenting them. Sometimes this is treated as though it were a stain on the ivory skin of objectivity. However, the complaint misses the point. Rightly understood, objective teaching is not forswearing every point of view—which is at any rate impossible. It is teaching enough—and well enough—so that even if the perspective of the teacher is askew, students will nevertheless be offered everything he can give them to set it right again. An objective teacher is one who makes the young a gift of the knowledge, the ability, and the encouragement to discover and try to correct not only their errors (though those too, and with his help), but also his own. This may be a teacher's deepest counsel of tolerance.

Now as to the other matter. As we saw earlier, the authoritarian program of education depends on certain assumptions about God. A contrasting view is sometimes taken of its counterpart, to the effect that the *liberal* program of education *cannot help but squeeze out* faith. This view arises not so much from the liberal emphasis on rational reflection as from a notion that often walks by its side: an idea that faith and rational reflection are mutually exclusive. That idea is what we shall examine. It is, I think a rather silly error, though one that some liberals do commit.

The very act of reasoning in order to learn about the world outside us presupposes that perception is not wholly an illusion, and that the consequence relation—"if this, then that"—corresponds to something in reality. The truth of these presuppositions cannot be proven. Accepting and acting upon them is therefore an act of faith. Moreover, no proof of anything at all can be so completely drawn as to eliminate its dependence, conscious or unconscious, on undemonstrable *givens*. Whatever one's *givens* may be, accepting and acting upon them, too, is therefore an act of faith. Therefore the real issue between authoritarians and liberals cannot be whether to have faith; it must be whether to have faith in this or that. A further point is this. If an individual may be said to follow as his "god" whatever it is to which he makes all else subordinate, whatever it is that constitutes his ultimate concern, then so-called secular philosophies are crammed not only with faith, but with "theology." Therefore the real issue between authoritarians and liberals is not even whether to have faith in a god, or in something other than a god; it is whether to have faith in this or that kind of god. It is, in other words, strictly analogous to the issue between believers in different religions.

We see that in giving a privileged place to rational reflection, liberal education does nothing to corrode faith in general. It might corrode certain kinds of faith: for if one believes that authoritarians believe in the right kind of god, he has no business being a liberal and ought to become an authoritarian; conversely, if one is convinced that liberalism is true, he apparently does *not* believe in that kind of god (whether or not he knows it) and must believe in another.

Although it is frank about its presuppositions, beyond this point liberalism presupposes very little.[9] Beyond it, what liberal education does about the choice between remaining candidates for the ultimate concern is simply to preserve its essential characteristic: the characteristic of being, precisely, a choice. There is, of course, one last presupposition even in this. The liberal educator presupposes that whatever concern might deserve to be called ultimate is of such a nature that it cannot be truly served *except* by choice. For if any educator believed the contrary, he could not conscientiously leave the choice open. He ought to realize that this belief is consistent with some creeds and inconsistent with others.

Willy-nilly, then, any program of education will uphold certain kinds of faith and corrode the rest. I have said nothing about the particular kinds of faith that our own education might uphold or corrode. But I do not claim that our own education is thoroughly liberal, either; if it were, there would be little need for this discussion.

Notes

1. A wholly different kind of authoritarianism believes that human beings are naturally good, but perverted by class society. Having dealt with this earlier I will not deal with it here; see my remarks on totalitarian ideology in Part Two.
2. Locke, *Second Treatise of Government*, section 6; Jefferson, *Declaration of Independence*, opening lines.
3. Of course, I do not mean to suggest that Aristotle was the first liberal or anything of that sort. For discussion of what parts of his theory are and are not consistent with liberalism, see "A Vindication of the Politics of Virtues" in the author's *The Nearest Coast of Darkness*.
4. Thomas Hobbes, *Leviathan*, esp. the first thirteen chapters.
5. James Fitzjames Stephen, *Liberty, Equality, Fraternity*, at 118; Bruce A. Ackerman, *Social Justice in the Liberal State*, at 3.
6. Stephen, ibid., at 70.
7. This conception is Aristotle's, though much of its development as represented in the following paragraphs is distinctive to liberalism. See his *Nicomachean Ethics* 2.1105b–06b.
8. Ibid., 2.1107a, 3.1115b–16a.
9. What little it does presuppose is further considered in the last part of the book.

7

How Neutralism Distorts Liberal Education

As Ackerman's theory shows us, neutralism distorts liberal education because, though approving it, it does not understand it. Sometimes these misunderstandings are subtle—less like sheer blunders than like aborted insights. Unfortunately, this does not diminish the gravity of their consequences.

Ackerman understands politics as a struggle to possess or control "power." Like Hobbes, who defined power as "the present means to any future apparent good," Ackerman uses the term very broadly; however, his usage is more like Nietzsche's than like Hobbes'. To him it seems to mean any resource which may help anyone to impose his or her will on the world.[1] Thus it may include wealth, property, personal liberties, access to other minds through speech and education, even the opportunity to influence the genetic endowment of the next generation. All of these are "power." Generally speaking, they are "scarce" in the sense that "total demand outstrips supply."[2] Their variety enables Ackerman to present as "power struggles" disagreements of many kinds that would not ordinarily be regarded in this light. For instance, to engage in controversy over the moral education of the young comes across as a purely will-driven pursuit of the access to their minds necessary to make many replicas of oneself—as we see shortly.

According to Ackerman, the principle of struggle holds no less for liberal politics than for any other kind. However, he regards liberal politics as unique in settling power struggles through a highly structured public conversation. The norms of this conversation are six in number.[3] 1. Everyone who lays claim to a resource may be challenged by anyone else. 2. Everyone who is challenged is obliged to reply.[4]

3. Every reply must take the form of a *reason* why the challenged person need not accept the challenger's claim. 4. Reasons given in reply to a challenge are to be disregarded unless they are consistent with reasons given in replies to previous challenges. 5. Claims of personal superiority to the challenger may not be given as reasons. 6. Nor may arguments based on conceptions of what is good for human beings.[5]

Through the fifth norm, political theorists of many different persuasions might agree with Ackerman. The parting of the waters comes with the sixth. This is where Ackerman declares his commitment to neutrality. We can be a bit more precise by consulting the exploded diagram of neutrality given in chapter 5: taken together with the others, norm six commits Ackerman to the eighth of the thirteen senses of neutrality, Blind Neutrality of Debate. However, at one time or another he drifts off into almost every one of the other twelve. This preserves the usefulness of his theory for illustration.

Ackerman begins his discussion of education and nurture with the arresting statement that children are born "radically incomplete." They do not enter the world already equipped with language and culture; their future development is open-ended, or, as Ackerman prefers to call it, "free." The term "free," of course, has evaluative as well as descriptive overtones. This is no accident; in Ackerman's case it is the residue of a logical fallacy. As David Hume pointed out, no valid "ought" statement can be derived from "is" statements alone. But from the premise that any child *can* learn to function in a "bewildering variety" of human cultures, Ackerman seems to conclude that we *should* regard the direction of the child's development with indifference. The sole premise expresses an "is"; yet the conclusion expresses an "ought."[6]

At any rate, to function in even one of these many possible cultures, the child depends on "models of behavior" that we, his elders, provide, and there's the rub. "The authoritarian," says Ackerman, "exploits the child's cultural dependence to limit his cultural freedom." In the authoritarian's view, "infancy is a time to plant the seed the seed in good moral ground; childhood is a time for the weeding and pruning needed to transform good young saplings into extra-fine timber." As a consequence, authoritarians think that "by maturity, a well-educated person can only look with contempt upon the stunted and deviant growths that, unaccountably, inhabit so much of the forest."[7]

Ackerman cannot help but regard all of this as wrong. It violates the "ought" that he has fallaciously derived from his "is." Yet now the "ought" changes. Rather than regarding the direction of a child's development with indifference, we are to *encourage* morally unguided diversity. "We have no right," he begins, "to look upon future citizens as if we were master gardeners who can tell the difference between a pernicious weed and a beautiful flower." And against that way of viewing them, he sets the system of liberal education. Rather than suggesting that some ways of leading a life are better than others, he says, liberal education "provides children with a sense of the very different lives that could be theirs—so that, as they approach maturity, they have the cultural materials available to build lives equal to their evolving conceptions of the good."[8] Ackerman believes that no other kind of education can be defended against the challenges that inevitably arise in the highly structured public conversation that he described earlier. For this reason, education of this kind, and no other, must be guaranteed to every child by the state.

Superficially, Ackerman's account of liberal education looks very much like the account I gave above. As in my account, so in his, liberal education is championed against authoritarian repression; and as in his account, so in mine, the basis of liberal education is found in a moral psychology emphasizing *choice*. But these appearances are deceptive. Earlier in this book the observation was made that in saying we wish to raise the young to make moral choices for themselves, we may mean either of two things:

a. that we want them to develop the qualities of character that will help them to recognize wrong and embrace right with as little external guidance as possible, or

b. that we want them to acquire all-purpose conceptual ingredients with which they can whip up their own unique versions of what counts as right and what counts as wrong.

What I mean is the former. With certain reservations prompted by the fear that children may grow up to be felons (as we see later), what Ackerman means is the latter.

This is an immense distortion of one of the deepest counsels of tolerance. Yet on a first reading of Ackerman's treatise, the difference between the two interpretations of the counsel is blurred. Three different clouds obscure it: the ambiguity of the phrase "conception of the good"; eccentric definitions of liberal and authoritarian education; and Ackerman's use of metaphor. Let us examine all three.

The first cloud has to do with the fact that when a person uses the phrase "conception of the good," he may be thinking of either a universal, or a particular ideal. The phrase may denote a conception of what is good for human beings *as such*—or it may denote a conception of what is good for a *particular* human being: the details of the life suited to his particular gifts and calling. Between the universality of the one idea and the particularity of the other there is, of course, no real contradiction. Courage, integrity, wisdom, love, and the other virtues are universal goods of character, but recognizing this does not prevent us from saying that they may find expression in many different cultures, callings, and personalities. Ackerman, unfortunately, confuses the two senses of the phrase. He treats conceptions of what is good for human beings *as such* as though they *were* sets of plans for the personal details of one's own life—but imposed upon the world at large. By doing so, he makes it seem as though the universal and the particular are enemies; as though to teach the meaning of goodness is to extinguish the varieties of goodness.

This is a shame. In fact, unless we admit what is the same for all, genuine diversity is impossible; to reanimate an earlier metaphor, life is like music, where the variety of melody depends on the principles of harmony. But Ackerman thinks that teaching scales and keys and time signatures and such is akin to mass-production. Rather than diversity of melody, he would have noise.

The second cloud that obscures the difference between the two interpretations of moral choice is Ackerman's eccentric way of using the terms "liberal" and "authoritarian." As my own account aimed to show, liberals and authoritarians alike bristle with moral ideals. They grow them like fur. They are covered with them. They rub them off on the young like dogs in summertime. If we wish to distinguish them we must mark with *which* ideals they bristle, and *how* they rub them off. These two distinctions are sharp and interdependent. Liberal ideals simply cannot be taught by authoritarian methods, nor authoritarian by liberal methods. Both distinctions are missed by Ackerman. As he uses the term, authoritarianism includes *any* attempt to teach the young the difference between good and evil. Naturally, this way of speaking makes the truly liberal just a special case of what he calls authoritarian; the chasms between these two programs of education disappear like wrinkles under vanishing cream. He has no reason to regret the passing of the former because according to his dictionary, truly liberal education is not, truly, liberal education. As an honorific term, "liberal education" is reserved for teaching that avoids ideals as though they were infectious diseases; only neutralism is liberal.

Avoiding all ideals is, of course, impossible. A *consistently* neutral education could not even accept the ideal of being educational, and so could not exist. Indeed, apparently Ackerman himself is too nearly a true liberal at heart to observe his neutralist vows with any real consistency. We find him on one page, for instance, explaining that educators must encourage "imagination," "independence," and (in the sense of rational scrutiny of conventional prejudices) "doubt." Though these qualities will "necessarily come in conflict with whatever moral ideals happen to dominate society at large," he insists that they be nurtured, come what may.[9] I read this as a confession that a truly liberal education *does* have ideals, and that they are worth defending against their adversaries.

One might almost say that Ackerman's thinking is redeemed by this unacknowledged inconsistency. But this would go too far: for his doctrine conceals bad as well as good ideals, and tends to cripple the good ones.

The third cloud that obscures the difference between the two interpretations of moral choice is Ackerman's use of metaphor—in particular, his image of moral education as a kind of "horticultural" tyranny. We've read this metaphor above. Let us break it down and examine it more closely.

The metaphor has three phases. In the first, Ackerman simply says that according to "authoritarians" (that is to say, everyone who is not a neutralist), "Infancy is a time to plant the seed in good moral ground." Not much need be said here. There is nothing particularly perverse about the idea of planting the seed in good moral ground—nor does Ackerman seem to expect it to strike anyone in that way.

But mark how he shifts the metaphor in phase two. From the language of planting and nurture, we move suddenly to the language of cutting and pulling up, for now "authoritarians" are said to believe that "childhood is a time for the weeding and pruning needed to transform good young saplings into extra-fine timber"; they think they can "tell the difference between a pernicious weed and a beautiful flower." The altered image must mean something; in fact, it is repeated for emphasis. Taken seriously, it suggests that teaching the young the highest and best of our ideals is a kind of purge, like the purification campaigns of Hitler, Stalin, and Pol Pot. Is this what a neutralist believes? Sometimes one does hear parents and teachers speak of training young branches, but never of "pruning" them—much less of "weeding" pernicious growths from the kindergarten! Surely Ackerman knows that liberals in my sense of the term (who are "authoritarians" in his) do not throw insufficiently virtuous children into gas chambers. But what else could such words mean?

After the genocidal allusions of its second phase, the third phase of the metaphor is almost anticlimactic. However, the vision it conjures is bad enough. "By maturity," says Ackerman, "a well-educated person can only look with contempt upon the stunted and deviant growths that, unaccountably, inhabit much of the forest." The insinuation here is very like Ronald Dworkin's thesis that anything short of neutrality is a violation of "equal concern and respect." Raising the young according to our moral ideals is a solid guarantee that in maturity they will be haughty, unreflective, unloving, and intolerant. Apparently this guarantee holds even if love, tolerance, reflection and humility are among the moral ideals we have taught them.

Obviously this is false. But suppose it were true. Still far from clear would be why, if teaching children about the good makes them so paradoxically wicked, allowing them to evolve their own "conceptions of the good" does not liberate still greater possibilities of wickedness.

Notes

1. Here, the assertion of will itself is the apparent good, though, for reasons shortly to be clear, Ackerman does not call it that.
2. Ackerman, *Social Justice in the Liberal State*, 3. At 113, Ackerman calls germ plasm an exception to the rule of scarcity because "each of us possesses more . . . than we can possibly use for our procreative purposes." However, this seems to be a mistake. The "power" for which he regards us as "struggling" in the field of genetic manipulation is not germ plasm *per se*, but control over its use.
3. Ackerman packages them differently than I do, as three "constraints" plus certain other understandings that he does not number. The first norm on his list, called

"Rationality," is third on mine. The second on his list, called "Consistency," is fourth on mine. The third on his list, "Neutrality," has two branches. Branch one is my sixth, and branch two is my fifth; but I give the name "neutrality" only to the former. In the latter, Ackerman employs the term in a sense irrelevant to present purposes. His discussion may be found in ibid., at 3–12.

4. But see ibid., at 5, note 1.

5. I am simplifying. Actually Ackerman uses two very different versions of norm six. In each version a certain kind of reply to a challenger is ruled illegitimate. The version most often used in the book (call it version one) stipulates that no one who replies to a challenge may rely in any way on conceptions of what is good for human beings. But another version (call it version two) is given in the introductory discussion (ibid., at 11) and used in the discussion of genetic manipulation. Version two is much more relaxed, stipulating merely that no one who replies to a challenge may claim that his conception of the good is *superior* to the challenger's. Apparently this leaves the defender free to employ the same conception of the good as the challenger did. (See James Fishkin, "Can There Be a Neutral Theory of Justice?") But then Ackerman stipulates that before a reply may rest on any conception of the good, *everyone* must accept this conception. The final stipulation preserves the meaning of version two only on the assumption that every member of society is a potential challenger, and that real and potential challenges are equally salient.

6. Ibid., at 139.

7. Ibid.

8. Ibid.

9. Ibid., at 162.

8

Neutralist Education in Closer Scrutiny

The next task is to examine the particulars of the educational program that Ackerman proposes. Its cornerstone is that the liberal regime is committed to a system of liberal education not "because it wishes to indoctrinate children in one vision of the good rather than another," but because it wishes them eventually to take their places as participants in the highly structured public conversation that regulates the struggle for power.[1]

Primary Education

The first step in the neutralist program for education and nurture is "primary" education, by which Ackerman means what goes on in the family before the child has reached the age of five—an age the significance of which will be clear shortly. Two assumptions guide him here. The first is the "multiplicity of paths to citizenship"; the second is the "need for cultural coherence."

Assumption one, says Ackerman, means that the state has no legitimate concern with how children are raised, so long as they acquire the ability to participate in neutral power talk. But he points out that if a child is exposed to an "endless and changing Babel of talk and behavior," developing such an ability is beyond the realm of possibility. The child will lack "a sense of the meanings that the noises and motions might ultimately signify." According to Ackerman this fact leads us directly to a "liberal theory of the family."[2] Before turning to assumption two, let us pause to look this over.

Though Ackerman does not present it systematically, his theory of the family seems to include four principles: 1. No child can be properly raised by a "random concatenation of grown-ups." 2. "Each citizen, *regardless* of his conception of the good, has the right to discharge his power of primary education over his children in the way that seems best" to him. 3. The state may intervene only if a family is "failing to provide the cultural coherence necessary for a child to develop the competences required for citizenship," which are the competences necessary to participate in neutral power talk. 4. Calls for such intervention should be treated "with caution" because of the potential for authoritarian abuse.[3]

These principles certainly demand more than casual scrutiny. Consider the fourth, for instance. To illustrate it, Ackerman explains that the state may intervene to protect a child, but not to protect a fetus. The distinction itself, of course, is controversial—but what concerns me here is the *reason offered* for it, which is rather astonishing. If a child is not taught the competences necessary for neutral power talk, says Ackerman, we will not know what to do with him as an adult because he will not be able to talk with us. By contrast, aborted fetuses present us with no such problems for the simple reason that they will never grow up.[4] Presumably, although we should not be permitted to hurt children and let them live, there would be nothing wrong with simply killing them, because then they would not grow up to cause us problems either. But let us leave this aside and return to more general considerations.

Of course, Ackerman is right to assert the central place of the family in liberal ideas of nurture, and right, too, to stress the liberal reluctance to intervene in the family's internal affairs: this is a counsel of tolerance. But we have a problem. The privileged position of the family is usually and properly defended in terms of the ultimate good of the child. But "this rough magic I here adjure";[5] the conscientious neutralist refuses all dealings with the good. How, then, can Ackerman concede so much to the family? Apparently he thinks his concession has nothing to do with the good. Rather, different families raise their children in different ways, and the multiplicity of families guarantees just that "multiplicity of paths to citizenship" with which he began. Thus his defense of the family is neutral after all.

Or is it? No, of course not. It clearly presupposes that being able to join in neutral power talk is a true good. That is what Ackerman means by "citizenship," and he is for it. Well, then, does a commitment to citizenship tell us *enough* about the good to be useful? No again. This comes out with limpid clarity in the principles that Ackerman gives to regulate family interventions. We may not intervene at all, he says, unless we have very strong reason to believe that the way in which the child is being raised will *not* leave him able to join in suitable public conversations as an adult. An example shows that this means less than it seems to. Traditionally, physical and sexual abuse have been accepted as reasons for intervention; apparently, Ackerman's principles would counsel us to reject them. For we know good and well that many abused children grow up perfectly capable of participating in all kinds of public conversations.[6] Later on, Ackerman does suggest that parents must be prevented from "forcing" incestuous relationships upon their children "in order to pre-empt the challenge of liberal education."[7] What a mighty blow for children is this. Presumably, the permissibility of incest would depend on the motives of the parents. Incest for the usual motives would have to be allowed; only that which aimed to "pre-empt the challenge of liberal education" would be prohibited. Let us make the example more extreme. Suppose the abuse of a child actually poses the risk of death. On Ackerman's principles, can we not *now* intervene? I am sure that Ackerman himself would say "Yes." But his principles leave no room for any answer but "No"—that is unless the child has *already* developed the ability to participate in neutral public conversation, so that he can neutrally protest. For as Ackerman's contrast between abortion and poor nurture reveals, we may not object to parental misconduct merely because it prevents a potential citizen from reaching adulthood. We may protest only when it brings someone to adulthood without the ability to be a citizen.

Another question arises as we read along in Ackerman. Granted that families provide a "multiplicity of paths to citizenship"; still, are they the only possible providers of these paths? This, apparently, is where Ackerman intends his second assumption to function—the "need for cultural coherence." No child can be properly raised by a "random concatenation of grown-ups." Ergo, families: "each citizen, *regardless* of his conception of the good, has the right to discharge his power of primary education over his children." In order to see what a dazzling non sequitur this is, we need to keep our attention on the part of the part of the sentence that follows "has the right" without being distracted by the seven words beginning with "regardless." Nowhere is this "right" submitted to the "test of neutral dialogue," and Ackerman does not seem to realize that it would be just as feasible on his principles to say that *no* citizen, regardless of his conception of the good, has the right to discharge his power of primary education over his children. How does neutrality allow counting them as "his" in the first place? And in view of the accidents of meeting and the vagaries of courtship, how is it that the parental pair is *not* just a "random concatenation of grown-ups?"

If we believe that it does children good to give cultural reinforcement to the biological bonds between them and their parents, we can reply to these questions easily enough. But there is that rough magic again; neutralism must adjure it.[8] Perhaps the neutralist should assign the responsibilities of nurture to state-run crèches instead of parents. (Some say we are moving in that direction anyway.) If each crèche were run by a small cadre of adults, carefully selected for compatibility of outlook, they might well provide less "random concatenation" and more "cultural coherence" than most of the families we know today. Taking a tip from Ronald Dworkin, we might put the whole scheme under judicial supervision to avoid any pollution by external preferences.

Enough of that. Let us turn to the next phase of Ackerman's discussion—the "decline of parental authority."

According to Ackerman, by the age of five a properly reared child can raise "the question of legitimacy" that every liberal is obliged to hold sacrosanct: "Parent, why are you entitled to boss me around?" After all, says he, parents are like other powerholders, and "the very act of questioning his parents' legitimacy begins to qualify the child under the dialogic tests for citizenship." What this seems to mean is that the power struggle between him and his parents has now moved in some sense into the public domain, where it is subject to the same rules of conversation that govern all public discourse. To wit: When challenged by the child, parents must reply by giving reasons to the child. These reasons must be consistent with reasons previously given, and they must not involve parental claims of personal superiority to the child. Finally, they must be neutral: they may not involve claims that the parents "know what's good for the child better than the child does himself." In fact, according to Ackerman only one reason is strong enough to overcome the child's new "prima facie right to act in the way that seems to him best." This is that unless the tot is subjected to further training, when he reaches adulthood he will be too aggressive to escape imprisonment for criminal behavior. That, the parents know, would be "yet more intrusive" than their own restrictions.[9]

The other half of this story is that as "control" wanes, "guidance" waxes. The assumption behind guidance is that "it is up to the child to decide" what he wants to do. But, aware of the child's "inexperience in the prudential judgments required in comparing means to ends," parents may find "ways of suggesting to the child that, *even when taken in his own terms*, he has misestimated the costs or benefits involved in the activity in which he has become interested."[10]

Again let us step back and study the figure that Ackerman has sketched for us. As before, the outline is right: liberals do believe that as the child grows, control should diminish in importance while guidance should increase. But the colors, lighting, and perspective of the sketch are all somehow wrong.

The colors of the sketch are off because although we should indeed give growing children more and more reasons and fewer and fewer commands, the rationale for this need not be what Ackerman says it is. In his view, the family simply presents a special case of power struggle, a microcosm of the war of all against all. Of course, this is a real possibility; families do harbor conflicts. But in ordinary families we also find genuine community of sentiment, interest, and concern, and it is a very deep mistake to take the pathological case as the norm.

Ackerman himself remarks that "the complex controls imposed by the family do not depend merely upon the superior force of the parents but upon their capacity to maintain the child's respect and affection,"[11] and worries that reconceiving the family "on individualistic lines"[12] will destroy proper as well as improper parental authority. But if all of this is true, why not admit that our reasons for shifting from control to guidance have very little to do with "the liberal's corrosive inquiry into the legitimacy of power?"[13] Ackerman sees the shift like this: Children must learn the basics of communication before they can learn to take part in neutral power talk. When children are very young, the state indulges the parental desire to foist on them a conception of the good, because this is a precondition of learning to communicate at all. Afterward the state withdraws the indulgence, and parents bow to the inevitable. The truth about the shift is more like this: Parents should never give up their concern for the ultimate good of their children. However, the best way to express this concern changes as children begin to mature. The goal is that in adulthood, they will conduct their lives in the way that befits mature human beings—wisely, after due reflection, making good moral choices and knowing why they make them as they do. Gradually shifting from control to guidance as they near this goal is the only way to lead them to it. The strategy here is the same as with every other counsel of tolerance: means are moderated for the sake of the end itself.

After the colors, the lighting of Ackerman's sketch is off because by and large—although to a diminishing degree as children grow in wisdom—parents *do* know what is good for their children better than the children do themselves. And, yes, there are times when parents must simply say so. Sometimes children do not understand the prudential issues involved in a course of action, and the costs of error can sometimes be too high to let them learn "the hard way." Sometimes they understand the prudential issues well enough, but not the moral issues. Sometimes they need to be protected from practices which, indulged, would pervert rather than enlarge their understanding. Sometimes, even, they do know what is good for them—but haven't yet developed the self-control necessary to execute their wills without swerving. And let us be frank: Ackerman is not *completely* wrong about power struggle. However they may love and respect their parents, children are crafty. What they have going for them is that the question "Why?" can always be asked one more time. That child must be rare to whom it has never occurred to manipulate the insecurities of adults by turning their willingness to give reasons against them.

Finally, the perspective of Ackerman's sketch is off because we can surely give children better reasons for our moral demands than he thinks—unless we are utter cynics. As we've seen, on his telling the only reason strong enough to overcome the presumption that the child may do as he pleases is that without further training, by adulthood he will be too aggressive to escape imprisonment for his crimes. But must we really tell Sonny that the only reason for being good is to keep from havin' to sing them jailhouse blues? Or shall we merely *think* this while giving him different reasons, thereby violating his supposed citizenship right to question the legitimacy of parental authority? For it is certain that this rationale for restricting his conduct could never survive the "test of neutral dialogue" with the child. One can imagine the following conversation:

SONNY: I think I'll go rip off Eddie's bike.

DAD: What will Eddie think when he sees you riding around on his bicycle?

SONNY: He won't think nothing. It looks just like a thousand other bikes.

DAD: All the same, you shouldn't take it, son. That would be stealing.

SONNY: Yeah, I know. So what? I'm as good as he is.[14]

DAD. And he's as good as you are. It doesn't sound as though you have much respect for your young fellow citizen.

SONNY: I respect him plenty. He's just as entitled to try'n stop me as I am to try'n take his bike away—if he sees me.

DAD: Sorry, I just can't let you do it.

SONNY: Look, old man, why are you entitled to boss me around?

DAD: [Sighs.] Do I have to answer that?

SONNY: Mr. Ackerman says so.[15]

DAD: Well, look at it this way. My restricting you now promises to minimize the overall weight of special restrictions imposed upon you through your whole lifetime.[16]

SONNY: Uh huh. Tell me another one.

DAD: No, really. If I let you learn thievery now, then some day, when you're all grown up, you might be caught.

SONNY: Not me. I'll be too smart.

DAD: That's what they all think, son.

SONNY: Awright, so maybe I will be caught. So what? I want the bike *now*.

DAD: Son, you just don't understand. The pain of eventual imprisonment would far exceed the present pleasures of purloining your good friend's bicycle.

SONNY: Sorry, Dad, you can't say that t'me.

DAD: Why not?

SONNY: Whadda *you* know about it? If I rate the present pleasures of bikin' higher than th' discounted future pain of imprisonment for similar offenses, that's my business.

DAD: Huh?

SONNY: I mean you don't necessarily know what's good for me any better than I do myself, old man.

DAD: Where did you learn to talk like that?

SONNY: I told you. From Mr. Ackerman.[17]

DAD: But I never heard you talk like that before.

SONNY: I never had t'engage in neutral dialogue before. So do I get to rip off the bike, or don't I?

DAD: Well, I gave guidance my best shot. Now it's up to you to decide.

SONNY: I decided ten minutes ago. Weren't you listening?

DAD: Then go to it, son. I'd hoped that you would be more like me, but I'm glad
   you're achieving your own self-definition.[18]
SONNY: Yeah, right. I mean, me too.

[*Curtain.*]

The lesson of the preceding conversation is that in so-called neutral
dialogue, merely prudential arguments against the commission of crimes
can always be cancelled out by counting pains and pleasures differently. But in a way, this is only icing on the cake. A much deeper irony
of Ackerman's position is that it undermines the distinction, supposedly much beloved of neutralists, between crime and sin. Using the
criminal code as the primary agent of moral instruction for the young
has serious and undesirable side effects that depending on parents does
not. But now, parents are given a program for instruction according to
which they should tell their children that *unless an act is against the
law, it's all right.* Either there are no sins — or else, every sin is also a
crime.

Secondary Education

By secondary education, Ackerman means that portion of the education of the child that takes place in schools rather than at home.
Because his discussion shifts back and forth between various "rights,"
"needs," "interests," and "projects" of children, parents, and other
interested parties, I can make my points more clearly in the context of
a schematic diagram of his argument than in the context of a mere
summary.

One of these "rights" might be called the right of cultural access to
the child. As we have seen, during primary education Ackerman would
allow only parents the right of cultural access. This he seems to view
as a sort of accommodation between the parents' greedy desire to make
the child in their own image, and the state's supposedly neutral aim of
providing him with cultural coherence so that some day he can join in
power talk. The parents get what they want, and by a fortuitous co-
incidence the child gets what the state wants him to have. But it takes
only four years for the child to achieve cultural coherence. In the fifth
year the accommodation breaks down, and a new need begins to take
over. Now the child needs — nay, is "entitled" — to receive the cultural

"materials" with which to "forge the beginnings of an identity that deviates from parental norms"; all this for the sake of eventual "self-definition."[19]

The reason this breaks down the old accommodation is that one cannot count on parents to provide the new "materials." Apparently, their only concern is to replicate themselves. They want the child to carry their own personalities into the next generation. However, a new accommodation can be brought about with the desires of other interested parties to make the child in *their* own images. Ackerman says that parents must increasingly recognize the "right" of others to provide the child with the cultural materials *they* desire, due to their own replicatory urges, to provide, and to let him know that his parents' view of his childish resistance to their authority "is not unchallenged within the liberal community."[20]

At this stage, then, what we witness is a grand transfer from parents to outsiders of the rights of cultural access to the child. These outsiders are collectively organized in the "school." Essentially, the school does nothing but mediate the transfer of cultural access rights. Education involves no more than that.[21]

But these access rights are not transferred all at once. Because the replicatory urges of outsiders rival those of parents, it isn't easy to let outsiders stir the tea at all without blowing the lid right off the pot. Parents do retain a "residual" authority and right of access, because of their continuing, and necessary, "project in aggression control" — which we have already examined. Parental efforts to keep their children from turning into jailbirds depends on "subtle ties" which "could not survive an environment in which parental models were subjected to constant ridicule and condemnation." This generates what Ackerman calls the "problem of liberal curriculum": "Given the continuing need to control access, how does one select among the different citizens who offer themselves as secondary educators?"[22]

Already there are serious problems with this account. Ackerman's approach to education is reminiscent of nothing so much as the Madisonian strategy for keeping the ship of state on an even keel: to pit ambition against ambition. The difference is those Nietzschean touches as to the nature of the ambitions: apparently parents and teachers want nothing but to load down children with their own desires, prejudices, and grudges; they want to make them what *they* were before them. This picture is truly frightening, and if things were as bad as all that, surely not even Ackerman's desperate remedies could give us any relief. If all parents really were seized by the will to power, his first accommodation would surely produce not "cultural coherence" but a random assortment of neurotics; if teachers were likewise seized, his second accommodation would finish the job by shattering the glassy psyches of the young into a thousand jagged shards. Now there is no need to pretend that parents and teachers are never moved by the sheer pride of playing God with the dust of childish humanity. They are at times—and so there is some real point in the introduction of checks and balances into the institutions of education. But Ackerman exaggerates. After all, quite a few adults are happy enough to see children grow up to be capable, knowledgeable, good, and true—and in this, they should be encouraged, not discouraged.

Ackerman does at times seem to remember himself and recognize that his strategies could not work unless besides the sheer pride of playing God, parents and teachers had some genuine concern for (dare we say it?) the good of the child. But even here he misses the point. On one page, for instance, he suggests that it may not hurt a child to be exposed to a few "intolerant" teachers, so long as they are not allowed to "envelope" him for very long. Insofar as this presupposes that *most* educators might *not* be intolerant, it seems to go a long way toward unravelling his Nietzschean psychology (and wiping out the rationale for the two accommodations). But he brings this good beginning to a different kind of ruin with an eccentric definition of "intolerance."

According to Ackerman, the essence of intolerance is to regard one's beliefs as "the" truth, and to be "wholeheartedly enthusiastic" about them.[23] Now what could this mean? Every proposition implies the falsehood of its contrary. If A is true, then not-A is false; if A is not "the" truth regarding these two alternatives, then the title must pass to not-A. Expressions like "my truth" and "your truth" might be ducky in singles bars and hip psychotherapy, but they will not pass muster in logic. True tolerance in matters of belief means teachers may believe things true, but must *forbear from suppressing all who believe differently than they*. By contrast, Ackerman evidently takes it to mean that teachers must speak to students like this: "Now, I do, in some sense, hold this belief, but you must understand that I don't do so because I think it true, and I certainly don't feel *strongly* about it—dear, no!"

All of this is connected with a strange euphemism in his discussion of the "self-definition" that secondary education should help the child to achieve. Ackerman refers at one point to the "peculiar joy that comes when, after moments of doubt and despair, a person discovers that there *is* a conception of himself which is worthy of his affirmation."[24] The reference to this joy is attractive, not only for its wording but for the complex insight that it suggests. The puzzle is that the insight is one that Ackerman's premises cannot bear.

I called the insight "complex." That is because one would like to take the reference to joy as involving three distinct ideas. First, it seems to presuppose that there is a certain very large class of lives— presumably, those that exercise the goods of character—that are objectively worth living. Second, it seems to presuppose that for each individual, there is at least one life in this class that suits his gifts and responds to his calling. Finally, it seems to tell us that the peculiar joy in question, while not the *reason* for leading this special life, is the natural ornament to its discovery and inauguration.

I accept all three ideas. But Ackerman cannot even accept the first without calling his whole theory into question. Once we recognize that his reference to "worth" is gratuitous, the rest of his meaning falls into place. The life "which is worthy" of a person's affirmation means simply the life *which he in fact affirms*; and the "joy" to which Ackerman refers comes not from affirming a life that is worthy of affirmation, but from affirmation as such. The satisfaction of the need to affirm one's life is evidently what Ackerman means by "self-definition."

The flaw in this is that there is no such thing as a need to affirm one's life. For comparison, think of a man with a pathological aversion to food. Because of his excessively strict diet, his body is wasting away. Naturally, the gnawing pain is his belly is good for him. It is the only thing that might get him to stop being foolish and eat. But he doesn't think of it that way. He doesn't say, "What I really need is food." What he says is, "What I really need is the joy of fullness." After searching high and low, he finds a special gimmick that gives him that joy of fullness without his having to eat. And, of course, it leads him to death by starvation.

Ackerman's theory is like that, but about worth, not about food. A man might have a pathological aversion to a life worth living. Because of his good-starved life, his soul is wasting away. Naturally, the gnawing pain in his heart is good for him. His doubt, his sense of ruin, and his nameless longing are the only things that might spur him to change his life. But he doesn't think of it that way. He doesn't say, "What I really need is a life worth living." What he says is, "What I really need is the joy of affirmation." After searching high and low, he finds a special gimmick that gives him that joy of affirmation without his having to change his life—the goal, I think, of many of our cultural fads. And, of course, it leads to his "death" by starvation.

To some it may appear that I am denying children's need for unconditional love. On the contrary! Children should not be left to find their way to the good through the wastelands. They need loving guides who can show them a better path. Yet there is something wrong with our love. We do not love too much, but too imperfectly. Two kinds of self-absorption are prevalent in our culture: self-hatred and self-infatuation. Middle-class educators are all too ready to think that our job is to replace the former with the latter. Perhaps neutralism would call this love. But if it is "love," it is false love, not true love. Children do not hate themselves because they are insufficiently infatuated with themselves, but because we have failed to teach them that the most estimable of all things are beyond Self. And the best way of teaching them this is, precisely, to love them unconditionally. Why? Because this is what true love is: a going out of Self, a concern for the good of the Other, which may inspire an echoing love by its example. Unconditionally loving children is not the same as unconditionally "affirming" everything about them. To affirm the inaffirmable is to tell a child that nothing about him matters; it is merely a form of contempt.

Despite all, it is not impossible to rescue Ackerman's program from the morass of neutralism. He makes four proposals for secondary education. They are not all wrong; with heavy editing, they can be salvaged. Let us see how.

Proposal one is that in order to protect the residual interest of parents in aggression control, "the early stages of the liberal curriculum will content themselves with the elaboration of life options relatively close to those with which the child is already familiar."[25] This sounds something like the "expanding horizons" approach that the public schools already follow; but Ackerman may have either of two different things in mind.

First he may merely be endorsing the *current* practice of "expanding horizons," whereby first the child is taught about neighborhoods, then about the city and state, later about the country and its history, and later still about other cultures. The *reason* for which Ackerman approves it is too thin—we have already seen the ethical poverty of what Ackerman calls "aggression control"—but it is not morally objectionable per se. We might reject it because it does not teach children enough, but that is a different matter.[26]

On the other hand, Ackerman's reference to "life options" may signal something different than current practice. It may mean that he has a sort of supermarket interpretation of expanding horizons in mind instead, whereby first the child is taught (for instance) that men and women get married and have children, then he is taught that he may prefer to have children outside of marriage, later that he may wish to consider group marriage, and later still that he might train for a career in prostitution. This, of course, would have to be repudiated. Not that teenagers could not be taught something about the arguments of opponents when learning the rational basis of our own family norms; in fact, they should.[27] But a supermarket approach is something else entirely. It replaces rational judgment with a taste test.

There is also a contradiction between this first proposal and a suggestion that Ackerman adds later to the discussion of the fourth: that an effort be made "to expose children with similar primary cultures to *different* secondary environments."[28] This may be merely an endorsement of bussing to achieve racial integration. However, the only cultural contrast he mentions is between the Amish and New Yorkers.[29] I assume, therefore, that his endorsement is intended for something more radical: that Christian parents should send their children to atheist schools, atheist parents to Christian schools, Marxist parents to rich-kid schools, and so forth. Taken in the light of his earlier admission that the relationship between parents and children "could not survive an environment in which parental models were subjected to constant ridicule and condemnation,"[30] this must be regarded as a Statist attack on the very institution of the family, and be condemned. Once again it shows us the directionless character of neutralism. It can simultaneously defend, and destroy the family. The only thing it *cannot* be—is neutral.

Ackerman's second proposal is that "the early effort must provide the child with skills that he may find useful in a variety of self-definitions."[31] As we have seen, the vague term "self-definition" carries a heavy and objectionable weight of ethical subjectivism. But we have an opportunity for editing here: had Ackerman instead said something like, "the early effort must provide the child with skills that he may find useful in a variety of callings, as well as the knowledge and capacities on which the exercise of virtue depends in all of them," no true liberal could complain.

Third, Ackerman proposes that "the child's responses during one year should guide the curriculum he receives in the next";[32] in other words, children are not all to be forced down the same path. This is half true and half false, but by adding a distinction (one which neutralism itself would not allow) we can make it all true. Being guided by the child's responses should mean something different in practical education than in moral education and the liberal arts. In practical education, we must be guided by the child's responses in the sense that not all children have the same gifts and callings, and that what a child's gifts and calling are will emerge only slowly through the responses of the child himself. Here, not every child need learn the same things. By contrast, *all* children should develop good character, and *all*—unless we wish to give up the republic—should learn something of such disciplines as history. This does not mean that even despite the entirely normal variations in their temperaments and talents, good character and civic understanding must be encouraged by precisely the same teaching techniques in every child. Provided that the reflective ideals of the liberal tradition are not abandoned, the choice between these different techniques might again be guided by the child's responses.

Finally we come to Ackerman's fourth proposal: that as the child gains "increasing familiarity with the range of cultural models open to him in a liberal society," the choice of his curriculum "should increasingly become his responsibility."[33] Again the proposal can be salvaged, but it needs two alterations. First, we should reiterate the distinction applied to his third proposal. Although surely the choice of the practical aspects of his curriculum should increasingly become the responsibility of the child, it should not be possible for him to opt out of the means by which the school develops character and civic understanding. Second, we should restate the condition for this transfer of control. Ackerman, as we saw, speaks only of "increasing familiarity with the range of cultural models open to him in a liberal society." But this is rather vague, and probably does *not* mean 'increasing familiarity with the variety of worthwhile lives, and increasing insight into his own gifts and calling." However, that is what it ought to mean. Otherwise we would be suggesting that mere exposure to various cultural influences—for instance, certain "heavy metal" apostles of suicide, Satanism, rape, and bloody mayhem—contributes to the ability of the young to make wise curriculum choices. We need not pretend before the young that lives like this do not exist. But some of the "cultural models" that are currently "open" to them in our liberal society would better serve as bad examples, and we are naïve if we do not admit it.

That sometimes the proposals of neutralists can be brought back from beyond good and evil is encouraging. Perhaps their authors can be persuaded to return to true tolerance as well.

Notes

1. Ackerman, *Social Justice in the Liberal State*, 159.
2. Ibid., at 141.
3. Ibid., at 141–43.
4. Ibid., at 144–46.
5. Shakespeare, not Ackerman.
6. Some legislators, in promoting laws to curb child abuse, have even confessed to having been abused as children. There they are: publicly conversing. Yet perhaps Ackerman would not regard discourse of this kind as sufficiently neutral to demonstrate the development of the capacity in which he is interested.
7. Ibid., at 156.
8. Ackerman does consider the idea that "the family is a 'natural' institution needing no further justification in larger political terms." However, in the next sentence he rejects it. Oddly, he does not say that it is false. Rather he says that neutralists will not easily find its implications "endurable," ibid., at 164. I daresay that is true.
9. Ibid., at 147–48.
10. Ibid., at 150.
11. Ibid., at 155.
12. Ibid., at 163.
13. Ibid., at 163–64.
14. "I'm as good as you" is the most characteristic conversation stopper in Ackerman's dialogues.
15. According to Ackerman, "Parent, why are you entitled to boss me around?" is the fundamental "question of legitimacy." Ibid., at 147.
16. Ibid., at 148. The full passage states that "authorizing special controls during childhood may increase the youth's capacity to remain free of the special restric-

tions imposed on aggressive adults by the criminal law. The task, in short, is to design a set of behavioral limitations *over a citizen's entire lifetime* which promise to minimize the overall weight of special restrictions." Ackerman adds that "Junior cannot protest special restrictions in childhood that free him from greater restrictions in later life." But if we hold Ackerman to his other statements, then once the passage from control to guidance has occurred, he can. The parent must also reply in the child's own terms. Ibid., at 150.

17. Ibid., at 147, where Ackerman announces, "a liberal political community cannot support the exercise of coercion when the only thing that can be said is that elders are intrinsically superior to younger citizens; nor can it flatly assert that parents necessarily know what's good for the child better than the child does himself. These moves are flagrant violations of the Neutrality principle."

18. Ibid., 154, 159.

19. Ibid., at 151, 153–54.

20. Ibid., at 153, 151, in that order.

21. Ibid., at 154–55.

22. Ibid., at 155–56.

23. Ibid., at 159.

24. Ibid., at 165.

25. Ibid., at 157.

26. The expanding horizons approach has come under some attack at professional meetings of educators and textbook publishers on the grounds of expecting too little. Critics point out that children already know they live in neighborhoods; they already know their parents shop in stores; they already know they go to school; and so forth. I thank John Lawyer, an editor for Holt, Rinehart, and Winston, for bringing this to my attention.

27. Some on the Right will argue that this is not an appropriate place to be liberal, because stable families are even more important than the reflective ideal. Suppose the premise true. Even so, during a period of cultural decay like our own, a blind prejudice that only one way is right can easily be replaced with a blind prejudice that anything goes. Therefore the only way to stabilize the family is to teach that it has a deeper warrant than prejudice. Perhaps these critics fear that it does not?

28. Ibid., at 158–59.

29. Ibid., at 159; he may have in mind the decision of the U.S. Supreme Court in *Wisconsin v. Yoder* (1972). This decision—further considered in Part Five—gave Amish parents an exemption from a state compulsory school attendance law in order to withdraw their children from public high schools which they considered morally corrupt and have them "learn by doing" in the Amish community.

30. Ibid., at 155.

31. Ibid., at 157.

32. Ibid., at 157–58.

33. Ibid., 158.

Part Four

The Special Case of Expressive Tolerance

Introduction to Part Four

On the spectrum of possible views about expressive tolerance, two positions mark the endpoints. The "ultraviolet," so to speak, is that everything that can be construed as expression should receive absolute legal protection. The "infrared" is that only those expressions that are true should be protected. Shortly will follow arguments that the path of true tolerance lies along a mean between these extremes. However, the extremes themselves deserve our interest for at least a moment longer, if only because of a pair of mistakes that might be made about them. Mistake one is that the "ultraviolet" position is dictated by ethical neutralism. Mistake two is that the "infrared" position is dictated by its rejection.

The first mistake is not really hard to see through. As we have found in Part Two, ethical neutralism is internally inconsistent. For this reason it cannot give exclusive support to any position at all; by the Law of Duns Scotus it supports, and at the same time rejects, them all. Mistake two is also fairly transparent. To reject neutralism is merely to reject a logical contradiction. Merely rejecting a contradiction can no more commit one to supporting a particular position than merely accepting the contradiction can.

9

General Counsels of Expressive Tolerance

The Mean

From the preceding remarks it follows that in order to know to what view of expressive liberty one truly is committed—"ultraviolet," "infrared," or something in between—one must know more than the mere fact that he rejects the logical inconsistency of neutralism, that is, that he is willing to make a rational choice among conceptions of the good. He must also know just what conception of the good he has rationally chosen—or, if he has not yet chosen one, he must do so.

In the liberal political tradition, a particular conception of the good is already embodied. Of all of its elements, the one central to the issue of expressive liberty is *the good of discursive reasoning.*[1] Discursive reasoning is regarded as a good of very high order for at least the following related reasons, against which I know of no convincing arguments:

1. Though not fail-safe, discursive reasoning is instrumental to possession of the good of truth (an intrinsic good).

2. Though not fail-safe, discursive reasoning is also both instrumental to, and a constituent of, the good of individual moral development (an intrinsic good). It is instrumental to it as a means to discovery of specifically moral truths; it is a constituent of it as belonging to the virtue of moral judgment.

3. Finally, discursive reasoning, though not fail-safe, is instrumental to struggle against political dictatorship. Dictatorial power, in turn, is regarded as evil not only because no checks prevent it from being used selfishly (to the detriment of prima facie goods), but also because, even when used unselfishly, it curtails the moral development of the citizens (to the detriment of an intrinsic good). It does this by limiting

opportunities for citizens (a) to learn concern for the public good, and (b) to exercise responsibility for acts they commit in the realm of public decision.

To accept these arguments, and to recognize the very high order of the good of discursive reasoning, obviously makes it impossible to accept the "infrared" position on expressive liberty. This is not a naïve optimism that without the suppression of the false, people will inevitably reason their way to what is true. We can be quite sure that sometimes we will not. Not only will we make random errors because our faculty of reason is *finite*, but also we will make systematic errors because our faculty of reason is *flawed*; it is, for instance—as James Madison observed—tied to self-love. Some of these errors may hurt us and hurt others.

Thus, liberty for discursive reasoning is a terrifying prospect. Nothing could be worse—except to suppress it. It seems that responsibility, that thing of terror, is one of the things we humans were made for. Short of divine grace, the only instrument we have for discovering the errors of discursive reasoning is more discursive reasoning, flawed or not. Remarkably, people do sometimes accept conclusions, against initial reasoning and against all inclination but the inclination to the true, because of better reasoning.

What commitment to the good of discursive reasoning implies about the "ultraviolet" position is not immediately obvious, but it becomes more clear when we reflect on what was just said about naïve optimism. Expression in general cannot be accorded the same high value as rationally discursive expression. Granted that the other faculties involved in expression, for instance imagination and desire, are not necessarily more flawed than the faculty of reason, they are certainly not less flawed, and they lack its self-critical ability. Reason *as such* can criticize a chain of reasoning. Imagination *as such* cannot criticize a stream of imagining, nor can desire criticize a cataract of desiring.[2]

The Location of the Mean

The tenor of these arguments is closely in line with what has been said about true tolerance throughout this book. What is contrary to the good must be tolerated in just those cases where its suppression would involve equal or greater hindrance to goods of the same order, or any hindrance at all to goods of higher order. In the case at hand, the good which sometimes suffers harm is truth itself, an intrinsic good, higher in order than merely prima facie goods. Sometimes it suffers this harm in the course of discursive reasoning, sometimes in the course of other forms of expression. The goods for the sake of which we must tolerate such harm are goods of the same order[3]: truth itself, and, directly and indirectly, individual moral development. Suppression of discursive reasoning would generally do equal or greater damage to these goods for the reasons given in the previous section. Therefore, tolerance of errors that arise in the course of discursive reasoning must be absolute. No such statement can be made in advance about other forms of expression; indeed, if unregulated they may undermine discursive reasoning itself. Therefore, the tolerance extended to other forms of expression should *never* be absolute. However it should not be arbitrary either: it must depend on a balancing of harms, the outcome of which will vary according to the form of expression in question and the circumstances under which it is indulged. We may call this "qualified" protection, within which further distinctions may be made as discussed in a later paragraph.

I concede that there may be exceptions to one of the previous paragraph's claims: the claim that the harm to intrinsic goods caused by suppression of discursive reasoning is equal to or greater than the harm to intrinsic goods permitted by toleration of error. How could one say there were not? As we will find again later, it is difficult to prove a negative. A hasty response to this admission might be to say that in *all* cases the amount of protection given to expression must depend on a governmental balancing of harms. This, I believe, would be incorrect. I do not mean to argue that there is not, in principle, any right place to strike a balance. The defect in the idea of balancing arises from practice, not from principle. By their nature, governments are not well able to *find* that "right place." They are systematically inclined to regard as untrue and unwholesome all views that put their own policies in a bad light, or that displease the informal elites from whom the governmental officers tend to be drawn. Popular republics, moreover, are apt to show an additional bias in favor of popular majorities—or at least in favor of those minorities which press their views so fervently as to give the appearance of being majorities.

The solution to which this drives us is likely to seem paradoxical.

Although in principle, balancing may be right and absolutism wrong, yet in practice there must be some absolute limits on what the government may do. A government constrained by certain absolutes is much more apt to strike the right balance than a government with no other burden than to strike balances. This does not imply a return to the "ultraviolet" position, because we can, after reflecting on governmental temptations, distinguish those forms of expression that are not at significant risk of being overregulated by a government intent on balancing, from those forms that are:

1. Philosophers would have to be kings, and kings philosophers, to eliminate the risk of overregulation were they to lay hands on discursive reasoning. In fact, they would have to be better philosophers than we have now, better than we have had before, and, given the limitations and flaws of the human faculty of reason, better than we have any prospect of getting.

2. A second area which would have to be granted absolute protection is the provision of *information*—not all information, but *that which may be needed in discursive reasoning about the government, by those outside it*—even if the information is not to be found in the course of an argument itself. This information might be construed as what is needed by the public to perform what Vincent Blasi calls the "checking function"—resistance to tyrannical abuses of governmental power. Alternatively this information might be construed as what is needed by the public for a more participatory kind of politics, like that envisioned by Alexander Meiklejohn. However, it may well be that exactly the same information is required in both cases.[4]

For convenient reference later on, I will call these two areas the "discursive reasoning" and "republican information" criteria for deciding which forms of expression deserve absolute protection.[5]

With other forms of expression—expression which is neither discursive reasoning nor the provision of republican information—balancing seems much less liable to systematic warp in the direction I have just described. Even so, in a republic like ours it would be prudent to take advantage of the separation of legislature and judiciary in order to make a procedural distinction *within* the category of expression that qualifies only for qualified protection. The reason is as follows: Societies are an embodiment of lessons drawn from generations of experience in the balancing of harms. Thus, although long-established mores are not inevitably justified, there should be a certain presumption in their favor. Even among those forms of expression which fail to qualify for absolute protection, the mores of our society support a more generous attitude toward some than toward others—for instance, toward the expressiveness of classical literature than toward the expressiveness of drunken singing in public places. Thus, one might afford the former "strong" qualified protection, and the latter "weak" qualified protection. The procedural device for this would be to allow courts to consider whether the legislature had, in fact, carefully balanced harms in cases covering the former, but not to allow them to do so in cases covering the latter. Ascertaining that the legislature had done its job, however, should not be confused with stepping into the legislature's place—with courts balancing harms on their own account.

Clarifications

Three categories of expressive activity have been identified: first, discursive reasoning and the provision of republican information; second, forms of expressive activity that are neither discursive reasoning nor the provision of republican information but toward which the mores of the society support a generous attitude; and third, forms of expressive activity that fall into neither of the preceding categories. Under the principles defended here, activity in the first category would receive absolute protection; activity in the second, strong qualified protection; and activity in the third, weak qualified protection.

These categories cut at right angles to the sorts of categories usually employed in discussions of expressive tolerance—"art," for instance. Arguments based on such catch-alls tend to shed more warmth than light. Consider a dramatic production that included (a) explicit discursive reasoning in the form of dialogue about the ethics of violence; (b) ordinary story; and (c) the actual murder of a member of the cast. There is nothing farfetched about this—so-called snuff films already circulate in the underworld.[6] The only difficulty is that the single designation "art" obscures the fact that the play includes three distinct forms of expression. Surely the ethical argument, taken by itself, should receive absolute protection; the story, taken by itself, strong qualified protection; and the murder, taken by itself, weak qualified protection (which would mean that legislatures could, if they chose—as surely they would—prohibit it without hesitation). The mere fact that all three might be staged simultaneously should not interfere with their distinction in a court of law. We would simply tell the defendants, "You aren't being tried for either the argument or the story, but for the murder."

One might worry, of course, that the penalties would have a "chilling effect" on legitimate theatre. However, this is like worrying that confiscation of narcotics concealed in powdered fruit drink mix would have a "chilling effect" on the production of Kool-Aid. It presupposes what is not true: in the one case, that the manufacturers cannot tell what they are putting in the package; in the other, that the producers cannot tell what they are putting on the stage. Then again, instead of worrying about "chilling effects," one might sanguinely assume that "nothing needs to be done—by itself, the good will drive out the bad." There is very little chance that the works of Jane Austen will "drive out" the works of the Marquis de Sade, because they appeal to very different desires—in the case of de Sade, compulsive desires. Worse, the tendency of the compulsion is to seek ever more brutal stimuli as the old ones lose their power to excite.

But the example of drama can also be used to generate a deeper objection to the categories I propose. One might argue that in the play, ordinary story, as well as discursive reasoning, warrants absolute protection. For language has not only a discursive function, but also a "pointing" function: some themes that are nearly impossible to catch in a flimsy net of propositions can be adumbrated by another, more oblique kind of narrative. They have no proper vehicle but story.

This is true—yet not a warrant for absolute protection. There are two reasons to think so. First: *Precisely because* of the obliquity with which story develops its themes, it is taken in, as it were, subliminally. We can be taught by both speeches and stories. The difference is that we are far less apt to know what we are being taught in the latter than in the former. Argument achieves its effects by moving the levers of logical consequence; story, those of pity, passion, and pleasure.[7] Second: If we admitted oblique expression to absolute protection, then we really would have a slippery slope—but not in the direction that the libertarian fears. The only way to admit it to absolute protection *consistently* would be to admit to absolute protection *anything that ex-*

presses a theme, and to disregard the problem of obliquity altogether. But any act might be said to express a theme in some way—in our example, the murder no less than the story.[8] Therefore, to embrace a "theme" criterion is merely to say that everything is permitted.[9]

I take it, then, that my crosscutting analysis of "art" is not unreasonable, and I would apply the same analysis to other conventional categories such as "entertainment" and "commercial expression," though here too the problem is complicated by side issues. Extended discussion of these side issues here would drive me from my central theme.[10]

Is This a Possible Constitutional Position?

In Part One I explained why, even though the arguments for true tolerance stand or fall irrespective of the U.S. Constitution, constitutional considerations cannot safely be disregarded. Such considerations did not play an important role in Part Three, about the first special case of true tolerance, because the Constitution is silent about education.[11] However, it is not silent about matters connected with expression.

We begin with the name of Alexander Meiklejohn. Meiklejohn is the most renowned exponent of the "political speech" theory of the First Amendment. More important for our purposes is something much less often remarked: he was also the first to stress that the Constitution provides for two distinct levels or orders of expressive tolerance, not one. It follows that for constitutional purposes, expression must be divided into two distinct categories—that expression which qualifies for first order toleration, and that expression which qualifies only for second. Though not following him in every respect, my presentation is indebted to Meiklejohn's.[12]

First order toleration is announced by the First Amendment. The category of expression that it privileges is made up of speech and press; the level of government to which it is addressed is federal,[13] although parallel guarantees are found in all state constitutions; and the degree of protection it promises is absolute. "Congress shall make *no* law," it says, "abridging the freedom of speech, or of the press." A possible sticking point is what the framers and ratifiers meant by freedom of speech and press. We will come back to that.

Second order toleration is announced by the due process clauses of the Fifth and Fourteenth Amendments. The category of expression that they privilege includes all expression that is not already privileged by the First Amendment; the level of government to which they are addressed is in the case of the Fifth, federal, and in the case of the Fourteenth, state; and the degree of protection they promise is qualified rather than absolute. The federal and the state governments may deprive persons of life, of property, or (what matters for present purposes) of "liberty," but only provided that they observe "due process of law." Just how much is meant by "due process of law" is contested, but it means, at least, that government must not act in an arbitrary fashion. To limit any liberty, including liberty of expressive activity, the government must base its action on a law, enacted through proper legislative procedures, and brought to bear on cases through proper judicial procedures. The contested point is whether, in this second stage, courts may second-guess the deliberative balancing of harms that proper legislative procedures are meant to facilitate. The earlier suggestion of a distinction between a "strong" and a "weak" form of qualified tolerance points to a possible resolution of this issue.

So far we can see a parallel between the treatment of expression under the Constitution, and the treatment of expression under the principles of true tolerance. Both provide for two orders of protection, one absolute, one qualified by deliberative balancing of harms (and in both there seems to be some warrant for dividing the second order into two suborders, but let us put this off for a moment). We know that under the principles of true tolerance, the category of expression that qualifies for absolute protection is discursive reasoning. The question is whether that is the same category of expression that qualifies *constitutionally* for absolute protection—or, to put it another way, whether that is the same category of expression that the First Amendment designates by the terms "speech" and "press."

At the very least, speech and press must have been taken by the framers and ratifiers to include spoken and printed criticisms of the government.[14] Probably we can say more, for Americans after independence experienced an explosion of debate and discussion of all sorts, and valued the experience highly. Yet the terms "speech" and "press" have a narrower extension than the current term "expression." It is ludicrous to imagine the framers and ratifiers using the First

Amendment to protect lewd pictures, for instance. No doubt absolute protection was intended in the founding generation to include more than spoken and printed criticisms of the government; but no doubt it was not intended to include more than what can be spoken or printed. Surely, all of the kinds of expression to which the First Amendment refers are kinds that require words.

Discursive reasoning uses words, but so do many other forms of expression. Because every one of the ratifying states subjected some of them to restrictions of one sort or another, we cannot say that they intended absolute protection for all of them. However, what the framers and ratifiers did and said provides insufficient grounds for determining for which of them they did intend absolute protection. It seems, then, that we can go no further in interpreting their intensions. *Within the limits* already sketched, we must *assign* a meaning to "speech" and "press."

I suggest as a fundamental principle of constitutional interpretation that even after we have gone as far as possible in interpreting the intentions of the framers and ratifiers, we are not at absolute liberty to assign to a term or clause whatever meaning we please. If the Constitution warrants respect at all, we must attribute to those who were responsible for it at least such intelligence as we credit ourselves in talking about them; and if the Constitution is at all a genuine limit on what we would like to do, then, unless we go to the trouble of constitutional amendment, we must accept their universe of ideas as normative. Thus, it is indeed permissible to ask which meaning, of all the meanings we could plausibly assign to a contestable clause, follows from the political argument that seems most reasonable to us; it is permissible, I say, but only if we go on to ask whether this argument could be intelligibly expressed *within the universe of ideas that the framers and ratifiers inhabited.*[15] Because the principles of true expressive tolerance can indeed be intelligibly expressed within the universe of ideas of the founding period, they do provide a possible Constitutional position.

Is This the "Official" Constitutional Position?

The Supreme Court's practice has deviated from the constitutional interpretation that I have proposed—and therefore from true tolerance—in two respects. First, the Court has not seriously distinguished between the absolutism of the First Amendment, and the latitude for balancing offered by the Fifth and Fourteenth. Instead, it has treated *all* expression as liable to balancing. Second, the Court has not consistently distinguished its own functions from the functions of legislatures. Therefore, it has done a great deal of balancing on its own account rather than merely ascertaining that the legislature has done it. Both deviations have had unfortunate results. The result of the second has been simple confusion. Case-by-case adjudication does not lend itself to coherent reconciliation of numerous considerations when very few of them are ever likely to have a significant bearing on any single case. The result of the first deviation has been more grievous. Often the Court has balanced its way to a *higher* level of protection than any legislature would be apt to concede; and on the other hand, often it has balanced its way to a *lower* level of protection than true tolerance demands. The problem is neither overprotection nor underprotection alone, but both, depending on the type of expression. The gravest overprotection has been called forth by the lewd and morbid. Into the gravest underprotection, on the other hand, the Court has been frightened by the efforts of political dissidents to organize during periods of patriotic hysteria.[16]

Overprotection and underprotection are, I think, equally serious lapses from true tolerance. While overprotection has contributed to the humiliation of the very idea of virtue, both civic and personal, underprotection has eaten away at the foundations of republican liberty. However, since most of my academic brothers and sisters are already acutely aware of the second danger, perhaps I may be of greater service by concentrating on the first. Here, indeed, the bulk of the academy is against my position; so much so, that one contributor to a reputable legal journal could hail the glorious advent of what he called "pornotopia" (porno-utopia) without even seeming to think himself ridiculous.[17]

Attacking overprotection is just as important to the cause of true tolerance as attacking underprotection. For the grimness and vacuity of what is overprotected may help to show, by contrast, what is really worth protecting. The Court's protection of many forms of expression that would once have been considered obscene by reclassifying them as equivalents of "speech"—nude dancing, for instance—has lent a stolen dignity to these vulgarities that alters and degrades the very "community standards" on the application of which the Court insists.[18] It elevates the esteem in which we hold filth, and—by grouping all forms of expression together—demeans and discourages the discursive practices through which the individual and the community become more truly free.

How True Tolerance Differs from "Conservative" Approaches

Neutralism is not the only plague on the liberal house today. Another is a kind of communitarian relativism. Both epidemics have spread into both the Left and Right wings of the dwelling; in the academy at least, neutralism has spread more rapidly on the Left, communitarianism on the less influential Right. At a number of points in my own discussion, I am obviously in debt to conservative critiques of neutralism, and do not fear admitting it. Moreover, while not a communitarian, I obviously do acknowledge that community traditions are important. Finally, I obviously concur with conservatives that obscenity is beyond the pale of true tolerance. These facts may predispose some readers to view my approach to freedom of expression as simply a recapitulation of conservatism.

Actually there are a number of positions that are called "conservative," and my approach differs sharply from most of them. In particular, my arguments forbid the suppression of expression on any of the following grounds:

1. solely on the grounds that the expression suppressed calls for a still broader suppression;
2. solely on the grounds that it counsels disobedience to law;
3. solely on the grounds that it attacks our form of government;
4. solely on the grounds that it attacks our way of life;
5. solely on the grounds that it supports beliefs that are considered false;
6. solely on the grounds that it supports beliefs that are considered bad for the community;
7. solely on the grounds that it gives offense or violates our mores; or even
8. solely on any combination of these grounds.

If my arguments are right, then to refuse to permit suppression solely on such grounds is a counsel of tolerance. Yet here I part just as sharply from the Left: for to say that expression may never be suppressed *solely* on such grounds is not to say that expression may never be suppressed *on such grounds*. The necessary condition for suppressing expression is that

A. it is not discursive reasoning;
B. it is not republican information, that is, a communication of information needed by the people in order to carry out their Constitutional responsibilities; and
C. a specific law authorizes its suppression for a reason that is not itself barred by the Constitution.

Provided that a form of expression contains neither discursive reasoning *nor* republican information, *any* of grounds one through eight might be admissible as a motive for such a law—although as I have stated, laws interfering with forms of expression that have traditionally been accepted by the community would be subject to judicial scrutiny to ensure that they were not capricious. (Here the division of second-order protection into two suborders reenters.)

In conclusion we may say that the approach proposed occupies the mean not only between the logical extremes regarding expression, but also between the positions actually current on the Right and Left wings of contemporary liberalism.

Notes

1. Expressive activity intrinsic to religion ranks no less highly, but for different reasons. I bring this, in Part Five, under the topic of religious rather than expressive tolerance.
2. Someone could object that reason *as such* is an abstraction—that in all concrete exercises of discursive reasoning, we reason, imagine, and desire all at once. But the objection, viewed more closely, is really a supporting argument. This is true: discursive reasoning never takes place without the cooperation of the other faculties. But so is this: often the other faculties do function without the cooperation of discursive reasoning. Permitted, *without* its correction, to acquire an unwholesome bent, they will twist it their way when on later occasions it calls them to its assistance. To put it more plainly, straight thinking can sound an alarm when the imagination begins to twist. But a man with an imagination that has already been twisted often cannot think straight either. It warps the deck of his mind, pulling all his thoughts to one side.
3. I do not consider the highest-order good, the ultimate concern, until Part Five. Nothing there weakens the argument here.
4. See Blasi, "The Checking Value in First Amendment Theory," and Meiklejohn,

Free Speech and Its Relation to Self-Government; compare Lillian R. BeVier, "The First Amendment and Political Speech: An Inquiry into the Substance and Limits of Principle."

5. Two matters of detail must be made as clear as possible. First, in saying that level one expression would receive "absolute" protection I mean that government would be prohibited from screening it according to its point of view. I do not mean that the government would be prohibited from devising reasonable regulations concerning the times, places, or manners in which it might take place. This would be permitted so long as the time, place, and manner regulations were not deliberately and successfully composed to keep certain points of view from being expressed. Second, I assume throughout this discussion that the level of protection to be accorded a particular instance of expression has nothing to do with the level of protection to be accorded other instances of expression with which it may happen to be connected. For instance, political arguments warrants absolute protection. Now suppose that publication of obscenity were deemed to warrant penalty; and suppose that one sentence in an article on politics fell under the definition of obscenity. I would not say that penalizing the obscenity somehow impaired the protection given to the rest of the article.

6. These films claim to depict actual murders. So far as I know, no one has ascertained whether the murders are real; on the assumption that the filmmakers know their market, however, presumably the viewers think they are, and desire to see them for just that reason.

7. See Aristotle, *On Poetry* and *Politics*, bk. 8, chaps. 5–7, for the classical discussion of the moral effects of poetry, drama, and music. A far more critical discussion of drama may be found in Jean-Jacques Rousseau's letter to d'Alembert, which Allan Bloom has attempted to revive in his *Politics and the Arts*.

8. Analogously, Marshall Cohen claims that pornography "makes a moral point." "Sade," he says, "may be read as a reply to Dante." And so he may, though this is not the clincher that Cohen supposes. See his untitled reply to Walter Berns, "Pornography v. Democracy: The Case for Censorship," at 41. Compare David A.J. Richards, "Free Speech and Obscenity Law: Toward a Moral Theory of the First Amendment," from which I quote in note 17.

9. Similar considerations must be kept in mind when applying the republican information criterion. Just as every act (obliquely) expresses a theme, every act (obliquely) communicates information. An act obliquely communicates information by serving as an intentional or unintentional basis for inference; for instance, the murder of X by Y provides me with a basis for the inference that Y did not want X to live. But oblique expression is not enough; murder does not qualify for absolute protection as an oblique communication of information, republican or otherwise. By the same token, neither does pornography. It does offer a vicarious experience from which a person might attempt to make an inference about direct experience. However, to allow absolute protection to everything that might count as "experience" would be the annihilation of law. Considerations like these are the basis for the much-maligned but essential distinction between speech and conduct in First Amendment law.

10. In the case of commercial expression, for example, an important side issue is what kinds of commercial entities are doing the expressing. All other things being equal, should commercial expression by corporations or by regulated utilities

enjoy the same level of protection as commercial expression by an ordinary person? For some purposes, of course, a corporation *is* a person in the eyes of the law. However, such personhood is highly qualified. It is a special privilege granted to groups of persons, the liberty of expression of each of whom is already separately protected. We do not grant this privilege on grounds that it is essential to the liberal conception of the human good, or on grounds that it is essential to liberal political institutions, but on grounds that it *contingently* promotes the *contingent* goal of commercial prosperity. The state could abolish the privilege altogether if it saw fit. In the meantime, as a direct consequence of the privilege, corporations are often able to accumulate resources for use in expression that ordinary persons can hardly imagine. Said John Milton in his *Areopagitica*, "though all the winds of doctrine were let loose to play upon the earth, so Truth be in the field, we do injuriously by licensing and prohibiting to misdoubt her strength. Let her and Falsehood grapple; who ever knew Truth put to the worse in a free and open encounter?" (*Areopagitica and On Education*, at 50.) But all other things being equal, the winds of doctrine blow more strongly at the backs those who can afford to take out full-page advertisements in the Sunday *Times*. On the face of it, then, there is no more reason to grant corporations the level of protection for commercial expression that ordinary persons would enjoy, than there would be to grant them rights to vote or hold office. For diverse perspectives on related issues, see Jerome A. Barron, "Access to the Press—A New First Amendment Right"; Lawrence H. Tribe, *Constitutional Choices*, 210–18; the majority opinion in *Miami Herald v. Tornillo* (1974), which in effect squelched Barron's proposal; and *Central Hudson Gas Company v. Public Service Commission* (1980), Justice Rehnquist, dissenting.

11. Future judicial activists might nevertheless claim Constitutional justification for some sort of educational doctrine. In their view, Constitutional silence is not an insuperable obstacle to the discovery of a Constitutional right, as witness the discovery of a Constitutional right of privacy in *Griswold v. Connecticut* (1965). Indeed, affirmation that education is a Constitutional right may not even be necessary, as witness *Plyler v. Doe* (1982), which concerns education for children of undocumented aliens. Justice Brennan, speaking for the Court, used an imaginative argument, resembling more-conventional suspect classification analysis, to justify the position that a government benefit which is not a Constitutional right may nevertheless have a measure of Constitutional protection.

12. See his *Free Speech and Its Relation to Self-Government*.

13. According to the Incorporation Doctrine, the First Amendment did not originally apply to the states, but came to do so with the ratification of the Fourteenth. Considering the difference in order of protection between the First and the Fourteenth Amendments under discussion here, this argument seems specious. A case might be made that the First Amendment applies to the states via the republican guarantee clause found in Article IV, Section 4; such an argument would face the obstacle that the republican guarantee clause is usually considered nonjusticiable. Alternatively a case might be made that the First Amendment applies to the states via the privileges and immunities clause in Article IV, Section 2; see appendix 2, note 5.

14. An objection can be drawn from the fact that in English common law, the phrase "freedom of speech" had a much narrower meaning. It did not put a certain *kind* of expression off limits for purposes of regulation; rather it put a certain *strategy*

of regulation off limits with respect to expression. For instance, it was not regarded an abridgement of freedom of speech for the government to prohibit "seditious libel," that is, speech critical of the government. Indeed, the truth of a criticism, rather than being a defense against the charge, was viewed as an aggravation of the offense. However, it *was* regarded an abridgement of freedom of speech for the government to practice prior restraint. In other words, it could punish seditious libel after the fact, but it could not prevent it by requiring all publications to be submitted to a licensing board beforehand. Certainly, *some* of the framers and ratifiers meant no more than this by the First Amendment, or the Alien and Sedition Acts could never have been visited on the early republic. On the other hand, some of them certainly meant much more by it. The Alien and Sedition Acts did not survive. More important, at the time of its framing and ratification, the First Amendment was a triumph for Anti-Federalists, not Federalists; Anti-Federalist views, therefore, are normative on the issue. Anti-Federalists who had agitated for the Amendment clearly intended its meaning to be more expansive than the old common law meaning of freedom of speech, for they counted on it to legitimate their criticism of the excessively powerful government they expected the Federalists to set up.

15. See appendix 2.
16. For an example of underprotection, see *Abrams v. United States* (1919). Examples of overprotection are discussed later in the text.
17. "Pornography can be seen as the unique medium of a vision of sexuality, a 'pornotopia'—a view of sensual delight . . . erotic celebration . . . easy freedom. . . . Pornography builds a model of plastic variety and joyful excess. . . . of the independent status of sexuality as a profound and shattering ecstasy": David A.J. Richards, "Free Speech and Obscenity Law: Toward a Moral Theory of the First Amendment," at 81.
18. For the classification of nude dancing as speech, see *Schad v. Borough of Mount Ephraim* (1981), at 65–66; for the various incarnations of the "community standards" criterion, see *Roth v. United States* (1957), at 489; *Memoirs v. Massachusetts* (1966), at 418; and *Miller v. California* (1973), at 24. All of these will be discussed later. In 1991, as I prepare this manuscript for publication, the Court has began to move away from the doctrine enunciated in *Schad*, but its ultimate fate is unclear.

10

Abuse of the Free Speech and Free Press Clauses: The State Involvement with Obscenity

The Meaning and Constitutional Status of Obscenity

The Supreme Court states that obscenity is "constitutionally unprotected." This is a dramatic but misleading way of saying something much more mundane: that obscenity warrants only level three protection, which I have called weak qualified protection. Judicial intervention is certainly considered proper if the penalties for obscenity are inflicted outside the law, or without a fair trial; also if the law involves constitutional issues beyond the narrow question whether obscenity may be regulated at all—for instance if the law provides for cruel and unusual penalties, or if it defines obscenity so broadly that forms of expression warranting higher levels of protection also come under its heel. The Court means merely that it sees no need to second-guess legislative balancing of harms in the regulation of obscenity per se.

That, of course, is as I think it should be. However, because the Court has never very firmly grasped what obscenity is, it has experimented, sometimes disastrously, with three different approaches to things in obscenity's neighborhood. Each of these has left some traces in the case law. A fourth approach has been proposed by feminists but has not yet reached the Court. Therefore, before proceeding I had better briefly state what I mean by the obscene.

To put the matter as simply as possible: I understand a form of expression as obscene if it would tend to excite morbid passions in its actual or intended audience; but only provided that this tendency *could have been averted*—by excision or modification—without removing an essential component of expression that warrants absolute protection.

By "morbid passions" I mean not only morally illicit sexual desire and prurient excitement in excretory functions, but also the desires to hurt, to debase, or to be hurt or debased. The adjectives in this sentence are important. I do not maintain, for instance, that all sexual desire is morally illicit, and grant the inevitability of debate over when it is and when it is not—as of debate over everything else in law.

The "Averting Proviso" is also very important. I hope that it will calm fears that the proscription of obscenity will have a "chilling effect" on forms of expression that do warrant absolute protection. Its purpose can best be explained through an example. Suppose a person were to write a pamphlet advocating that the laws against the sexual abuse of children should be repealed, and developing reasons for doing so. So far, it would be entitled to absolute protection for two reasons. In the first place, it would constitute discursive reasoning. In the second, since it would concern the work of elected representatives, it would constitute a communication of republican information. Either of these reasons would be sufficient. There are, of course, some people who might find the pamphlet morbidly exciting just because of the topic that it addressed. However, the Averting Proviso would prevent us from classifying it as obscene solely on this ground. Why? Because this would involve us in the proscription of discursive reasoning and republican information *in themselves*—not in the proscription of something contingently associated with them. But now let us modify the example. Suppose that, interlaced with the argument, the author had included lewd descriptions of sensations experienced during sexual acts involving children. No doubt, by arousing morbid passions, these descriptions might make some people more willing to accept his conclusions. However, this kind of "information" forms no essential part of what the public might need to know to make the decisions for which it is constitutionally responsible, and this kind of "persuasion" forms no essential part of discursive reasoning. Since its excision or modification would have done no injury to any expression that did warrant absolute expression, there would be no barrier to considering it obscene. Circulating this obscenity could be penalized despite the fact that it was interlaced with material that was not itself obscene.

An examination of my definition will also show that obscenity is not the same thing as the mere sponsorship of immorality, even though the reason for the proscription of obscenity is, of course, moral. Recently a newspaper item in my city mentioned that a man arrested for the sexual abuse of children had written and distributed a pamphlet entitled "How To Have Sex With Kids." Whether the pamphlet were obscene would be a question of fact to be determined by applying the criterion given above. One can—just barely—imagine such a pamphlet having been written in such a way that despite its gross immorality, it was purely pragmatic and would not tend to excite morbid passions in its actual or intended audience. In that unlikely but not altogether impossible case, it would not be obscene. I do not say that it could not be proscribed; but if it could, its proscription would have to be justified on other grounds.

It may well be, of course, that other grounds would not be hard to find. Then again it may not. I am assuming that this pamphlet was nothing but a technical manual for the commission of a crime. As such it would certainly lack absolute protection. For it would not constitute discursive reasoning about sexual ethics; it would not constitute discursive reasoning about the law; and it would not provide information that the public would need in order to engage in discursive reasoning about the government. It would not say, "Here is why the act is right and should be legal," or even, "Here is a principled argument for open civil disobedience." Rather it would say, "Here is how to commit the act in secret and get away with it." And if this assumption about the pamphlet were wrong? Yes, arguments of the types that I assumed it did not contain *would* warrant absolute protection. As John Stuart Mill observed, a rational confrontation with our foes may be illuminating even if it does not convert us. It may convert *them*; and it may help us to an *active* understanding of a truth that, formerly, we had believed only in an indolent way.[1] In the meantime, the act itself is still illegal, and knowing, now, who approves it, we are better able to protect our children from them.

Caseline One: Standard Obscenity

"Standard" obscenity is the name I will give to that (flawed) understanding of obscenity and its constitutional status in which the

Supreme Court has invested the greatest portion of its labors. It begins, interestingly, in a case that does not directly involve obscenity at all—*Chaplinsky v. New Hampshire*, decided in 1941. Chaplinsky, a Jehovah's Witness, had one day been distributing tracts in the streets and (according to witnesses) denouncing all religion as a racket. That, by the principles of true tolerance, was his right. But an ugly crowd gathered. After a disturbance began, a police officer began to escort Chaplinsky to the station. He did not arrest him, merely warning him that he was in danger from the crowd. So far no violation of the Constitution was alleged. But then, Chaplinsky supposedly told the officer "with force and arms" that he was a "God damned racketeer" and a "damned Fascist" and that "the whole government of Rochester are Fascists or agents of Fascists." For this, Chaplinsky was charged with violating a state statute against what came to be called "fighting words." In his defense, he challenged the statute on grounds that it violated the First Amendment.

After various appeals Chaplinsky's conviction was upheld by the Supreme Court. Said Justice Murphy,

> Allowing the broadest scope to the language and purpose of the First Amendment, it is well understood that the right of free speech is not absolute under all times and under all circumstances. There are certain well-defined and narrowly limited classes of speech, the prevention and punishment of which have never been thought to raise any constitutional problem. These include the lewd and obscene, the profane, the libelous, and the insulting or "fighting" words—those which by their very utterance inflict injury or tend to incite an immediate breach of the peace. It has been well observed that such utterances are no essential part of any exposition of ideas, and are of such slight social value as a step to truth that any benefit that may be derived from them is clearly outweighed by the social interest in order and morality.[2]

Just why this decision was used as a precedent in later obscenity cases is clear. The nature of Justice Murphy's argument is not clear. On the one hand, it seems to suggest that except for certain narrowly defined categories of expression, the protection of the First Amendment is indeed absolute. But the way in which it establishes just which forms of expression are to be categorically excepted is not the way that the absolute language of the First Amendment permits—that is, to define *what, within that language, counts as "speech."* Rather it assumes that *even the forms excepted* are "speech"—justifying their exception by weighing their social value as "steps to truth" against the social value of "order and morality." Two wholly different approaches to protection are confused.

This confusion is revealed with particular clarity in the final sentence of the passage quoted. That "such utterances are no essential part of any exposition of ideas" could have served a categorical-exception approach by defining what counts as "speech" within the language of the First Amendment. But that is not how the idea is used, for the next part of the sentence reverses it. Instead of saying that such utterances are *no* part of discursive reasoning in the interests of truth, it says that they *do* form a part, albeit one that is so slight that it can be outweighed by other considerations. Clearly Justice Murphy does assume that "steps to truth" are precisely the social value that the Amendment is intended to promote. But if he thinks that this value can be balanced against others, then clearly in his view it is *not* constitutionally absolute— and that means that he is really following not a categorical-exception approach, but a balancing approach. Whether he knew that he was doing this is another question; his rhetoric suggests that he did not.

Unfortunately, this confusion between a categorical-exception and a balancing approach persists in later cases which deal directly with obscenity. While claiming that obscenity is categorically excepted from First Amendment protection, the Court has incorporated balancing tests in its definition. Besides this, in various cases involving both obscenity and other matters, the Court has persisted in its confusion about the constitutional meaning of "speech":

- In *Chaplinsky*, as we have seen, the Court dropped a hint that speech might be the exposition of ideas, but declined to follow up with a definition.
- In *Winters v. New York*, a 1948 case involving a magazine devoted to stories of "bloodshed, lust, and crime," the Court announced that "We do not accede to appellee's suggestion that the constitutional protection for a free speech applies only to the exposition of ideas."[3]
- In *Joseph Burstyn v. Commissioner of Education*, a 1952 case involving the censorship of motion pictures, the Court held that entertainment deserves First Amendment protection because it *is* an exposition of ideas—then, seemingly unaware of the discrepancy, called on the authority of *Winters*.[4]
- In *Roth v. United States*, the 1957 case in which the Court offered its first definition of obscenity, it returned to the idea that obscenity has no First

Amendment protection because—being no part of an exposition of ideas—it is utterly without redeeming social value. To back this up, it quoted from *Chaplinsky*.[5]

And so on, until finally,

- In *Shad v. Borough of Mount Ephraim*, decided in 1981, the Court ruled that the First Amendment protects coin-operated mechanisms that allow customers to watch nude dancers perform live behind glass panels—on the grounds that nude dancing, being entertainment, does not have to be an exposition of ideas to have social value.[6]

But I am getting ahead of the argument. Let us return to *Roth*, and see how the standard approach to obscenity evolved.

Justice Brennan, writing for the Court, undertook in *Roth* a broad survey of the guarantees of freedom of expression in effect in the states which had ratified the Constitution by 1792. He showed quite clearly that freedom of expression was not then construed as protecting every utterance, and in particular, that laws everywhere proscribed obscenity. Not resting with this, he showed that obscenity was still decisively rejected by community mores, observing that it was illegal in every one of the states and had been addressed by Congress twenty times from 1842 to the year in which *Roth* was heard. To further illuminate the real object of freedom of speech and press, he quoted from a letter of the Continental Congress sent to the inhabitants of Quebec in 1774:

> The last right we shall mention, regards the freedom of the press. The importance of this consists, besides the advancement of truth, science, morality and arts[7] in general, in its diffusion of liberal sentiments on the administration of Government, its ready communication of thoughts between subjects, and its consequential promotion of union among them, whereby oppressive officers are shamed or intimidated, into more honourable and just modes of conducting affairs.[8]

He explained that the touchstone of obscenity is whether the material has a tendency to excite lustful thoughts. However, construction of a definition suitable for judicial use is slightly more complicated. "The early leading standard of obscenity," developed in a British case in 1868, "allowed material to be judged merely by the effect of an isolated excerpt upon particularly susceptible persons." Some American courts adopted this standard, but later decisions, said Brennan, rejected it and substituted another, which he and the majority of his colleagues approved:

> whether to the average person, applying contemporary community standards, the dominant theme of the material taken as a whole appeals to prurient interest.[9]

In view of the meticulous historical presentation that preceded this announcement, Justice Brennan's failure to give a careful justification for the definition itself is rather surprising. Even the contrast with its British predecessor leaves most of the argument to the reader's power of filling and smoothing ellipses. An attempt to develop such an argument might have revealed that the new definition and the rules for applying it had serious flaws. Perhaps this is not so bad; flaws, great or small, are all but inevitable in any first attempt to construct an authoritative judicial standard. Later cases might have been expected to bring these flaws to the surface, where they could have been seen and eliminated. Unfortunately, that is not what happened. In later cases they did come to the surface, but they were not eliminated. Instead they were exacerbated. First let us see just what these flaws are.

The first flaw is not in the definition itself, but in the rules for its application; they do not reckon with the paradox that "to the pure all things are pure." As the judge of prurient interest, the decision established "the average person, applying contemporary community standards." What Brennan intended this provision to remedy was the British error of allowing material to be judged by its effect on "particularly susceptible" persons. That was indeed an error; but this provision merely replaced it with another. In one sense, of course, "contemporary community standards" are quite appropriate to the determination of obscenity. In a community in which no one ever wore clothing, nudity per se could not be obscene because it could never excite lust; in another community, it might. The difficulty, however, is that Brennan intended the average person to apply these contemporary community standards to *himself*. An example will show how this misses the point. In an average person—at any rate, in a morally healthy person, who may or may not be average—the photographic exhibition of children performing sexual acts would not arouse lust. Rather it would arouse pity, and an indignation against the photographer. For that matter, lust is not the predominant response of a morally healthy person even to the photographic exhibition of adults performing sexual acts. The predominant response is shame over the exhibition of what ought to be an intimate and sheltered exchange of tenderness. Of course he will turn away from the dreary spectacle, partly *lest his interest should* turn into lust; the experiment of finding out what he will feel if he does continue to look is not one he wants to undertake, nor one the Court should require of him. Thus if the average member of the community were morally healthy, a Brennan juror, assuming this character, could never find either of these exhibitions obscene. Only if the average member of the community were a voyeur or worse could he agree, "Yes, this appeals to my lust; it is obscene."

This first flaw would be eliminated had Justice Brennan simply made the determination of obscenity depend on the tendency of material to arouse lust in *its actual or intended audience*. We can see that this would have hit the target in our example: voyeurs, ordinary and pedophilic, are precisely the market for the two kinds of exhibition mentioned. Moreover, by framing the rule in this way, everything that really needed to be admitted about the importance of contemporary community standards would already have been presumed.

The nearest the Court has ever come to eliminating the flaw in question was in *Ginzburg v. United States*, decided in 1965, and *Ginsberg v. New York*, decided in 1968. In the former, the Court allowed the fact that material was openly advertised as having prurient appeal to be admitted as presumptive evidence that it did, in fact, have prurient appeal and was therefore obscene. In the latter, the Court upheld the conviction of a man for selling a 16-year-old boy a "girlie" magazine that was *not* alleged to be obscene as regards adults. At the time, commentators claimed that the Court had shifted to a "variable" obscenity standard. If true, this would have been a significant advance. However it was not true. In neither case did the Court adjust the definition of obscenity (which had by then undergone other revisions) to provide, in general, for the effect of the material upon its audience rather than upon the presumably normal juror. Nor in the latter case, as Justice Fortas noted in his dissent, did it provide a supplementary definition of obscenity as regards minors—resting instead on the observation that "the power of the state to control the conduct of children reaches beyond the scope of its authority over adults."[10] This was true, of course, but not a remedy for the flaw that I have described. Two great opportunities for its remedy had been missed, and the precedential value of the decisions was never clear.

The second flaw in *Roth's* doctrine is its reliance on the narrow concept of "prurient appeal." As Justice Brennan explained, material has prurient appeal only if it has a tendency to excite lustful thoughts, and by lust, he meant sexual lust.[11] This way of characterizing obscenity is surprising because, as his own historical survey had made quite clear, far more than ordinary sexual lust was covered by the traditional concept of obscenity. Moreover, a great (and by all accounts, increasing) proportion of the material which is sold to morbidly obsessive people excites passions which do not meet this standard: for instance, a vigorous market presence is enjoyed by photographs and films of men and women being covered with urine and feces, mutilated, and killed. We may agree, on the testimony of Sigmund Freud, that all of these somehow have a sexual basis; overtly, however, they are not sexual.[12]

Although, since *Roth*, the Court has declined to *exclude* the other morbid passions from the standard of obscenity—and has sometimes even glanced in their direction—the issue they pose has been squarely faced only by those members of the Court who have *opposed* the regulation of obscenity! For instance Justice Douglas, in his *Ginzburg* dissent, remarked that "Some like Chopin, others like 'rock and roll.' Some are 'normal,' some are masochistic, some deviant in other respects." He then asked, "Why is it unlawful to cater to the needs of this group?" The answer, of course, is that it is not unlawful—but that it should be. Nothing becomes a "need" merely because it is desired. No one "needs" what inflames his desire to torture and be tortured. One quails at Justice Douglas's enclosure of the word "normal" by quotation marks. But Justice Brennan himself, toward the close of his career, was no longer far from this position, opposing all regulation of obscenity except for what was aimed at minors and unconsenting adults.[13]

The third and last flaw in the *Roth* doctrine is its insistence that obscenity be determined only with respect to the "dominant theme of the material taken as a whole." This was a fundamental departure from precedent, and a grave mistake. The correct approach to mixed materials, I suggest, was taken in *Valentine v. Chrestensen*, decided in 1942. A municipal ordinance of New York forbade the distribution in the streets of printed handbills containing commercial advertising. The respondent, Valentine, owned a former U.S. Navy submarine. When he attempted to distribute a handbill advertising that the boat would be exhibited to visitors for a fee, Police Commissioner Chrestensen informed him that distribution of advertising handbills was prohibited by the ordinance. Valentine responded by preparing a proof of the same handbill, this time with a political message on the other side. With it, he returned to Chrestensen. The commissioner explained that Valentine would be perfectly free to distribute handbills bearing the political message alone, but not handbills bearing the political message on one side and the commercial advertisement on the other. Valentine printed the handbill anyway, and attempted to distribute it. When the police interfered, he filed suit, claiming a violation of his First Amendment rights. Two issues are involved here. The first is whether commercial advertising is constitutionally protected. Whether the Court was right or wrong about that does not concern us here, except insofar as its finding that commercial advertising is *not* constitutionally protected enabled it to consider the second issue, which does concern us. That issue is whether a valid prohibition of constitutionally protected material becomes void in cases where constitutionally *un*protected material is inseparably attached to the same instrument of expression.

The Court said "No," firmly sealing off the route of escape from prohibition that Valentine had attempted to take. "If that evasion were successful," said Justice Roberts for the Court, "every merchant who desires to broadcast advertising leaflets in the streets need only append a civic appeal, or a moral platitude, to achieve immunity from the law's command."[14] He was right—and his observation may also be applied more generally. If the evasion were possible in the case of commercial advertising laws, there is no reason why it should not be possible in the case of laws involving libels, fighting words, or obscenity. Yet, unaccountably, Justice Brennan reopened the escape hatch when he surveyed obscenity. The "dominant theme of the material taken as a whole" provision allows a distributor to escape any and all prohibitions by interlacing his filth with lectures on abnormal psychology, packaging it as an account of unusual sexual customs, or appending a platitude to "avoid following these bad examples."

Why we should be more solicitous of pornographers than of advertisers is very hard to fathom. Possibly Justice Brennan was concerned that the proscription of obscenity might interfere with the circulation of material that really does deserve absolute protection. For instance, someone might claim that a legitimate textbook on anatomy or discussion of the ethics of sex is obscene because some readers find the topic intrinsically arousing. *Valentine* seemed to suggest that legitimate expression could be protected by focussing on the *intent* to evade; however, criteria based on intent alone are often difficult to apply, and Justice Brennan may have concluded that some other strategy for protection was needed. If so, he simply settled on the wrong one. For we have already considered this problem. No more would be needed than to add a single clause to the definition of obscenity: to say that a form of expression is obscene if it would tend to excite morbid passions in its actual or intended audience—but only provided that this tendency could have been averted, by excision or modification, without removing an essential component of expression that warrants absolute protection. Unlike the "dominant theme of the material taken as a whole" provision, this would not render all obscenity laws unenforceable.

To conclude this discussion of *Roth*: we see in Justice Brennan's definition a serious effort to come to grips with obscenity, but one that is utterly (and needlessly) useless for doing anything about it. With this we turn to *Memoirs v. Massachusetts*, more colloquially known as *Fanny Hill* after the main character of the book that it concerned—the second of the three most important obscenity cases, decided in 1966.

Far less need be said about *Memoirs* than about *Roth*, because it was essentially a transitional decision. The plurality opinion was joined by only three Justices, and the remaining five—some concurring in the judgment, some not—were split several ways as to how obscenity should be understood. What is noteworthy about *Memoirs* is that although it presented its definition of obscenity as nothing more than *Roth's* definition, as elaborated by subsequent decisions, the definition was in fact brand new. Writing for the plurality, Justice Brennan said that for material to be judged obscene,

it must be established (a) that the dominant theme of the material as a whole appeals to a prurient interest in sex; (b) the material is patently offensive because it affronts contemporary community standards relating to the description or representation of sexual matters; and (c) the material is utterly without redeeming social value.[15]

These criteria were to be satisfied *independently*, and unless all three were satisfied, material could not be considered obscene.

The first point to be noted is that the new definition does not remedy even one of the three flaws of the *Roth* doctrine. The second and third of these flaws—reliance on the narrow concept of "prurient appeal" and insistence that obscenity be determined only with respect to the "dominant theme of the material taken as a whole"—are merely reproduced in *Memoirs* condition *a*. Apparently the first of the three flaws is reproduced as well; for although we are not told for whom the material is supposed to have its prurient appeal, the presumption seems to be that once again, this appeal is for the average person rather than for the actual or intended audience of the material in question.

The second point to be noted is that in *Memoirs* condition *b*, the *Roth* concept of "contemporary community standards" is put to use in a new way—a way that was not anticipated in *Roth*, that has nothing to do with morbid passion, and that makes the unenforceability of obscenity regulations even more a foregone conclusion than before. Suddenly we are told that material must be "patently offensive" in the light of these community standards before it can be judged obscene. *Roth* had told us that material may not be judged obscene unless ordinary people find it arousing; without withdrawing that requirement, *Memoirs* now tells us that it may not be judged obscene unless ordinary people also find it distasteful. Of course they are unlikely to find distasteful what they already find arousing, so we have a neat Catch-22.

The third point to be noted is that in *Memoirs* condition *c*—that in order to be judged obscene, material must be "*utterly* without redeeming social value"—the confusion between a categorical-exception approach and a balancing approach, which was inherited through *Roth* from its ancestor, *Chaplinsky*, finally becomes malignant. As Chief Justice Burger remarked seven rueful years later in *Miller v. California*, "the *Memoirs* plurality produced a drastically altered test that called on the prosecution to prove a negative, . . . a burden virtually impossible to discharge under our criminal standards of proof."[16] That under an *unconfused* categorical-exception approach, material found obscene would have been deemed *by definition* utterly without value of the kind contemplated by the First Amendment, is of no avail here. For one of the great lessons of *Memoirs* and subsequent cases is that scholarly "experts" can always be found in plenty to testify to the social value of anything whatever: no matter how worthless, no matter how vile.

Judge Clark seemed to take it upon himself to prove this thesis. In his dissent he carefully described both the book whose Constitutional status was at issue in this case, and what the experts said about it. Its full title was *John Cleland's Memoirs of a Woman of Pleasure*. An account of the sexual activities of a bawdy house through the eyes of a 15-year-old prostitute named Fanny Hill, it was described by the defense—note well, by the *defense*—as "the first deliberately dirty novel in English."[17] Of course, the defense was trying to make a point: that a book that is not merely dirty, but dirty and old, cannot possibly be *"utterly* without redeeming social value"; that the antiquity of its dirtiness redeems it. In much the same vein, a certain portion of the testimony was devoted to showing that the book was "well-written."[18] From a review submitted by the defense: "Yet all these pangs of defloration are in the service of erotic pleasure—Fanny's and the reader's. Postponing the culmination of Fanny's deflowering is equivalent to postponing the point where the reader has a mental orgasm."[19] If this is what constitutes good writing, it does not redeem dirtiness; it increases it.[20] But the soaring zenith of scholarly fatuity is reached by a witness who calls the central character "what I call an intellectual . . . someone who is extremely curious about life and who seeks . . . to record with accuracy the details of the external world, physical sensations, psychological responses . . . an empiricist . . ."[21] Just what sorts of "details" is this "intellectual," this "empiricist," concerned to "record" so "accurately"? As Justice Clark observes, in each of the more than two dozen bizarre, perverse, and often gory sexual scenes that make up almost the whole of the book, "the exposed bodies of the participants are described in minute and individual detail. The pubic hair is used for a background to the most vivid and precise descriptions of the response, condition, size, shape, and color of the sexual organs before, during, and after orgasms."[22]

There is much more of this, but one suspects that Justice Clark was speaking to a chamber that was, if not wholly empty, at least not full. For his part, Justice Douglas was more interested in endorsing the thesis of a Unitarian minister who had compared *Memoirs of a Woman of Pleasure* with a book by the Rev. Norman Vincent Peale on the subject of *Sin, Sex, and Self-Control*. The point was that "at the present point in the twentieth century," both of these two books "symbolize the human quest for what is moral" in a high and inspiring way.[23] Justice Douglas reproduced the entire text of the minister's sermon in a lengthy appendix to his concurring opinion.

We turn, finally, to the last of the three key decisions in the standard obscenity caseline: *Miller v. California*. Decided in 1973, this case gave us yet another definition of obscenity, and this one was destined to last. But what is most wondrously strange in *Miller* is that despite its harsh criticism of *Memoirs* and high-flown rhetoric about returning to the approach pioneered in *Roth*, its definition bears little resemblance to *Roth's* and is almost identical to the one offered in *Memoirs*. Speaking for the majority, Chief Justice Burger declares that

> The basic guidelines for the trier of fact must be: (a) whether "the average person, applying contemporary community standards" would find that the work, taken as a whole, appeals to the prurient interest; (b) whether the work depicts or describes, in a patently offensive way, sexual conduct specifically defined by the applicable state law; and (c) whether the work, taken as a whole, lacks serious literary, artistic, political, or scientific value.[24]

He also makes clear that henceforth, "community" is to mean the local community, not the nation as a whole.[25]

Component by component, let us see what this definition offers. As to *Miller* condition *a:* This is the same as *Memoirs* condition *a*, except in one respect. *Memoirs* condition *a* reproduced two of the three flaws of the *Roth* doctrine explicitly, and one only apparently. By contrast, *Miller* condition *a* reproduces all three explicitly. And the fact that the contemporary community standards which the average person is to apply are now specified as being local rather than national does nothing to ameliorate flaw number one (the only one to which it might be relevant): for this average person is still to apply them in the wrong way. "The" prurient interest means *his* prurient interest, not the prurient interest of the actual or intended audience.

As to *Miller* condition *b:* This merely reproduces the flaw of *Memoirs* condition *b*, a flaw newly invented in *Memoirs* for which *Roth* was not to blame.

And as to *Miller* condition *c:* This differs from *Memoirs* condition *c* in two respects. The first is that the "value" which, in the case of filth, is held to be redemptive, is now called "literary, artistic, political, or scientific" instead of "social." But these two descriptions seem equally inclusive; for instance they both require us to say that the venerably filthy, the skillfully filthy, the contentiously filthy, the knowledgeably filthy, and the intriguingly filthy are not filthy. The second difference between *Miller c* and *Memoirs c* is that the threshold under which value must sink before it ceases to be redemptive has been lowered: instead of requiring that material must be "utterly" without value in order to be judged obscene, it requires only that the material lack "serious" value. But this change is mostly cosmetic. One reason for saying so is that any importance it might otherwise have had is vitiated by yet another application of the phrase, "taken as a whole." The other is that—as the Chief Justice amazingly overlooks—the new requirement *still* requires the prosecution to discharge the "virtually impossible" task of proving a negative. That is precisely the defect of *Memoirs* about which he had most bitterly complained. This illustrates once again the folly of confusing a categorical-exception with a balancing approach. The former would permit no such requirement.

Let us conclude this section. Obscenity, the Court says, is constitutionally unprotected. Yet the Court protects it by rendering the proof of obscenity almost impossible. Hardly can a jury turn in a conviction without defying its instructions and applying common sense instead of the legal definition. Hardly can an appeals court uphold a conviction without doing the same. Thus the Court almost requires judges and jurors to be liars in order to do what, by its own reiterated teaching, the law requires and the Constitution does not forbid. Because most of our judges and jurors do not want to lie, the least effort to limit the distribution of the morbid and degrading is so difficult that many if not most of our communities no longer even try. Chief Justice Burger himself had to scramble for an argument that evaded the definition he had written in *Miller* when, eight years later, in *Schad v. Borough of Mount Emphraim*, he found himself in the minority—though perhaps he did not explain it to himself in that way.[26] This was the case in which the Court classified coin-operated machines that permit customers to view live gyrations of genitals and other body parts as media of protected "speech."

That this goes on in the name of republican liberty beggars the imagination. How has the Court responded to the explosive spread of the obscene? By putting the blame on the nature of obscenity rather than on its own defective doctrines. We may witness three reactions, besides the dominant reaction of grimly staying on course.

First, there have been those dissenters, such as the late Justice Douglas, who advocated the complete abandonment of any effort to set constitutional standards for obscenity. This jurist quite frankly admitted that he saw no reason why lewd materials should not be available even to children.[27]

Second, there have been the disillusioned, such as Justice Brennan, who in *Miller* complained of "institutional stress" without recognizing that it was self-induced.[28] Concluding that obscenity is impossible to define, he finally declared that it should be regulated only to protect children and unconsenting adults. But as Chief Justice Burger remarked in *Miller*, there is no reason to think that it can be defined for children and unconsenting adults if it cannot be defined for consenting adults.[29] In much the same vein as Justice Brennan's proposal, there have been suggestions ever since *Roth* that the Court should give up the effort to define obscenity in general, and instead permit the regulation of only "hard-core" obscenity. But as Chief Justice Warren asked with Justice Clark in a dissent to the 1963 case *Jacobellis v. Ohio*, who can define "hard-core" obscenity with any greater clarity than "obscenity"?[30] Or to put a different twist on this remark: Why should we expect Justices to see what is involved in the former when they have failed to see what is involved in the latter? The cogency of the question is pointed up by the fate of the *Miller* decision. One of the arguments that Chief Justice Burger advanced in its favor was that at last, it *did* narrow the focus of the *Roth* doctrine to "hard-core" obscenity.[31] Yet clearly this was false: for it allows all obscenity to get by, be its "core" a "hard" one or a "soft." In the meantime, the jaded public is losing both the ability and the interest to make distinctions.[32]

Third, the Court has raised a new Constitutional doctrine alongside the old, which I will briefly examine in the next subsection but one: "child pornography." By this means it has permitted the regulation of one small class of material that the standard definition was expected to reach, but cannot reach. Yet the need for supplementary doctrines is very hard to gauge when the standard doctrine itself is so badly in need of repair; and this particularly supplementary doctrine has certain peculiarities of its own, as we will see.

Unlike common sense about some things, common sense about obscenity is not repugnant to the Constitution; it is merely more and more in decay. The Court should never have attempted to do without this common sense; instead it should have tempered it. There would have lain the path of true tolerance.

Caseline Two: Indecency

I call the clutch of cases that deal with indecency a "caseline" mostly for the sake of parallel with the titles of the other subsections in this section. Even the term, "indecency," does not appear in all of them. Their logical connections are not well developed in the decisions themselves, and, although the Burger Court showed a glacial drift in the direction of less protection rather than more, these decisions show very little in the way of evolving doctrine. For purposes of my argument, two contrasting cases will serve quite well. Because I do not have a great deal to say on this topic, we will move swiftly.

Cohen v. California was decided in 1971. The action begins when the aponymic gentleman is witnessed in a corridor outside the Municipal Court in the County Courthouse, wearing a jacket on which the words "F--- the Draft" are plainly visible. In the corridor are women and children. Cohen is arrested, charged, and convicted of violating a California law which prohibits maliciously and willfully disturbing the peace or quiet of any neighborhood or person by offensive conduct. The gist of his defense is that he did not perform any violent act; that he did not threaten to perform any violent act; and that the jacket itself had not incited anyone to perform, or threaten to perform, any violent act. He states that he wore the jacket merely to inform the public of the depth of his sentiments against the selective service law and the war in Vietnam. The state court is not impressed, and affirms the conviction. It reasons that "offensive conduct" means conduct with a *tendency* to provoke others to commit violent acts and disturb the peace, and that Cohen could reasonably have foreseen that a jacket bearing the legend "F--- the Draft" might produce this effect.[33]

FCC v. Pacifica Foundation was decided in 1978. Here the action begins when a radio station owned by licensee Pacifica broadcasts a prerecorded monologue entitled "Filthy Words." The monologue, which is presented as comedy, lists and reiterates a large number of colloquial uses of what it calls "words you couldn't say on the public airwaves." As the monologue comes on the air, a father is driving in an automobile with his little boy, their radio turned to the Pacifica station. The broadcast upsets him, whereupon he complains to the Federal Communications Commission. In response, the FCC determines that the monologue is indecent even though not obscene, and therefore falls under U.S. law prohibiting the transmission by radio of "any obscene, indecent, or profane language." Without punishing the station immediately, the FCC puts its declaratory order in the station's file. Pacifica files suit. Treating "indecency" and "obscenity" as different terms for the same thing, it argues that because the broadcast did not appeal to prurient interest, it could not have been indecent.

These two cases resulted in opposite decisions by the Supreme Court. Cohen was given the right to use indecent words on a jacket; Pacifica was denied the right to broadcast them over the radio. Let us reason as lawyers do and see whether we can find any differences in the circumstances of the cases that would rationalize their different outcomes.

There appear to be two such differences. One is that Cohen's jacket used indecent language in order to express a political slogan, while Pacifica's broadcast used indecent language merely in an attempt to entertain. But this distinction is hardly to be taken seriously. If anything, it should have cut the other way. For the Court has often made clear its view (whether or not this view is correct) that forms of expression do not lose their constitutional protection merely by being entertainment, and it has never (whether or not it should have) claimed that entertainment is entitled to less protection than political speech. Thus, the question should have been the same in both cases: Could the indecent language have been eliminated without impairing a protected element of expression? In *Cohen*, it could have; in *Pacifica*, it could not. Cohen could have expressed the same political view, with the same clarity, even with the same emotional intensity, without using offensive language—the contrary view of Justice Harlan, speaking for the *Cohen* majority, notwithstanding. All he would have lost would be a *way* of expressing emotional intensity—one which said, in effect, "I feel so strongly about this that I don't care about *your* feelings; in order to prove it, I am even willing to use language that injures you." By contrast, without the indecent language, the comedy of the Pacifica broadcast would have lost its point—the comment by Justice Stevens, speaking for the *Pacifica* majority, that it was not part of an expression of ideas, notwithstanding. Freud explained about this in *Jokes and their Relation to the Unconscious*: indecent jokes produce pleasure by releasing inhibitions. But one need not study the Father of Psychoanalysis to get the idea. One need only read the transcript of the broadcast. Such as it is, the humor of the monologue is produced by sheer, grinding repetition. Without its "Filthy Words," nothing would be left but shreds and scraps of connective tissue.

The second difference is that Cohen displayed indecent language in the corridor of a public building, while Pacifica broadcast indecent language over the public airwaves. But again, the difference is hardly to be taken seriously. The *Pacifica* opinion called attention to two distinctive features of radio broadcasts as justifying their scrutiny for indecent content. The same two features distinguished Cohen's exhibition of his jacket. First, since a broadcast audience "is constantly tuning in and out, prior warnings cannot completely protect [the listener from] unexpected program content."[34] But the employees and other citizens in the Courthouse corridor were constantly *walking* in and out. Making matters worse, many of them, either because of their official duties or because of their legal business, had no choice but to be there. Of course, Justice Harlan asserted that "those in the Los Angeles courthouse could effectively avoid further bombardment of their sensibilities simply by averting their eyes."[35] But as Justice Stevens remarked in reply to the analogous assertion, "to say that one may avoid further offense by turning off the radio . . . is like saying that the remedy for an assault is to run away after the first blow."[36] Second, said the *Pacifica* Court, "broadcasting is uniquely accessible to children."[37] But as the record showed, children were present in the Courthouse corridor as well; and while public buildings may not be "unique" in their concentration of juveniles, one ought to bear in mind that where parents have no choice but to go, children often have no choice but to follow.

The fact is that the differences in the outcomes of *Cohen* and *Pacifica* were not due to differences in their circumstances. They were decided on different theories. Both theories allowed that there are categorical exceptions to First Amendment protection, but:

- Justice Harlan said that the kind of language that was later to be called "indecent" did not fall into any of the categorical exceptions that the Court had already established; Justice Stewart said that for circumstances like those under consideration, a new categorical exception should be established.
- Justice Harlan said that indecent utterances are "necessary side effects of the broader enduring values which the process of open debate permits us to achieve"; Justice Stewart said that they are "no essential part of the exposition of ideas."[38]
- Justice Harlan said that any theory which could support the proscription of indecent language under circumstances like those under consideration would "effectively empower a majority to silence dissidents simply as a matter of personal predilections"; Justice Stewart said that "at most," the proscription of indecency as defined by the FCC would "deter only the broadcasting of patently offensive references to excretory and sexual organs and activities."[39]

Justice Stewart had by far the stronger side of this argument. For Justice Harlan's claim about "necessary side effects" serves him much less well than it seems to; it gains apparent force only through the ambiguity of the word "necessary." To be sure, in the white heat of political argument, with tempers going off like signal flares, a certain amount of indecent language inevitably does leak past the civilized inhibitions that help us to stay on the subject, think clearly, and keep from killing each other. That hardly diminishes the value of a public commitment to keeping these inhibitions in good repair. Nor does necessity in the sense of inevitability imply necessity in the sense of a requirement: we do not need to prime ourselves with indecency in order to begin a discussion of politics, and indecency does not heighten the rationality of the engagement once begun. As to Justice Harlan's wild speculation that prohibiting the use of the word "f---" around children who have no choice but to be present would somehow commit us to the suppression of political dissidents—to put this plainly is sufficient to refute it.

Or is it? Justice Harlan said that there is no way to distinguish the word on Cohen's jacket from any other offensive word. We have seen that argument before: it is a version of our old friend, the Slippery Slope Slogan. But Justice Harlan gives it a new twist, which we might call the Bad Faith Variation. "Governments," he warns, "might soon seize upon the censorship of particular words as a convenient guise for banning the expression of unpopular views."[40]

They might indeed. But then, so might they seize upon the proscriptions of libel or of "fighting words" for this purpose; in fact, that would seem by far the more likely, because it would be easier and because there is precedent for it.[41] Shall we get rid of them too? It would serve no purpose; for *no* construction of *any* constitutional guarantee is proof against its abuse by an unchecked government acting in bad faith. The Court, however, is empowered to act as a check. That is a function of judicial review. The important question, then, is not whether an abuse of a doctrine permitting the proscription of indecent language can be imagined; it is whether the doctrine invites such abuse.

If the doctrine were fashioned after *Pacifica*, the answer would be "No." In the first place, the Court's opinion did not approve any form of regulation more stringent than that applied by the FCC to Pacifica Foundation. That regulation did *not* require "censorship" in the narrow sense; it did not involve prior screening of broadcast material by FCC officials. Moreover, even its proscription of indecent language was less than absolute. The FCC wished to treat indecent language in a fashion analogous to the law of nuisance—which channels offenses, rather than prohibiting them. For instance, the FCC directed attention to the time of day during which children were most likely to be in the audience.

In the second place and even more important: even in the act of accepting the FCC's definition of indecent speech as "patently offensive" and its decision to regulate on that basis, Justice Stewart issued warning. "The fact that society may find speech offensive," he said, "is not [by itself] sufficient reason for suppressing it. Indeed, if it is the speaker's opinion that gives offense [rather than the manner in which he expresses it], that consequence is a reason for affording it First Amendment protection."[42] Thus, like a two-edged knife, the concept of the offensive must cut both ways. Words may lose protection through offense, but opinions must be protected all the more.

For these reasons, there would be no need to object to a general indecency doctrine modelled after *Pacifica*. But what relation has all this to obscenity? *Had the Court defined obscenity properly in the first place*, there would be no relation. We would then have two distinct categorical exceptions to the absolute protection of the First Amendment. One would single out forms of expression that do nothing but excite the morbid passions; the other would single out forms of expression that do nothing but offend the community. Both would be consistent with the same understanding of what it is that the promises of free speech and press protect: discursive reasoning and the communication of republican information. And both would be phrased in such a way that these promises were not diminished.

However, the inclusion of a *separate* "patent offensiveness" criterion in the Court's definition of obscenity is a blurted confession of the Court's inability to see that phenomenon clearly. In order to be what it is, says the Court, indecency must be only what it is. But in order to be what *it* is, obscenity must be something else as well.

Caseline Three: Child Pornography

With a single stroke of the modelling knife, the 1982 case *New York v. Ferber* carves a complete new approach to the regulation of obscenity. A Victorian writer might speak of Athena springing grown from the forehead of Zeus, but the simile would not be helpful: for Zeus was wise, and Athena flawless. *Ferber*, by mischaracterizing the standard approach to obscenity, evades the difficulties in the relationship between the father doctrine and the daughter doctrine; and in the same great arc of reasoning in which it damns the sexual abuse of children, it specifies conditions under which that abuse would have to be allowed.

It is a bad decision. Yet it is better than *Miller*; and thus it raises the painful question whether bad law can be justified by its tendency to ameliorate some of the defects of even worse law. I think that, at least in some cases, the answer to this question is "Yes." Had the standard caseline defined obscenity properly in the first place, *Ferber* would have been unnecessary. But beggars can't be choosers, and given the sorry state of the standard approach, we are better off with this flawed child pornography doctrine than without it.

Here are the facts of the case. The New York legislature passed a statute prohibiting persons from knowingly promoting sexual performances by children by distributing material which depicts such performances. "Sexual performances" were defined as performances including actual or simulated sexual intercourse, deviate sexual intercourse, sexual bestiality, masturbation, sadomasochistic abuse, or lewd exhibition of the genitals. Ferber was convicted for selling films of young boys masturbating. The New York Court of Appeals reversed his conviction, but the U.S. Supreme Court reinstated it.

Now the Court could have upheld this conviction on far sounder grounds than it actually offered. One such warrant might have been explained in this fashion: Even an absolutist approach to First Amendment protection does not forbid regulations that concern merely the time, place, and manner of expression. The guiding principle here is that protected expression loses its protection when the manner in which it is carried on violates the rights of others. For instance, the protection to which I am entitled in criticizing your political views does not guarantee me the privilege of writing my objections in spray paint on the walls of your house. In the same way, protected expression loses its protection when it is carried on in a manner that involves the sexual abuse of children.

The second way in which the Court might reasonably have upheld Ferber's conviction might have been explained like this: Just as the absolutist approach to First Amendment protection permits the promulgation of time, place, and manner regulations, so it permits the identification of forms of expression that are categorically excepted from absolute protection. Here too there is a guiding principle: only those forms of expression are "speech" or "press" which either form an essential part of discursive reasoning, or communicate information needed by the public in order to make the decisions for which it is Constitutionally responsible. But surely lewd depictions of sexual performances by children are not "speech" or "press" in either sense.

These two warrants for Ferber's conviction are mutually compatible, although the first is stronger. One might, after all, argue that the second warrant could not be applied across the board because not all depictions of sexual performances by children are "lewd." In order to merit this description, they would have to have a tendency to excite morbid passions in their actual or intended audience. But consider a possibility raised by Justice O'Connor: "clinical pictures of adolescent sexuality" might be included in "medical textbooks."[43] Would such pictures necessarily tend to excite morbid passions in their actual or intended audience? Possibly not, so the second warrant would not apply. Yet still—notwithstanding the unexplained doubts of Justice O'Connor—*the pictures could not be produced without the sexual abuse of the child models*. Therefore they must be suppressed, and here the first of the two warrants takes up the slack in the second.

The *Ferber* opinion includes arguments that resemble both of the grounds that I have offered, but it develops them in an illogical and self-defeating manner.

First, Justice White, speaking for the Court, explained that the standard obscenity doctrine had been "an accommodation between the State's interests in protecting the 'sensibilities of unwilling recipients' from exposure to pornographic material and the dangers of censorship inherent in unabashedly content-based laws."[44] This, of course, was false, for the Court had never held that the willingness of recipients limited the government's power to regulate the distribution of pornography. In fact in the 1973 case *Paris Adult Theatre v. Slaton*, and over the objections of Justice Brennan, the Court had flatly rejected the idea that obscene films acquire Constitutional protection "simply because they are exhibited for consenting adults only."[45]

At any rate it was clear in *Ferber* that the standard obscenity doctrine did not reflect the state's compelling interest in ensuring the welfare of children threatened with sexual abuse. So for this second point, Justice White explained that even the *distribution* of depictions of child sexual performances hurt the children depicted, and hurt them in two ways. One of these was that the circulation of permanent records of the children's participation exacerbated the harms that they had already suffered through being made to perform. The other was that the abuse of making them perform could never be prevented so long as the network for the distribution of the product was still open.[46] Now both of these points were valid, and both of them were important. One regrets only that as he made them, Justice White missed an opportunity to revise a related doctrine. Here, he stressed the co-dependence of production and distribution. However, this dyad is really a triad: production, distribution, and consumption. Distribution and consumption are co-dependent for the same reason that production and distribution are co-dependent: without purchase, there is no point in distribution; without distribution, there is no point in production. Yet the Court had taken pains to ignore the co-dependence of distribution and consumption in *Stanley v. Georgia*, a 1968 case which gave constitutional protection to a man's possession of obscenity even though it could not lawfully have been sold to him in the first place. *Stanley* had struck an especially strange note in its suggestion that the possession of obscenity must be protected because it is somehow essential to "man's spiritual nature."[47]

Third—and here is where the vessel strikes the shoals—Justice White said that the *method* for allowing the regulation of child pornography should be the relaxation of selected components of the standard formulation of obscenity. To wit,

> The *Miller* formulation is adjusted [for application to child pornography] in the following respects: A trier of fact need not find that the material appeals to the prurient interest of the average person; it is not required that sexual conduct portrayed be done so in a patently offensive manner; and the material at issue need not be considered as a whole.[48]

What this adjustment left intact was the very last requirement of the *Miller* formulation. Before the depiction of sexual performances by children could be judged pornographic, it would still have to be shown lacking in "serious literary, artistic, political, or scientific value." Said Justice White, "How often . . . it may be necessary to employ children to engage in conduct clearly within the reach of [the New York statute] in order to produce educational, medical, or artistic works cannot be known with certainty"; but, he declared, the occasions of such necessity could be identified "through case-by-case analysis of the fact situations," and wherever the necessity was shown, the statute would have to be set aside.[49]

What this really means is that child sexual abuse must be permitted when it is deemed necessary for the achievement of educational, medical, or artistic ends, a doctrine the likes of which has not been heard since the passing of the Third Reich. Not a shred of doubt as to its wisdom was raised by any member of the Court. Indeed, several Justices, in concurring opinions, went out of their way to stress that, albeit no doubt rarely, cases in which sexual performances by children were necessary for the production of works in enduring value would certainly arise. Let not the Right grimly shake its head. We are speaking of *both* of the ideological wings of the Court. Justices Brennan and Marshall made the point in an opinion written by the former; so did Justice O'Connor in an opinion written by herself.

Justice Brennan's is the more despicable of the two opinions, if only for the evasive way in which it speaks of "depictions of children" when what it really means is "depictions of child sexual performances":

> But in my view application of [the New York statute] or any similar statute to depictions of children that in themselves do have serious literary, artistic, scientific, or medical value, would violate the First Amendment. . . . The First Amendment value of depictions of children that are in themselves serious contributions to art, literature, or science, is, by definition, simply not "*de minimis*." At the same time, the State's interest in suppression of such materials is likely to be far less compelling. For the Court's assumption of harm to the child resulting from the "permanent record" and "circulation" of the child's "participation" lacks much of its force where the contribution is a serious contribution to art or science.[50]

The last observation is particularly interesting. Let us recall just what sorts of "performances by children" had been listed in the New York statute. Who would have guessed—had not Justice Brennan informed us—that the harm resulting to a child from his being made to submit to sadistic torture would be diminished by his learning that he had contributed to a moving picture that the experts called "art?" Who would have guessed—had not Justice Brennan informed us—that the harm resulting to a child from his being made to have sex with animals could be overbalanced by his learning that he had contributed to a program of experimentation that the experts called "science"? And let us remember the great lesson of *Memoirs v. Massachusetts*: even in this fragile republic, even these many years from Nazi art and medicine and these many miles from the nightmare of Soviet psychiatry, experts of the type required can *always* be found.[51]

Caseline Four: Sexual Subordination

As I suggested earlier, despite its flaws we are better off with the *Ferber* doctrine than without it—and there is hope, however this dark age may waylay it, that its flaws might be healed in future decisions. But there is another issue besides the cure of what ails it. That other issue is its expansion. For children are not the only people victimized in the production of pornography. So are adult women, and even adult men. The objection we may anticipate to changing the *Ferber* doctrine in such a way as to protect adults along with children is, of course, that children cannot meaningfully consent to their own commercial debasement and abuse—but that adults can. To this there are two replies.

First, we must bear in mind that very few adults can ever be expected to agree to the kinds of debasement and abuse that were listed in the New York statute at issue in *Ferber*. Consequently, we should not be surprised to learn that many of the individuals who are supposed to have consented to being pornographic subjects have actually been coerced. At hearings in Minneapolis over a proposed antipornography ordinance, testimony was heard from Linda Marchiano, the woman who appeared in the well-known film *Deep Throat* under the name Linda Lovelace. Speaking of how she was beaten and threatened, she commented that "So many people say that in *Deep Throat* I have a smile on my face and I look as though I'm really enjoying myself. No one ever asked me how those bruises got on my body." Every time people view the movie, she said, "they're seeing me being raped."[52]

Second, we have to ask whether an agreement to perform such acts on camera is not, in itself, proof of the performer's inability to give meaningful consent. It is not for nothing that our legal traditions limit the recognition of consent. Consent of the victim is not an allowable defense for murder, for instance, and in most places, a promise to perform meretricious services is not enforceable. The consent of the worker is not even enough to allow that he be employed for less than a certain wage, or for more than a certain number of hours—as fixed by statute. Aren't being mutilated, raped, prostituted, bestialized, or otherwise degraded on camera equally egregious "conditions of employment"?

In the last few years, some women in the feminist movement have organized around this issue. Yet there is something peculiar in their strategies. Surely, passing *general* pornography statutes, modelled on the New York child pornography statute, would have been their most promising strategy had promoting the welfare of women abused by pornography been their primary goal. The attribution of intentions to people on the basis of their actions alone is a very risky business, but the very different strategy that they have actually pursued suggests that promoting the welfare of women may have been significantly less important to them than raising consciousness. For one can raise consciousness just as well (and maybe even better) while losing all the battles, and the loss of this battle—with prejudice to all later battles—was a foregone conclusion. Instead of promoting the expansion of an already established categorical exception to First Amendment protection, this particular feminist faction has insisted on the establishment of a new categorical exception—one that would not only let a great deal of genuinely pornographic material past the gate, but that would probably also penalize material that, while *not* pornographic, does not happen to be consonant with feminist ideology.

The ordinances announcing this new categorical exception deserved to be repudiated by the courts, and they have been. What is more, they have been repudiated by other feminists. Unfortunately—because of the superficial similarity between the strategy that I have proposed, and the strategy that has so rightly been spurned—the chances of getting the *former* past the judicial gauntlet are now probably much reduced.

All of the elements of the strategy that I am criticizing—good as well as bad—are contained in a model antipornography ordinance drafted by Andrea Dworkin and Catharine A. MacKinnon. The most well-publicized versions of this model ordinance were passed in 1983 and 1984 by the Minneapolis and Indianapolis City Councils, respectively. The Minneapolis version was vetoed by the city's mayor, passed again by a new council, and again vetoed. The Indianapolis version was challenged in court by a coalition of booksellers, and found unconstitutional both in District Court and in the U.S. Court of Appeals. Part of the model ordinance was also incorporated into a Senate bill introduced in 1984 by Arlen Specter, a Pennsylvania Republican, who called it the Pornography Victims Protection Act.

The model ordinance begins with a statement of policy in which it characterizes pornography as "sex discrimination," a "systematic practice of exploitation and subordination based on sex that differentially harms women." It then proceeds to a formal definition, which runs as follows:

1. *Pornography* is the graphic sexually explicit subordination of women through pictures and/or words that also includes one or more of the following: (i) women are presented dehumanized as sexual objects, things, or commodities; or (ii) women

are presented as sexual objects who enjoy pain or humiliation; or (iii) women are presented as sexual objects who experience sexual pleasure in being raped; or (iv) women are presented as sexual objects tied up or cut up or mutilated or bruised or physically hurt; or (v) women are presented in postures or positions of sexual submission, servility, or display; or (vi) women's body parts—including but not limited to vaginas, breasts, or buttocks—are exhibited such that women are reduced to those parts; or (vii) women are presented being penetrated by objects or animals; or (ix) women are presented in scenarios of degradation, injury, torture, shown as filthy or inferior, bleeding, bruised, or hurt in a context that makes these conditions sexual.

2. The use of men, children, or transsexuals in the place of women in (1) above is pornography for purposes of this law.[53]

Now I have no difficulty with what this definition *seems* to mean. The problem is that what it seems to mean and what it means are two different things. Let us begin with what it identifies as the key element in pornography. It does not take the key element of pornography to be the excitement of lust in the narrow sense, as in the standard approach to obscenity; this the authors of the model ordinance scorn as "moralistic."[54] It does not take it to be the excitement of morbid passions in general, as in the amendment of the standard approach that I recommend. Nor does it take it to be harm to those employed in production, as in the child pornography doctrine—though the authors of the model ordinance do oppose that too. Rather, the key element of pornography is found in something quite novel: "subordination of women through pictures and/or words." Two things in this phrase need study. One is what is meant by subordination; the other is what it means to subordinate.

Dworkin explains subordination as "a social-political dynamic" consisting of four parts. The first is *hierarchy*, which means that some people have a lot of power while others have little or none. The second is *objectification*, which means that the people at the bottom of the hierarchy are treated as falling short of the human ideal, an ideal which the people at the top are taken to epitomize. The third is *submissiveness*, which refers to the tendency of people who are deprived of power and treated as less than human to defer to both the expressed and the anticipated wishes of the powerful. The fourth is *pervasive violence* directed by the people at the top of the hierarchy against the people at the bottom, "so widespread that it's normalized."[55]

In this sense, though, "subordination" is a noun, referring to a condition. By contrast, the definition of pornography offered in the model ordinance uses the term "subordination" for the *act* of subordinating. Neither its authors nor its advocates tell us what act this is. Presumably, a *particular* man "subordinates" a *particular* woman by depriving her of power, treating her as less than human, and hurting her, so that, in return, she submits to him; there are the four elements. But what does it mean for a particular woman, or women in general, to be "subordinated" *by words or pictures*? The only clue we have is that Dworkin, MacKinnon, and the advocates of the model ordinance persistently analyze pornography in terms of its social consequences. Following this lead, we must conclude that when they speak of words or pictures "subordinating" women, they mean that the words or pictures *reinforce the social condition* of female subordination; that is, that they give men a pretext to maintain this condition, or encourage women themselves to submit.

This idea is not very discriminating, and that is worrisome. There is nothing wrong with wanting to do something about men who deprive women of power, treat them as less than human, and hurt them: on the contrary! But at the very least, a definition of pornography motivated by such concern should distinguish between these two things:

1. material which offers information or discursive reasoning in which men might find either direct or indirect pretexts for their abusive treatment of women; and
2. material which contributes neither information, nor discursive reasoning, but which might lead men to treat women abusively by exciting the sheer lust to hurt or humiliate.

Material in the second category has no value, and deserves no special consideration. On the other hand, for reasons explained earlier in the discussion of expressive tolerance, prohibiting the circulation of material in the first category would be a grave mistake. Unfortunately, the concept of "subordination" treats both categories in the same fashion.

We haven't yet got to the bottom of the barrel. According to the model ordinance, subordination isn't a sufficient condition for classifying material as pornographic; it is only a necessary condition. In order to be pornographic, words or pictures that "subordinate women" must also have at least one of the nine other features listed in the definition. So we ask the question: does this additional requirement give us a basis for distinguishing between materials in the two categories distinguished above?

In order to answer this question we have to look at the list of features itself. Feature one, for instance, is that "women are presented dehumanized as sexual objects, things, or commodities." Clearly, pictures of women of the sort that we ordinarily call pornographic do "present" them in this way. But that is not the point; we must turn the sentence around. Does everything that "presents" them in this way approach the pornographic? Suppose that a team of reporters from one of the networks put together a documentary about the social problem of prostitution. Nothing in the topic demands that it be developed in a salacious manner, although of course it could be. The interviewers might treat the prostitutes themselves with compassion and respect. By any reasonable definition of pornography, this would not be pornographic. By the definition offered in the model ordinance, however, it would. For in the first place it is hard to see how the interviewers could avoid "presenting" the women "dehumanized as sexual objects, things, or commodities," because that is precisely the condition to which their profession reduces them; and in the second, some male viewers of the documentary would inevitably view the dehumanization of prostitutes as justifying the way in which they "subordinate" them. Thus, both the ordinance's requirements would be satisfied.

Or consider the second on the list of features—that "women are presented as sexual objects who enjoy pain and humiliation." Again, a great deal of pornography satisfies this description, but not everything that satisfies it approaches pornography. Feminists often apply the description to Freud's theory of feminine masochism, which they consider intrinsically "subordinating." Now his theories may be wrong, they may be ignorant, they may be mean spirited, they may even be products of his own neuroses; but can we reasonably call them pornographic? One hopes that we cannot; yet given the feminist view of Freud, it is hard to see how we could do otherwise.[56] As to the other seven features on the list—perhaps these would be less likely to stigmatize materials that were not really pornographic, but even here one wonders. For since we are speaking of "words" as well as "pictures," one would like to know what is meant by the persistent phrase, "presented as." Likewise, we know what it is to excite lust—but since, as we have seen, the authors of the model ordinance disavow any "moralistic" concern with that sort of thing, just what they mean by presenting conditions "in a context that makes [them] sexual" is completely obscure. Mysteries like these in a work of legal craft should make us watchful and suspicious.

Of course, one might argue that I am being unfair; that the authors of the model ordinance never intended that its phrases be applied in such ludicrous fashion as I describe. On the contrary, their intentions are much more clear than the ordinance itself. MacKinnon states bluntly that "existing standards of literature, art, science, and politics, viewed in a feminist light, are remarkably consonant with pornography's mode, meaning, and message."[57] These words portend a purge—and the methods to be employed in this purge are not even original. The basic technique is to twist the meanings of terms in ordinary speech. What do we call a political or scientific theory, possibly wrong, possibly right, but that does not happen to view the world "in a feminist light"? In the ordinary description, "argument"; in the revisionist description, "pornography." What do we call a filmed exhibition of live sexual performance, calculated to excite lust, but produced with the woman on top? In the ordinary description, "pornography"; in the revisionist description, "feminist erotica." This is the same technique Lewis Carroll attributed to Humpty Dumpty when he made him say to Alice, "When I use the word, it means exactly what I say it means, neither more, nor less." More to the point, it is the technique George Orwell discussed in his classic essay on politics and language, and attributed to totalitarian movements everywhere.

I think that I have said enough to justify my earlier statement that the approach to pornography pioneered by the authors and advocates of the model ordinance should be repudiated. However, that does not mean that they have failed to raise or resurrect any interesting issues. One such issue is whether, by influencing the attitudes and behavior of men, pornography promotes harm even to women who are *not* involved in its production.

Perhaps it may seem that I have already disposed of this issue, for I have argued that statements like "This material might prompt people who use it to harm others," do not provide good reasons to deny First

Amendment protection to material that would warrant protection otherwise. But what about material that would *not* warrant it otherwise? There the balancing of risks by legislatures is quite proper. Nor is there any reason why legislatures ought to limit themselves to considering the risk of harm to women. They also ought to consider the risk of moral wreck that pornography brings about in the very men who use it, by encouraging morbid obsessions and by cultivating warped attitudes toward the female of the species.

MacKinnon and Dworkin, as I say, have raised this issue, but they have also confused it in a number of ways beyond even the ones already discussed. One of the most peculiar is their inclusion of "assault or physical attack due to pornography" in the third section of their model ordinance under the rubric "unlawful practices." What makes this peculiar is that including a causal factor in the definition of the crime ignores the difference between the standards of proof that ought to be employed in showing that a law should be enacted and the standards of proof that ought to be employed in showing that an enacted law has been violated. Many sex offenders are found to have pornographic materials on their persons at the times of their assaults.[58] Legislatures might reasonably take this as suggesting that habitual use of pornography makes men more apt to commit violence against women. However, to try to show guilt on the presumption that *this* picture or book in *this* man's pocket made him commit *this* assault is not reasonable at all. If we try to be more reasonable by abandoning the presumption and *proving* the causal link in each case, then contrary to MacKinnon and Dworkin's intention, we will simply have no convictions. Why should we bring that consequence upon ourselves, when physical attack and assault are already illegal even when they are *not* "due to" pornography?

To turn to another issue: The most difficult objection for those concerned about the harms brought about by pornography is that "nothing has been proven." This objection is a bit misleading, so here we need to pause and survey the state of current knowledge. When we do this, we find that we know much more about some aspects of the problem than others. This is inadvertently reflected in an article MacKinnon has written to justify the model ordinance. She is able to devote some pages of the article to experimental evidence that exposure to pornography produces strong effects on attitudes. Concerning the other side of the question—whether these attitudes have any influence at all on subsequent behavior—even though some of her evidence is striking, it is all circumstantial.

That so much experimental evidence has been accumulated in support of the first proposition, linking pornography to attitudes, is surprising, considering the limits of experimental method in dealing with human subjects. Typically, a psychologist administers an attitudinal test to young males, some time later shows them a pornographic movie, and still later tests their attitudes again. As MacKinnon observes, these experiments have shown that exposure to even a single pornographic movie is associated with a significant difference in attitude. After viewing, subjects "more closely resemble convicted rapists attitudinally."[59] Perhaps these results really come as a surprise to no one. Experimental psychologists Edward Donnerstein describes the research by saying, "we just quantify the obvious."[60]

Most of the circumstantial evidence MacKinnon adduces in support of the second proposition, linking attitudes to behavior, comes from the hearings on the model ordinance that took place in Minneapolis. For instance, she notes that emergency rooms reported an increase in the number of throat rapes after the exhibition of *Deep Throat*, and that prostitutes reported increasing demands for oral sex. MacKinnon comments, "most concretely, before 'Linda Lovelace' was seen performing deep throat, no one had ever seen it being done in that way, largely because it cannot be done without hypnosis to repress the natural gag response. *Yet it was believed*. Men proceeded to demand it of women, causing the distress of many, and the death of some."[61] A great deal of testimony from other victims of sexual violence is also discussed: from wives abused by their husbands, young women abused by their dates, and so forth.

In a somewhat different vein were testimony:

- from a director of a rape crisis center, that "pornography is the permission and direction and rehearsal for sexual violence";
- from the director of sexual assault services at a school for behavior therapy, that pornography "is often used by sex offenders as a stimulus for acting out";
- from a therapist who works with sex offenders, that pornography "is a way in which they practice" their crimes; and

● from a psychotherapist specializing in services for men, that because pornography "is reinforcing, [and leads to sexual release, it] leads men to want the experience which they have in photographic fantasy to happen in 'real' life."[62]

These statements illustrate a new interpretation of clinical experience, sharply different from the interpretation more common a generation ago. The old interpretation was that because pornography provides sexual release, it offers a substitute for action. Its presupposition was that potential sex offenders are bursting with sexual desires that must have an outlet—if not through pornography, then through rape. The new interpretation, though, finds potential sex offenders to be bursting not so much with lust, as with anger and resentment. Pornography gives that anger a direction. By arousing lust and then relieving it, it makes the idea of action all the more attractive. Hence with the new interpretation, we move from the simple idea of blowing off steam, to the more complex ideas of permission, reinforcement, and rehearsal. Ironically, this is a sophisticated return to the "common sense" that prevailed in the generations before the older interpretation was offered.

Like the old, the new interpretation is handicapped by the fact that it is based on anecdotes—clinical in origin, but anecdotes nonetheless. To be sure, the general theories of motivation behind the new interpretation have a great deal of experimental evidence behind them. However, their application to sex offenders does not. We have no more "proof" for the hypothesis that pornography is rehearsal for action than for the hypothesis that it offers a substitute for action. What is worse, we have little prospect of getting such "proof." Human beings are notoriously difficult to study in natural settings.[63]

Three considerations demand voice in this matter. Two have already been anticipated.

The first is simply that even without a demonstration that attitudes like those of rapists lead to rapes, the fact that exposure to pornography does produce attitudes like those of rapists is a sufficient demonstration of harm. It is harm *to the man so influenced—moral* harm. If pornography makes a man think of women as "whores," it has done more than enough already. Whether or not he ever lifts a violent finger, it has unnaturally twisted his feelings toward half the human race.

The second is that although social science and public policy are both concerned with truth, they necessarily weigh the risks of error differently. For as statisticians tell us, there are two types of error. "Alpha" error is accepting a hypothesis as true when it is really false. This is the kind of error that traditional social scientists try hardest to avoid; they would rather have no findings than a mistaken finding. It is also the kind of error we try hardest to avoid in criminal trials; better to let ten of the guilty go free, we say, than to let one of the innocent be hanged. Yet as this proverb recognizes, beyond a certain point reducing the risk of alpha error tends to increase the risk of "beta" error: treating a hypothesis as false when it is really true.[64]

Granted that there are many situations in which we ought to be willing to swallow a large risk of beta error in order to commit as few alpha errors as possible, still, in many other situations this is not appropriate. For instance the shoe is on the other foot when we are trying to formulate policies to protect the public from harm. Consider the licensing of a new drug. Shouldn't the burden of proof be on the drug company to show that the drug is *not* harmful, rather than on the Food and Drug Administration to show that it *is*? Suppose a drug company were to offer an argument like this:

> The data suggests a strong likelihood that our drug does, in fact, have exceedingly dangerous side effects. However, because the data are not as strong as they might be, that conclusion carries a 20% risk of alpha error. In other words, there is a one-in-five chance that the experimental results are a fluke, and that the drug is really harmless. These odds are too short. Standard scientific practice is to reject a hypothesis unless the risk of alpha error is 5% or less. Therefore, we think that we should be allowed to market the drug as "useful and not proven to cause harm."

Surely the Food and Drug Administration should reply, "We understand your point, but this is not standard scientific practice. This is public policy, and lives are at stake. Your odds are long enough."

The same point applies to the controversy over the harm of pornography. Concerning whether attitudes like those of rapists lead to rapes, all of our evidence is circumstantial, most of it coming from clinical experience. Any conclusion based on this sort of evidence carries with it a higher risk of alpha error than would be tolerated in pure social science. But as in the regulation of drugs, this is not pure social science. This is public policy, where alpha and beta error need to be balanced against each other. Though alpha error is nothing to sneeze at, one should hope to persuade legislatures—to whom the task of balancing should fall—that in this context, beta error is the more dangerous of the two. Put another way: Given the fact that pornography does not warrant First Amendment protection in the first place—and given the fact that our traditions have never found in pornography any special value—we should be much more concerned about treating it as harmless when it is really harmful, than about treating it as harmful when it is really harmless. In the absence of hard experimental data, legislators should not hesitate to depend on circumstantial evidence and common sense. As in most matters of public policy, that is all they have and all they have any prospect of getting.

Third, last, and briefest—although not least in importance—where is it written that the only harm to women about which we have a right to be concerned is harm through assault to their bodies?[65] If—on such evidence as we find satisfactory—we are convinced that men who learn to think of women as "whores" will treat them with contempt and make bad husbands and fathers, isn't that enough?

Conclusion

Earlier in the book the general concept of tolerance was clarified by centrifuging our intuitions and discarding the neutralist impurities. As we have seen, the special case of expressive tolerance is particularly muddy. But is it muddy with the same kind of mud? So far in Part Five, I haven't said anything about neutralism.

The reason for this is that the term is not often used in the cases which we have considered. Why not? Because judges are not impressed with the idea? On the contrary. All too often they take it for granted. They have no more need to use the term than to remind themselves to breath. The few instances in which they do employ the term bear this out.

Uses of the term "neutrality" in free speech cases fall into two classes. In one, the term designates indifference as to what is good and bad; in the other, indifference as to what is true or false. Let us take these in order. A good example of the first is found in *Paris Adult Theatre I v. Slaton*, where Chief Justice Burger, speaking for the Court, announces that

The states have the power to make a morally neutral judgment that public exhibition of obscene material . . . has a tendency to injure the community as a whole, to endanger the public safety, or to jeopardize . . . the State's "right . . . to maintain a decent society."[66]

Had the Chief Justice been thinking more clearly as he wrote, perhaps he would have recognized that the state's concern for the "safety" and "decency" of the community is precisely what shows that its prohibition is *not* "morally neutral"; it identifies goods and evils.[67] Just what sorts of goods and evils the Chief Justice had in mind is still more clearly brought out in *Schad v. Borough of Mount Ephraim*. Dissenting this time, he argued that communities may use their regulatory powers to ban nude dancing within their boundaries, and his strongest language— surprisingly—was borrowed from *Village of Belle Terre v. Boraas* (1974), where Justice Douglas had written for the Court that the community regulatory power is "ample to lay out zones where family values, youth values, and the blessings of quiet seclusion and clean air make the area a sanctuary for people."[68] Safety, decency, family values, youth values, quiet, seclusion, even cleanliness—if there is anything "neutral" about this litany of "blessings," something very strange has happened to the English language.

A good example of the other use of the term "neutrality" is found in a passage from *FCC v. Pacifica Foundation*, part of which I have quoted before. States Justice Stevens,

But the fact that society may find speech offensive is not a sufficient reason for suppressing it. Indeed, if it is the speaker's opinion that gives offense, that consequence is a reason for affording it First Amendment protection. For it is a central tenet of the First Amendment that the government must remain neutral in the marketplace of ideas.[69]

The last sentence reflects a much more interesting mistake than the one made by the former Chief Justice. Justice Stevens has just been telling us why the government may keep "filthy words" off the public airwaves. He stresses that they are no essential part of an exposition of ideas, and reassures us that the government is prohibited from treating some expositions of ideas less tolerantly than others simply because it does not like the ideas whose expositions they are. All of this is as it should be. But does it really make the government "neutral" between ideas? It does not.

This claim may seem preposterous. But consider: There are some ideas that simply do not stand up well in discursive reasoning. One who wishes to get people to believe in them will have far greater success if he resorts to the irrational and subliminal methods of persuasion. Reduced to propositions, the messages his music and pictures convey are farcical—for instance, that men will be tough and resemble cowboys if only they smoke Marlboros, or that women will be leisured, glamorous, and self-possessed if only they smoke Virginia Slims. That is why advertisers rarely do reduce their messages to propositions. They know how to reach their markets.

Pornographers know this even better. It isn't really easy to make the case in argument, fair and square, that women like to be raped. But a movie of a willing victim who emits just the right type of groan and sigh is worth more to this point of view than an army of debaters. Not because it presents a counterexample—the victim is an actor—but because it moves the levers of lust and desire to humiliate.

This being so, the mere fact that a government does not discriminate *among instances of discursive reasoning* on the basis of the opinions they champion does not put all opinions on the same footing—especially if the government *does* distinguish between discursive reasoning on the one hand, and other forms of expression on the other. For making that distinction helps to ensure that ideas that cannot stand up well in discursive reasoning are at a disadvantage relative to those that can.

Now the plot thickens. What would happen if we gave all forms of protection the *same* level of protection? Would we be neutral among ideas *then*? No, not even then! For, given the weakness of human nature, irrational and subliminal methods of persuasion are far more powerful than discursive reasoning—and what is worse, the narrowest and most brutal ideas are just the ones with which these methods work best. Were we ever really to throw the field wide open, then whatever is true, whatever is honest, whatever is just, pure, and lovely would be the loser.[70]

No approach to expressive freedom is neutral. Every approach tilts the odds in a certain way. True expressive tolerance means tilting them in favor of real discourse, *rational* discourse, with a special indulgence for the communication of information that citizens—under a form of government designed to keep the ideal of rationality alive—might need.

Notes

1. John Stuart Mill, "On Liberty," chap. 2.
2. *Chaplinsky v. New Hampshire* (1941), at 571–72.
3. *Winters v. New York* (1948), at 510.
4. *Joseph Burstyn v. Commissioner of Education* (1952), at 501.
5. *Roth*, at 485.
6. See chap. 9, note 18.
7. "Arts" referred to useful occupations demanding skill and technique, not avenues of aesthetic experience—the work of the artisan, rather than of the "artist" as understood today.
8. *Journals of the Continental Congress*, vol. I (1974), at 108; quoted in *Roth* at 484. The last part of this quote also has some bearing on the later controversies over the Alien and Sedition Acts, which were briefly discussed in chap. 9, note 14.
9. *Roth*, at 488–89.
10. The quotation is from the majority opinion in *Ginsberg v. New York* (1968), at 638, where the Court in turn quotes from *Prince v. Massachusetts* (1944), at 170. Justice Fortas' objection is found in his dissent to the former, at 673. *Prince* did not concern expressive tolerance.
11. *Roth*, at 487, note 20.
12. To be sure, at ibid. Justice Brennan did say that "We perceive no significant difference" between the Court's new definition of obscenity, and the definition proposed in the American Law Institute's Model Penal Code—which he goes on to quote as mentioning "shameful and morbid" interests not only in sex and nudity, but also in excretory functions. But in the first place, Justice Brennan himself tended to focus on the former two elements alone, and in the second place, the Model Penal Code does not, by the mere mention of excretory functions, capture more than a short arc of the curve of morbid passions. Compare M.C. Slough and P.D. McAnany, "Obscenity and Constitutional Freedom—Part II," at 454–55.
13. See for instance his dissent in *Paris Adult Theatre I v. Slaton* (1973); but see also Chief Justice Burger's critique of Justice Brennan's position in *Miller*, at 26–27.
14. *Valentine v. Chrestenson* (1942), at 55.
15. *Memoirs*, at 418.
16. *Miller*, at 22.
17. *Memoirs*, at 449 (Justice Clark, dissenting).
18. Justice White concentrated on this point in his own dissent.
19. *Memoirs*, at 447, note 3 (Justice Clark, dissenting).
20. Though some of the other illustrations of allegedly good writing are simply ridiculous. One expert praised the author for his description of a fat prostitute by pointing out that he used the verb "waddles" rather than "walks." Justice Clark offers this tidbit in ibid., at 449.
21. Ibid., at 447.
22. Ibid., at 446.
23. *Memoirs*, at 443 (appendix to Justice Douglas, concurring).
24. *Miller*, at 24.
25. Ibid., at 30–32.

26. Said he in *Schad* at 85: "At issue here is the right of a small community to ban an activity incompatible with a quiet, residential atmosphere." The former Chief Justice did not explain how such a right could survive a finding that nude dancing is "speech."
27. See, for instance, his dissent in *Memoirs*.
28. *Miller*, at 92 (Justice Brennan, dissenting).
29. See note 13.
30. *Jacobellis v. Ohio* (1963), at 201 (Chief Justice Warren, dissenting).
31. *Miller*, at 25.
32. *Hustler* magazine, for instance, is very widely considered merely "soft" porn. Yet this is the magazine which featured on the cover of one of its 1978 issues a color simulation of a nude woman being fed into a meat-grinder and emerging as hamburger. For further discussion, see note 58.
33. Offensive conduct is a violation of mores that arouses indignation in others. Unlike "fighting words," it need not have a tendency to incite violence in order to be what it is. Despite the Court's rejection of Cohen's claims, it clearly joined in his confusion of offense with incitement. But where Cohen insisted that only actual incitement counted as an infraction of the law, the Court thought that a tendency to incite was enough.
34. *FCC v. Pacifica Foundation* (1978), at 748.
35. *Cohen v. California* (1971), at 21.
36. *Pacifica*, at 749.
37. Ibid., at 749.
38. *Cohen*, at 25; *Pacifica*, at 746.
39. *Cohen*, at 21; *Pacifica*, at 743.
40. *Cohen*, at 26.
41. As discussed in chap. 9, note 14, the concept of "seditious libel" was used as an engine of oppression in English and early American history.
42. *Pacifica*, at 745.
43. *New York v. Ferber* (1982), at 775 (Justice O'Connor, concurring).
44. *Ferber*, at 756.
45. *Paris I*, at 57.
46. *Ferber*, at 759.
47. The original source of this phrase is *Olmstead v. United States* (1928), at 478 (Justice Brandeis, dissenting). *Stanley v. Georgia* (1968) applied it to obscenity at 564. As I prepare this manuscript for publication in 1991, the Court shows signs of retreating from the idea that consumption is sacrosanct even though publication and distribution may be penalized. Whether the idea will be abandoned in standard obscenity as well as child pornography cases remains to be seen.
48. *Ferber*, at 764.
49. Ibid., at 773–74.
50. Ibid., at 776 (Justice Brennan, concurring).
51. In this context it is worth mentioning recent proposals that the experimentation records of the Nazi death camps be made available to American research workers in order to expand the fund of knowledge on the physiology of the human body under extreme and abnormal conditions.
52. Quoted in Mary Kay Blakely, "Is One Woman's Sexuality Another Woman's Pornography? The Question Behind a Major Legal Battle," at 40.
53. Catharine A. MacKinnon, "Pornography, Civil Rights, and Speech," at 21.

54. See Catharine A. MacKinnon, "Not a Moral Issue."
55. Quoted in Mary Kay Blakely, ibid., at 46, inset.
56. I have no evidence that MacKinnon or Dworkin think either that Freud should be censored, or that he should not. My point, rather, is that censorship of Freud seems to be entailed by their theories.
57. MacKinnon, "Pornography, Civil Rights, and Speech," at 21.
58. Other kinds of anecdotes suggesting that pornography encourages violence to women can easily be produced. In note 32 mention was made of the issue of *Hustler* magazine which featured a color simulation of a woman being fed into a meat-grinder. The circumstances which brought this to my attention was as follows. In 1978 I was a student, working as a welder. A co-worker brought the issue to work to show it during lunchtime. Discussion spontaneously turned to violence against women, whereupon the fellow who owned the magazine launched on a vociferous, and completely gratuitous, defense of his self-admitted abuse of his wife. On the use of anecdotal evidence, see below in the text.
59. Though as she wryly adds, "as a group they don't look all that different from them to start with." Ibid., at 53.
60. Ibid., at 55.
61. Ibid., at 35.
62. Ibid., at 45.
63. Even more so when methods for the study of human subjects are properly circumscribed, as both ethics and recent law demand.
64. The same point is stressed by social scientists who use Bayesian rather than traditional statistical methods.
65. See Stanley Kauffman's untitled response to Walter Berns, "Pornography v. Democracy: The Case for Censorship." For further discussion see Susan Mendus, "Harm, Offense, and Censorship."
66. *Paris I*, at 69.
67. His thinking might also have been clear but disingenuous. The pretense of neutrality may have helped him to gain a majority of the Court.
68. *Village of Belle Terre v. Boraas* (1974), at 9; quoted in *Schad*, at 86. The former was not an obscenity case. Justice Douglas was well known for thinking obscenity perfectly consistent with "family values" and "youth values."
69. *Pacifica*, at 745–46. The notion of this "marketplace of ideas" finds its first judicial expression in *Abrams v. United States* (1919), at 631 (Justice Holmes, joined in dissent by Justice Brandeis).
70. Compare William Galston, "Defending Liberalism," 627: "Social competition is no more reliably benign than economic competition. Indeed, a kind of social Gresham's Law may operate, in which the pressure of seductively undemanding ways of life may make it very difficult, for example, for parents to raise children in accordance with norms of effort, conscientiousness, and self-restraint." See also the works by Walter Berns listed in the bibliography, but note the very great differences between his approach to political argument and provision of republican information, and that taken here.

Part Five

The Special Case
of Religious Tolerance

Introduction to Part Five

What we make of the virtue of tolerance is the acid test of whether the liberal political tradition can be rescued from its foundations crisis. But the test is not really acid until tolerance is thrown into the strongest of all caustics. That caustic is religion. This is where the ultimate concern is roused, and where all that it cannot suffer must suffer deliquescence.

Yet the very notion of tolerance—of tolerance as a virtue, rather than a vice—arose as a religious idea. This may seem strange. Once one accepts something as the ultimate concern, whether what some call God, or some other "god," then its claims are by that fact acknowledged utterly superior to all others. They cannot be overbalanced by other scruples. If one of its claims is "Enforce the faith" and tolerance says "Refuse," then tolerance is a sin. That is why Nietzsche believed that if men still took God seriously, they would still be burning heretics at the stake. What is the truth of this difficult matter?

11

Tolerance and the Ultimate Concern

To find out the truth we need to examine some of the different concerns for which people claim ultimacy and what they tell us about tolerance. The following section examines the one forwarded by the religion most prominently practiced in our own culture, and relates it directly to the question of tolerance.[1] Then, after a brief digression on the meaning of secularism, we turn to five different secular creeds.

Tolerance and Ultimate Concern in Christianity

Tolerance was an issue in early Christianity because Christians were on the defensive. Their refusal to participate in the official ruler cult made them objects of suspicion. For pagans, participation was not a problem. Though in theory some sort of divinity was the ultimate concern for pagans too, it was, in their view, fissured. Their divinities were not jealous; there was always room for another god, demigod, or hero. So it was that the god Augustus, later joined by other Caesars, took his place first in Eastern pantheons, then in Rome itself. Jews too refused participation in the ruler cult; for them, as for Christians, there was no god but God. But they had already been awarded with official tolerance as a recognized ethnic minority. Christians, who were very puzzling to Rome—were they a new kind of Jew, or were they atheists?—sought a similar privilege for their own worship.

The great difficulty was that Christians and their imperial rulers subscribed to different ultimate concerns. Early Christian apologists tried to persuade the rulers to tolerate the ultimate concern of Christians as part of their service to the rulers' own ultimate concern, the

223

divinized cause of the Empire. Thus Melito of Sardis, Athenagoras, Justin, and other stressed the political loyalty of Christians and the civic usefulness of their moral teaching. They reminded Rome that they prayed, indeed not to the emperor, but certainly for him, even under persecution. Thus Tertullian: "A Christian is no-one's enemy, far less the emperor's. Knowing him to be appointed by God, he must love and reverence and honor him with the rest of the Roman Empire as long as time endures. . . . That is how we pray for the emperor's welfare: by invoking it from Him who can provide it."[2] Tatian made a similar appeal to one of the subject peoples: "Why, O Greeks, do you wish to rouse other religions against us, as is done in a wrestling contest? If I do not wish to avail myself of the religions of others, why should I be hated for it as though I were a criminal? If the emperor wishes to raise tributes, I am ready to pay them. If my master wishes me to administer and serve, I acknowledge his service."[3]

But we must not forget the apologetic purpose here. For a Christian *in* authority, the question of tolerance would present a different face than for a Christian *under* authority. There is nothing cynical about this; it is entirely principled. Before, one tried to elicit tolerance for one's own ultimate concern by appealing to others in terms of theirs. Now, one must decide whether the toleration of their ultimate concerns is consistent with service to one's own. Clearly the answer to this question must depend on the nature of the Christian's ultimate concern; for appeal to concerns that are less than ultimate—civil peace or what have you—is admissible only if, and in such ways as, the ultimate concern allows it.

What answer did the Christians give? That Christians in authority actually have often practiced religious intolerance is notorious. Thus many contemporary writers take for granted, like Nietzsche, that true Christianity is indeed inconsistent with tolerance. For example Walter Berns and Harvey C. Mansfield, Jr., in separate works, try to show that concerning religion, Madison, Jefferson, and other American founders had two goals. The first was to *transform* intolerant Christianity—to turn it, tame it, make it "reasonable"; to make it something that was no longer really Christian, but to do so in such a way that the citizens would not notice the difference; to make it something that was consonant with the needs of a state organized according to a secular theory of natural right instead of leaving it prone to dangerous religious enthusiams. The second alleged goal was to make of this new, surro-Christianity an American civil religion. Berns goes on to argue that the project was a success, and that we owe our civil peace to its victory.[4]

What most Americans call Christianity today may or may not be a pretender. So might what most Americans called Christianity in the days of the founding. But the deeper question, for us, is whether Berns and Mansfield are right about the authentic faith. For the fact that Christians in authority *have* often practiced religious intolerance does not settle the question of whether, in doing so, they were following the authentic faith, or rather perverting it.

To find a warrant in the Gospels for political enforcement of the true religion would be difficult indeed. Jesus, asked by Pilate whether he was the King of the Jews, said that his kingdom was not of this world. If it were, he said, his followers would take up arms for it.[5] This statement would seem to be as clear as anyone could wish: the Kingdom of God is not of such a kind that it can be promoted by force. And considering Who Christians take Jesus to be, his statements are necessarily authoritative for them.[6]

In later centuries, as need arose, some Christians developed the theological basis for religious tolerance further. As Lord Acton remarked, "very soon after the time of Constantine it began to appear that the outward conversion of the empire was a boon of doubtful value to religion." More than this, earnest Christians doubted that the new official establishment could be reconciled with the will of God. "God does not want unwilling worship, nor does He require a forced repentance," said St. Hilary of Poitiers. But if that is true, then when Lactantius reflected that "There is nothing so voluntary as religion," he was not departing from Christian teaching, but elaborating it.[7] We are inclined to think it novel of John Locke to have declared thirteen centuries later, in his first letter on toleration, that enforcing a faith on the unwilling is contrary to a gospel of love; we are inclined to believe that he too much have been trying to tame the faith rather than expound it.[8] But his teaching was not new; say rather that it had notoriously been forgotten.[9]

And if that, then say too that it has lately been restored. See for instance Thomas Merton: "You cannot be a man of faith unless you know how to doubt. You cannot believe in God unless you are capable of questioning the authority of prejudice, even though that prejudice may seem to be religious. Faith is not blind conformity to prejudice—a 'pre-judgment.' It is a decision, a decision that is fully and deliberately taken in the light of a truth that cannot be proven. It is not merely the acceptance of a decision that has been made by someone else."[10] Stated so categorically, this must hold even if that "someone else" is the government.

The key to this theology is that tolerant Christians regard their tolerance as required by God himself. It is that God is of such a nature that nothing exacted by threats could truly serve Him. Were their ultimate concern of a different nature, then by very reason of its ultimacy it would have to be served otherwise. So it is in some other religions, as indeed among intolerant Christians. As it were, they give a different god the name of God.

But notice: the same ultimate concern which, for its own sake, demands tolerance, also, for its own sake, sets the limits to what is tolerated. This is no more than we have seen in the less-than-ultimate concerns discussed earlier in this book, although their less-than-ultimate character may have made the consequences of possible error less terrifying there than here. Here as there, tolerance does not mean tolerating every evil, out of indifference to ends, but tolerating some evils, for the very sake of these ends.

A distinction may help to make this clear. To tolerate someone else's ultimate concern means in part to tolerate his faith in it, and in part to tolerate the services that it demands of him. If "God does not want unwilling worship," then the Christian's tolerance must be absolute with respect to permitting what others believe. But it does not extend to *honoring* what they believe, except insofar as their gods are more or less blurred and faulty images of his own. This, in turn, places limits on his toleration of the services which they render to their gods. He claims the right to say that there are evil services which nothing that deserved to be ceded ultimacy could demand, and the correlative right to try to stop anyone who attempts them.

For instance: whatever claims of conscience the Christian may honor, he cannot allow a person to plead reasons of conscience in justification of murder. "God told me to kill anyone who got in my way" cuts no ice with him; nor is the case different when other ultimate concerns, other gods, are pleaded in place of God. The Defense of the Revolution, The Greater Good of the Whole, The Purity of the Race, the

Hunger of Moloch—neither these nor any other claimants to ultimacy are accepted as justifying the sacrifice of innocents. "Even conceding your God-given right to honor another god," says the Christian, "that right concerns your own soul only. I will not permit you, in its service, to inflict harms which my own God abhors and forbids."

A Brief Digression: What Does it Mean to Be Secular?

Before we can speak of secular creeds we need to establish what we mean by secularism. It isn't enough simply to distinguish it from religion, for then we must ask what we mean by religion.

A widespread prejudice among political theorists is that secular creeds depend on reason while religions depend on faith. Both halves of the prejudice are mistaken. Many of the creeds conventionally called "religions" give a very high place to reason indeed. Likewise, many of the creeds conventionally called "secular" expect blind acceptance of dogma. Most decisive is the point explained in Part Three: the exercise of reason itself depends on faith.

Ordinary speech has it that secularists are those who do not believe in God. But this usage too is clearly unsatisfactory. Buddhists do not believe in God, yet we call Buddhism not a secular creed, but a religion.

One might reply to this objection that though Buddhists do not believe in God, they do believe in gods. But this is not satisfactory either, since Buddhist deities are merely incidental to Buddhism; they are not its ultimate concern.

This too prompts reply. For though Buddhist deities are not its ultimate concern, Buddhism does have an ultimate concern—in this sense a "god." Its ultimate concern is escape from suffering, which in its view arises inherently from desire and ultimately from very existence. A very different concern is ceded ultimacy in, say, Christianity and Judaism, but at least they have in common that each professes an ultimate concern.

Very well, take it that Buddhism is a religion because it professes an ultimate concern; that whatever professes an ultimate concern is by that fact a religion. But in this case, *any* system of concerns, even if

not a religion proper, has, at least, religious implications. For even if
its ranking of these concerns is incomplete so that none is yet professed
as ultimate, it at least carries implications for what *could or could not*
be professed as ultimate.

It begins to look as though so-called secular creeds are nothing other
than incomplete religions—when not, indeed, complete.

But, but, but—! Is this plausible? Is it credible? Where, for example, are the temples of utilitarianism? What are its sacraments, what
are its hymns? Who are its prophets, its martyrs, its priests? The point
is well taken, but not profound. On the whole, the various secularisms
do lack the outward trappings of the various religions. But is that
important? After all the difference does not hold across the board.
Marxism has never wanted for prophets, scriptures, shrines, or martyrs. Neither would positivism have wanted for them, had Auguste
Comte had his way. At most we might say that the concerns of the
creeds we are most at ease in calling "secular" lend themselves to
somewhat different modes of affirmation than the concerns of the
creeds we are most at ease in calling "religious."

And why is that? The most plausible explanation for this difference
is simply that it arises from the other. Not every secularism affirms its
concerns in "religious" fashion because not every secularism has finished ranking its concerns. Though these concerns inevitably carry
implications for what *could or could not* be ceded ultimacy, the final
decision may not yet have been made. By contrast, in a secularism
which *has* finished ranking its concerns, a secularism in which a
particular concern *has* been ceded ultimacy—for instance, Marxism—
the difference in modes of affirmation tends to disappear.

To conclude this section: Not every secular creed is a religion, but
none is without religious implications. In the sphere of the ultimate
concern as in every other, tolerance may be possible but neutrality is
not. Most secularists who propound ethical and political philosophies
do not realize that every such system presupposes a complete or incomplete theology. In fact, I am not here prepared to say whether any
realize this; my concern is simply that they come to realize it. Still less
do I argue *here* that their theologies are wrong.[11] They may be wrong;
they may be right. However, that question cannot even be discussed
until they lay down their Voltairian prejudices and recognize that it is,
in fact, a question.

Tolerance and Ultimate Concern in Classical Utilitarianism

One of the commonest secular philosophies is utilitarianism. Utilitarianism is based on the view that all of the real issues in ethics and politics come down to the question of how to make the sum total of the community's pleasure as great as it can possibly be—this sum total to be calculated by adding together all of the quanta of pleasure experienced, no matter with which individuals they originate. The rhetoric of the earliest utilitarians, such as Jeremy Bentham, dwelt scornfully on the "metaphysical" character of earlier theories that posited natural rights and natural duties—rights and duties allegedly not merely invented, but discovered—rights and duties that applied to us for some such cosmic reason as our relation to a creator God who was Himself the ultimate concern. This scorn was quite unfair. A pleasure, after all, is a subjective sensation. As such, if this pleasure is viewed apart from the person experiencing it, it ceases to be intelligible as a pleasure. No sense can be made of adding together the pleasures of two or more persons to make a sum unless these two or more are not strictly persons at all; unless, instead of being truly distinct, they are parts of some super-subjectivity. For any consistent utilitarian, the community is just such a super-subjectivity. It is, in fact, the *only* person—the only true person; strictly speaking, we who call ourselves "persons" are no more than its manifold organs of sensation. Obviously, such ersatz persons as we are can no more have claims against the community than the nose or eye can have claims against the body, and if we seem to have claims against each other, this merely means that some arrangements of the body's organs are more conducive to its pleasure than others. This body, this community, is the utilitarian god—whether we are speaking of the local community, the community of all human beings, or the community of all sentient life.[12]

Now as to tolerance: the utilitarian does not state categorically that all must believe in the same god as he. He does require that, whether knowingly or unknowingly, they act as it demands. That is, he requires that their beliefs promote social order and otherwise lead them to act in ways that maintain the aggregate happiness of the community at the highest feasible level. One consideration he must take into account is that some belief systems have this effect to a greater degree than others. But another is that sheer change in belief systems, not to mention competition between them, may be disruptive to social order and therefore to social happiness.

In each concrete situation the utilitarian must balance these considerations against each other. So, tolerance may sometimes be justified; generally speaking, however, whenever the prevailing religion is reasonably conducive to order and (in this and other ways) to happiness, he finds that the power of the state should be brought to bear to enforce its observances. Thus the nineteenth-century utilitarian James Fitzjames Stephen argued that the Romans were right to persecute the Christians on behalf of the ancient religion, but that once the Christians came to power it became their utilitarian duty to turn the tables.[13]

Tolerance and Ultimate Concern in Millian Utilitarianism

The utilitarianism of John Stuart Mill might seem to provide an exception to the generalizations of the previous section. However, in view of Mill's qualitative distinction between "higher" and "lower" pleasures in the essay "Utilitarianism," and his definition of utility as what is in the "permanent interests of man as a progressive being" in the essay "On Liberty," I think it fairer to say that Mill is sui generis, hardly a utilitarian at all; for the first concession makes the arithmetic summation of pleasure impossible, while the second deprives pleasure of any special status at all. Not that I wish to evade the task of identifying his theology. Perhaps we should describe Mill's god as precisely the promotion of these "permanent interests." As he does not fully identify or rank them for us, this theology seems incomplete. Even as it stands, however, it does have some implications for religious tolerance.

Mill believed religious tolerance to be in "the permanent interests of man as a progressive being" because of his confidence that truth emerges from creedal competition. Indeed, he has come to be regarded as the classical expositor of this view; "On Liberty" has replaced such earlier works as Milton's *Areopagitica* in popular estimation. However, he believed that creedal competition has this salutary effect only in the culturally advanced societies. Backward societies, rather than requiring religious tolerance, require tutelary regimes. These would promulgate, not indeed truth, but such watered-down versions and images of the truth as their subjects were so far able to understand and believe.[14] The more general point here is not that he distinguished between backward and advanced societies, but that the when and how of religious tolerance (as of all other varieties of tolerance) depended on the efficiency of creedal competition as a filter for truth.

Tolerance and Ultimate Concern in Rousseauan Contractarianism

In some of its versions, secular social contract theory worships the same god as Benthamite utilitarianism, although its theology differs from the utilitarian theology in emphasizing its god's will rather than its god's pleasure. Rousseau gives us a good example of this. Each of the collective entities in terms of which he frames his theory—the state, the sovereign, and so forth—is explicitly described not as an abstraction, but as a genuine person capable of both deliberation and will. The fact that it exists by convention rather than by nature does not, for Rousseau, detract from its personhood. Moreover this person is presented as distinct from the persons whose consent to the contract brings it into being; hence the distinction between the "will of all," which is a mere aggregation, and the "general will," which is the real, unitary will of the sovereign. Note well: Rousseau says, "Just as nature gives each man absolute power over all his members, the social compact gives the body politic absolute power over all its members, which as I have said bears the name sovereignty. . . . It is agreed that each person alienates through the social contract only that part of his power, goods, and freedom whose use matters to the community; but it must also be agreed that the sovereign alone is the judge of what matters."[15] Thus the sovereign is the ultimate concern. Just so long as the sovereign lasts, it is god. That is why Rousseau dares to think he has a right to propose a civil religion in the place of—or by way of taming—the revealed religions.[16] Those religions are wrong; his religion is right.

His general theory of religion distinguishes four kinds. 1. "Natural" religion, identified with the Gospels, is in his view bad because by severing the affections of the people from earthy things and dividing their hopes from earthly events, it undermines the intrinsic force of convention and denies it the augmenting force of piety. 2. Priestly

religion is bad because it brings about a state of war between competing sovereigns, one represented by the civil state and the other by the
ecclesiastical hierarchy. 3. Primitive civil religion is bad because, by
making religious differences appear to be offenses to God rather than
offenses to sociability, it puts the population "in a state of natural war
with all others, which is very harmful to its security."[17] 4. Only one
alternative is left: civil religion proper, in which an invented "God" is
worshipped for the sake of sociability and so becomes, in effect, an
extension of the true god, the sovereign.

Ideally, there would be no sects at all other than the state cult;
however, as a practical second-best, there would be a great many
subsects, all existing under the umbrella of the state cult.[18] Civil piety
is readiness to follow the mandatory observances of the state cult and
profess its articles of civil faith. By the logic of the social contract the
state cannot obligate anyone to believe them; but by the same logic it
may banish anyone who does not, and kill anyone who pretends.[19]
Enforcement may seem to present a problem because the state cannot
look into the citizens' hearts. However, Rousseau is satisfied that it can
make inferences from their conduct.[20]

Civil tolerance, the obverse of civil piety, is indifference among all
diversities of faith and observance so long as these are consistent with
the state sect itself. Withholding it from faiths outside the state umbrella is a logical corollary of extending it to those within.

Tolerance and Ultimate Concern in Lockean Contractarianism

Locke's theology is less consistent than Rousseau's. We can see this
by contrasting his *Second Treatise* with his first letter on toleration. In
the former, although he does not go so far as to commit himself to
Christian theology, he does rest his theory on the existence of a God of
the sort that a Christian could acknowledge as bona fide. This comes
out most clearly in his discussion of equality of rights. In the first
place, he points out that we share the same human nature; differences
among us are quantitative, so to speak, rather than qualitative. Now in
itself, our community of nature proves nothing about how we ought to
treat each other. It would prove something, however, if we were the
works of a creator God, because in this case our similarity could
reasonably be taken as a sign of His intentions for us.[21] But can we

know whether we are, in fact, the works of a creator God? Apparently we are in luck. Locke believes that natural reason can find sufficient proof of a creator God in the order of the universe. Therefore, says Locke, we must assume that we are made for His purposes, not for those of one another. In his own words, "men all being the workmanship of one omnipotent and infinitely wise Maker—all the servants of one sovereign master, sent into the world by his order, and about his business—they are his property whose workmanship they are, made to last during his, not one another's pleasure; and being furnished with the like faculties, sharing all in one community of nature, there cannot be supposed any such subordination among us that may authorize us to destroy one another, as if we were made for one another's uses as the inferior ranks of creatures are for ours."[22]

For its main thesis, the first letter on toleration accepts this theology. Indeed it goes further: Locke declares for Christianity and, as we have seen earlier, argues that religious intolerance is contrary to a Gospel of love. But tolerance never means tolerating everything. Logically, in describing what is not to be tolerated Locke should have drawn his bearings from the same concern as in urging tolerance in the first place; for any other concern would be less than ultimate. We saw in the discussion of Christianity how this could be done. Instead, here he draws his bearings from a different source—as it were, from a competitor for godhood: the security of the commonwealth. By this means he justifies withholding of toleration from all faiths that demand submission to a foreign sovereign.[23] He gives Islam as an example here because he thinks believers are obligated to submit to "the Turk." Almost certainly, however, he is thinking of Roman Catholic submission to the Pope as well. Now the expediency of such suppression is clear enough. I do not deny that Roman Catholics may have posed a serious threat to the English constitution at the time Locke wrote. But insofar as he rests his case on grounds of expediency without inquiring whether these grounds would have been acceptable to God, he has shifted the burden of ultimacy from one concern to another.

An argument based on God's will rather than expediency might have been available to him. He may have believed that Catholics desired the installation of an absolutist monarchy that would enforce their beliefs. Not only because he thought these beliefs wrong, but even more important because he thought that God Himself abhors intolerance, it might follow that the state could legitimately refuse to accommodate Catholicism. However, this is not what he said.

Tolerance and Ultimate Concern in Neo-Kantianism

More recent social contract theories, like that of John Rawls, take us into the broader field of Kantianism and neo-Kantianism—which wants to be tolerant but has some difficulty explaining why or in what sense. Kant, of course, is well known for having believed in the possibility of religion "within the bounds of reason." But completely aside from his explicit statements on the subject of religion, a theology of sorts may be inferred from his ethics alone (which have been more influential), and it is not altogether clear that this theology is consistent with his other. The critical moment would appear to come with the announcement of the second formula of the Categorical Imperative. According to Kant, we ought always to act in such a way that by our actions we treat others never only as means to our ends, but always also as ends in themselves.[24] At first this sounds just like Locke's statement in the *Second Treatise*, quoted above. However, the two statements are really quite different. Locke and Kant do agree that we are not made for one another's uses. However, whereas for Locke the reason is that we are made for God's uses, for Kant the reason is that we are ends in ourselves—that is, made for our own uses. In Kant's thinking we are each, as it were, little gods.

Kant faces a problem that Locke does not: how to bring order to this burgeoning multiplicity of ultimate concerns when he is forbidden to rank them further. To be sure, he thinks that a person can be true to his nature as a rational being only when he recognizes the equal ultimacy of each of the others. However, insofar as this supposes that an end "in itself" can nevertheless be limited by other ends, his solution does not seem to be altogether stable.

Of the many attempts to manage this instability, John Rawls' theory will serve as an illustration. As we saw in Part Two, his method of making each person recognize the equal ultimacy of every other is to put representative individuals in an Original Position in which each forgets the things that distinguish him from every other. There they are assigned the task of formulating principles of justice which they will have to follow when they return to the world. Naturally, one of the things Rawls makes the parties in the Original Position forget is their particular religions. Nevertheless they know that in the real world they may have religions, and may even care about them deeply; therefore, the principles of justice they draw up provide for the most extensive possible system of equal religious liberties.

Unfortunately, just *how* extensive this system is the reader is left to determine for himself. The difficulty is that the reader cannot even determine whether the parties in the Original Position would really agree to it. As Albert Weale has pointed out, they might well disappoint Rawls by drawing up the principle that those in the real world who feel deeply about their religious opinions should always be permitted to suppress the opinions of those who are only lukewarm.[25] Because Rawls assures us that the parties in the original position would be risk-averse, another possibility in this vein is that they would wish to minimize the maximum offense they could feel in the real world. In this case, they would doubtless make it a principle to visit even the smallest religious nonconformities with grave penalties. Evidently, the ambiguity of Rawlsian religious tolerance is a consequence of the fact that he leaves Kant's theology in the incomplete condition in which he found it.

Notes

1. To examine these issues from the perspective of Judaism would also be extremely valuable. However, any interpretation of Judaism that I could give would be a Christian interpretation of Judaism, and I wish to avoid examining sectarian controversies except where my theme demands it.
2. *Liber ad Scapulam* (To Scapula), 2, cited in Dvornik, *Early Christian and Byzantine Political Philosophy*, vol. 2, chap. 9, at 582.
3. *Oratorio ad Græcos* (Oration to the Greeks), 4, cited ibid., at 586–87.
4. See Berns, *The First Amendment and the Future of American Democracy*, chap. 1, and Mansfield, "Thomas Jefferson."
5. John 18:33–38, esp. verse 36.
6. A similar idea is contained in his precept to give to God the things that are God's, and to Caesar the things that are Caesar's: Matthew 22:21, parallel texts in Mark and Luke. The statement is enigmatic in that it does not say what things are Caesar's, or in what sense. Considering the context in which it was delivered, this is not surprising: see the same chapter, verses 15–22. However it does clearly distinguish the two kingdoms, and became a cornerstone of Christian political thought.

7. These passages from Hilary of Poitiers, *To Constantius*, and Lactantius, *Divine Institutes*, are cited in Lord Acton, "Political Thoughts on the Church," at 24. The edition is J. Rufus Fears, ed., *Essays in Religion, Politics, and Morality*, which is vol. 3 of his *Selected Writings of Lord Acton*.

8. For his argument, see his first letter on toleration, at 6. Locke was indeed heterodox in certain other respects, notably his attitude toward the Trinity.

9. Readers who wish additional support for this claim may consult appendix 3.

10. Thomas Merton, *New Seeds of Contemplation*, at 105. Note well: the "doubt" that Merton endorses is not doubt *in* God, but doubt *in the name of* God. His tolerance is not driven by his skepticism; rather, both of these qualities are driven by what he is *not* skeptical about. This illustrates the analysis of skepticism and tolerance offered in Part One and repeated in various places since.

11. Though, as a Christian, I obviously have views about the matter.

12. See his *Introduction to the Principles of Morals and Legislation*.

13. See his *Liberty, Equality, Fraternity*.

14. For the former point, see his essay "On Liberty"; for the latter, *Considerations on Representative Government*.

15. *The Social Contract*, bk. 2, chap. 4, at 62.

16. Rousseau's is the classical argument for civil religion; see ibid., bk. 4, chap. 8. Democratic theory picks up the theme through Alexis de Tocqueville, *Democracy in America*, esp. bk. 2, pt. 1, chap. 5; functionalist sociology picks it up through Max Weber, *The Sociology of Religion*; Emile Durkheim, *The Elementary Forms of Religious Life*; and Talcott Parsons, *The Structure of Social Action*. Perhaps the best-known contemporary advocate of civil religion is sociologist Robert N. Bellah, esp. *Beyond Belief: Essays on Religion in a Post-Traditional Age; The Broken Covenant: American Civil Religion in a Time of Trial*; and (with Richard Madsen, William H. Sullivan, Ann Swidler, and Stephen M. Tipton) *Habits of the Heart: Individualism and Commitment in American Life.*. The phrase "habits of the heart" comes from Tocqueville.

17. *The Social Contract.*, bk. 4, chap 8, at 128.

18. This must be inferred from Rousseau's analysis of "partial associations" in another chapter and context: ibid., bk. 2, chap. 3, at 61. Compare Madison's arguments about the competition of factions in *Federalist* #10.

19. *The Social Contract*, at 120–31.

20. Ibid. As I understand the text, this allows any crime at all to count as evidence of impiety.

21. Clearly Locke does not agree with Hobbes that God's sovereignty arises from his power alone.

22. *Second Treatise of Government*, chap. 2, sec. 6, at 5–6. See also Locke's treatise "On the Reasonableness of Christianity."

23. First letter on toleration, at 46–47.

24. Immanuel Kant, *Groundwork of the Metaphysics of Morals*.

25. Weale, "Toleration, Individual Differences, and Respect for Persons."

12

True Tolerance (Again)

We've now examined six creeds, one religious and five secular. Others could have been examined, but these will be sufficient for us to proceed. Let's summarize our findings. In every case, whether a creed tolerates other ultimate concerns depends on the nature of its own ultimate concern. It is in the nature of some ultimate concerns to demand tolerance, and in the nature of others to forbid it. But tolerance means different things in different creeds. This is because tolerance never means tolerating everything, and what is *not* tolerated also depends on the nature of the ultimate concern.

True tolerance of other ultimate concerns would mean tolerance based on that concern which *truly deserved* to be regarded as ultimate. But here we have a problem. The various creeds are in competition. They do not agree about the truth; they do not agree which concern deserves to be regarded as ultimate. And neutrality is impossible.

To be sure, certain of these creeds would like to end the competition. For the reasons given earlier, classical utilitarians would probably end it in favor of whatever religion happened to prevail already, provided that the conduct demanded by this religion were reasonably close to the conduct demanded by utilitarianism itself. Rousseauian contractarians would end it in favor of a made-to-order civil religion.

But those who call themselves adherents of the liberal tradition in politics, a tradition emphasizing broad liberties and constitutionally limited government, reject both of these creeds. Each of the various creeds that liberals do profess either (a) cedes ultimacy to a concern whose nature forbids the enforcement of an Official Religion, or at least (b) denies the ultimacy of those concerns whose service would demand such enforcement. Notwithstanding the fact that the ambiguity of several of these creeds (Millian utilitarianism, Lockean contractarianism, and neo-Kantianism) on the subject of the ultimate concern makes this denial less than robust, enforcement of an Official Religion is unlikely, and so creedal competition is likely to endure for some time. So long as it does endure, then professors of each of these various creeds stand in the same relation to one another that Christians once stood to the Roman government. That is to say, each must speak to the other in its own terms. They must find common ground. *Not* compromise: true compromise is possible only between lower goods, for the sake of another higher than both. By very reason of its ultimacy, an ultimate concern cannot submit to true compromise. All it knows is tactical compromise, which is not true compromise but a step toward ultimate victory.

Can common ground be found? Some can. In fact one element of common ground has just been given: Liberals agree in denying the ultimacy of those concerns whose service would demand the enforcement of an Official Religion. Enforcement of an Official Religion, in turn, seems to mean at least three things: (1) coercive enforcement of belief in an officially approved ultimate concern; (2) coercive enforcement of outward acts of affirmation of such belief; and (3) coercive enforcement of outward acts for the support of an organization officially designated for promulgating these beliefs. All three would be prohibited.

Note that none of these three prohibitions forbids liberals to *accommodate* outward acts in the service of ultimate concerns (or, for that matter, less-than-ultimate concerns) which they do not share; in fact, their spirit encourages the accommodation of such acts whenever possible. However, "possibility" here does not mean physical possibility. Which outward acts they *could* and *could not* accommodate would depend on the nature of their own ultimate concerns. For this reason we need to find out whether they share any more common ground concerning the nature of the ultimate concern than has just been stated.

One more element of common ground can, perhaps, be found. Like the other, it is negative. All of the creeds conventionally called "liberal" seem to agree that some goods are merely prima facie. They may disagree about which goods these are, although the suggestions I offered in Part One might meet with a wide measure of agreement. But no creed could cede ultimacy to a good it regarded as merely prima facie. If any goods are considered merely prima facie by *all* of the liberal creeds, then by that fact they also agree that none of them merits ultimate concern. This is part of their common ground. Beyond this point they will disagree. Some liberals *do* cede ultimacy to one or another of the *intrinsic* goods, such as virtue or truth. These may be the goods Mill had in mind when he spoke of the "permanent interests of man as a progressive being." Other liberals cede ultimacy to God, regarded not as an intrinsic good—like other intrinsic goods except higher—but as the very Ground of their goodness. Notice that in this case, intrinsic goods are, at least, less blurred images of the ultimate concern than prima facie goods are.

How far does this additional piece of common ground take us toward the resolution of the "accommodation" problem? It clearly settles some issues. For instance, nothing in the natures of the concerns ceded ultimacy by any of the creeds conventionally called "liberal" rules out accommodation of a person's desire to wear special clothing emblematic of his ultimate concern. The rule, therefore, would be that such dress *should* be accommodated so long as it is not unduly burdensome to the *less*-than-ultimate concerns which their own ultimate concerns allow.[1] Likewise, all of the creeds conventionally called "liberal" would agree that no concern that deserved to be ceded ultimacy could possibly require the sacrifice of infants to Moloch. The rule, therefore, would be that such sacrifice should *not* be accommodated.

There, for those who rightly crave them, are some "practical implications of the theory." But the additional piece of common ground just as clearly leaves some issues open. The notorious example is abortion. According to some of the creeds that share the "liberal" common ground, abortion is like the wearing of religious insignia. These ultimate concerns are not of such a nature as to forbid abortion. They may even be of such a nature as to demand that it be allowed; at any rate, its accommodation is not unduly burdensome to the less-than-ultimate concerns which they allow. But according to some of the other creeds that also share the "liberal" common ground, abortion is like the sacrifice of children to Moloch. Their ultimate concerns *are* of such a nature as to forbid abortion: to forbid it as the sacrifice of innocents.

To know whether or not abortion falls within the scope of true tolerance, one would have to know which of these competing concerns truly deserved to be treated as ultimate. The language of "choice," "privacy," or "autonomy" is of no help here. It is just another way of reaching for the square circle of neutrality. For whether abortion is one of the choices that people should be allowed is precisely the point at issue. Would the language of "choice" be persuasive if children *were* being sacrificed to Moloch? Abortion either is, or is not, the murder of innocents. Among all creeds which require that the murder of innocents be forbidden, those who also say abortion truly is the murder of innocents logically cannot regard its accommodation as falling within the scope of true tolerance. Those who say it truly is not, logically can. Unless one of the two groups can *convert* the other, that is, persuade it that it has been wrong all along about the ultimate concern, one of the two groups will simply have to win the political battle. And that is a "practical implication of the theory," too.

Note

1. Cases in which such accommodation might be considered unduly burdensome to such other concerns are not difficult to imagine. Suppose, for instance, that the clothing a government-employed firefighter wished to wear as an emblem of his ultimate concern were too bulky to permit the donning of a fire-retardant oversuit required in the performance of his duties.

13

Is This a Possible Constitutional Position?

In this chapter we are not asking about the constitutionality of true tolerance as such, but about the constitutionality of the common ground. This common ground is merely that portion of true tolerance about which adherents to a certain group of ultimate concerns can agree.[1] Unavoidably, the section includes some repetition of principles, and some multiplication of examples, but in a fashion suited to their new contexts. As we have seen, adherents to all of the creeds conventionally designated "liberal" can agree to each of the following prohibitions:

1. Government should be prohibited from coercive enforcement of belief in an officially approved ultimate concern.
2. Government should be prohibited from coercive enforcement of outward acts of affirmation of such belief.
3. Government should be prohibited from coercive enforcement of outward acts for the support of an organization officially designated for promulgating these beliefs.
4. Government should accommodate outward acts in the service of various ultimate concerns wherever possible.

The match between these four agreements and the constitution appears to be quite close: Agreements 1, 2, and 3 are unequivocally supported by the First Amendment's establishment clause, and Agreements 1, 2, and 4 by its free exercise clause.[2] Indeed Agreements 1 and 2 had already been partly supported by Article VI's prohibition of religious tests as qualifications for federal offices and public trusts, which the First Amendment made redundant.

However, the free exercise clause is sticky for the same reason that Agreement 4 is sticky. In prohibiting interference with the free exercise of religion, the Framers could not possibly have had in mind accommodation of such religious practices as the one mentioned earlier—sacrifice of infants to Moloch. Yet no doubt, had they all been Moloch-worshippers they would have thought otherwise. The point is that they were not Moloch-worshippers. To explain this in the language of Agreement 4, a creed can interpret when accommodation is "possible" only in the light of its own ultimate concern. No creed could agree to accommodate a practice which its ultimate concern abhorred. For that matter, even if the practice were *not* abhorrent to its ultimate concern, no creed could agree to its accommodation if such accommodation were—by its own measure—unduly burdensome to the *less*-than ultimate concerns which its ultimate concern allowed its adherents to recognize.

Thus, *Agreement 4 yields determinate results about what to accommodate only when all of the creeds that share the liberal common ground also agree about what is not abhorrent and about what is not unduly burdensome.* Any Constitution that overlooked this would be straw, because for its adherents, the ultimate concern—whatever it is—would necessarily trump all merely constitutional considerations.

It would be sensible, then, to interpret the free exercise clause as *requiring* accommodation—and thereby permitting the judicial enforcement of such accommodation—only when the italicized condition is met; only when judges can truly say, "all of the lovers of religious liberty within the tradition that shaped our institutions—whatever the various springs of their love—agree."[3] In all other cases, the decision over whether or not to accommodate must be left to be fought out in legislatures.

Can we flesh out this abstraction? To do that means to make some guesses concerning which practices the creeds within the liberal common ground could agree about, and concerning which others they would disagree about. The more agreement, the more latitude for judicial enforcement of accommodation; the less, the more latitude for legislative discretion concerning accommodation. I do not think such guesses are impossible. Here, for example, are two domains of practice about which the creeds within the common ground would probably, at length, agree:

- Both the desire of some public school students to pray and the desire of other public school students not to pray must be accommodated; therefore, prayer in public schools may be neither compelled nor prohibited. Implementation of this pair of agreements might not be easy. Still, those who insist that public school students be led in prayer by teachers, and, at the other extreme, those who would prohibit public school authorities even the option of scheduling periods of silence in which the students could pray or not, according to conscience, would seem alike to be arguing from illiberal principles.
- Both the desire of the adherents of various creeds to offer public witness to their own faith, and the desire of adherents of other creeds not to be taxed to support competition from the former, ought to be accommodated. Again, implementation of this pair of agreements might not be easy. Still, those who insist that their communities use public funds to erect displays explicitly endorsing the particular tenets of a single creed, and, at the other extreme, those who would prohibit local authorities even the option of setting aside a public place in which the adherents of various creeds could erect displays at their own expense, would seem alike to be arguing from illiberal principles.

Judges should enforce accommodation in cases where such agreement is reachable; if I am right that it can be reached in the domains of practice just described, then in them, among others, courts may pronounce it.

But here are two other domains of practice, in one of which the liberal creeds could certainly *not* agree, and in the other of which such agreement is at least extremely unlikely:

- They could certainly not agree whether to accommodate the practice that one side calls "aborting a fetus" and that the other side calls "bringing about the death of an unborn child." This is because they agree about neither who (if anyone) is a person, nor how much moral weight (if any) such personhood commands in the light of the ultimate concern.[4]
- They could probably not agree whether to accommodate the practice that one side calls "acknowledging the massive confirmation of natural selection as the exclusive mechanism for the origin of species" and that the other side calls "ignoring the bona fides of creationism as a competing attempt to account scientifically for the same facts." This is because they agree about neither the method of science, nor the substantive presuppositions that it requires, and they think, at least, that their differing methodological and substantive assumptions are tied to their differing ultimate concerns.[5]

In all such cases where there is creedal disagreement even within the common ground, the baton should pass from courts to legislatures. The practical question being no longer "Do the liberal creeds agree?", it must become "Which creeds are strongest?"

About some practices, of course, lengthy debate might be necessary even to determine *whether or not* the creeds within the common ground can agree. Hence I do not claim that settling accommodation issues in the way proposed would be easier than settling them in other ways; only that it would be right.

Abuse of the Concept of Establishment

Many textbooks from the elementary grades through college stress that the establishment clause builds a "wall of separation" between church and state. This metaphor has a venerable history.[6] We first encounter it in a letter written by one of the great figures of the Baptist and Puritan movements, Roger Williams. Says he,

> [T]he faithfull labours of many Witnesses of Jesus Christ, extant to the world, abundantly proving, that the Church of the Jews under the Old Testament in the type, and the *Church* of the Christians under the New Testament in the Antitype, were both separate from the world; and that when they have opened a gap in the hedge or wall of Separation between the Garden of the Church and the Wildernes of the world, God hath ever broke down the wall it selfe, removed the Candlestick, &c. and made his Garden a Wildernesse, as at this day. And that therefore if he will ever please to restore His Garden and Paradice again, it must of necessitie be walled in peculiarly unto himselfe from the world, and that all that shall be saved out of the world are to be transplanted out of the Wildernesse of the world, and added unto his Church or Garden.[7]

Williams believes that when the church becomes enmired in the world, it is no longer true to God, and that God responds to this desertion by withdrawing His grace. Government being a chief part of the enmiring world, the church must utterly refuse official sponsorship. To do otherwise would be to depend on the state instead of on God.

The metaphor reappears in a brief note written by Thomas Jefferson to the Danbury Baptist Association in 1803, almost a decade and a half after the drafting of the Bill of Rights. The critical passage is simply, "I contemplate with solemn reverence that act of the whole American people which declared that their legislature should 'make no law respecting an establishment of religion, or prohibiting the free exercise thereof,' thus building a wall of separation between church and state."[8]

In 1879 (on Jefferson's authority, not Williams'), the metaphor of the "wall" finds its way into the decision of the U.S. Supreme Court—oddly, not in an establishment case, but in a free exercise case, *Reynolds v. United States*.[9] In 1947, the Court in turn cites *Reynolds'* use of the metaphor to gild its decision in an establishment case, *Everson v. Board of Education*.[10] Everson then becomes one of the sources of a doctrine which is handed through a chain of cases including *Abingdon School District v. Schempp* (1963), *Board of Education v. Allen* (1968), *Walz v. Tax Commission* (1970), and finally *Lemon v. Kurtzman* (1971).

Finally, in a dissent to *Wallace v. Jaffree* (1985), one of the cases in which this doctrine has been applied, Justice (later Chief Justice) Rehnquist vigorously attacks the metaphor. He points out, among other things, that Jefferson was in Europe during the debates on the Bill of Rights and hence was hardly qualified to expound the intentions of those who wrote the First Amendment.[11]

The peculiar thing about all of this is that whatever role the metaphor may have played in the origins of contemporary establishment clause doctrine, it does not accurately describe that doctrine. Separation of church and state, yes; a *wall* of separation, no. In fact, the misleading character of the metaphor has been recognized over and again by the Court itself. Said Justice Douglas in *Zorach v. Clauson* (1952), for example:

> The First Amendment . . . does not say that in every and all respects there shall be a separation of church and state. Rather, it studiously defines the manner, the specific ways, in which there shall be no concert or dependency one on the other. That is the common sense of the matter. Otherwise, the state and religion would be aliens to each other—hostile, suspicious, and even unfriendly. Churches could not be required to pay even property taxes. Municipalities would not be permitted to render police or fire protection to religious groups. Policemen who helped parishioners into their places of worship would violate the Constitution.[12]

Likewise, former Chief Justice Burger, writing for the Court in *Lemon*, observed that "the line of separation, far from being a 'wall,' is a blurred, indistinct, and variable barrier depending on all the circumstances of a particular relationship."[13] Because, in the words of *Walz*, "rigidity could well defeat the purpose" of the establishment clause (not to mention its companion free exercise clause), the Court, rather than observing a "wall," has attempted to plot a "course"—no less than a "course of constitutional neutrality."[14]

"Neutrality"! We have seen that term before.

The first judicial reference to religious neutrality is found in a case concerning the Ohio Bill of Rights, decided by Ohio Superior Court in 1870. At the time, the Ohio Bill of Rights provided that "religion, morality and knowledge . . . being essential to good government, it shall be the duty of the General Assembly to pass suitable laws, to protect every denomination . . . and to encourage schools and the means of instruction." Judge Taft, dissenting from the majority, remarks that "The government is neutral, and, while protecting all [religions], it prefers none, and it *disparages* none." Ninety-three years later in *Schempp*, a case arising not under the Ohio but under the federal Constitution, Justice Clark quotes Judge Taft's remark with grave approval.[15] Without comment, he also extends the meaning. Henceforth the government is to be neutral not only between the various sects conventionally designated "religions," but also between religion and irreligion.

The doctrine that *Lemon* finally established in pursuit of this mysterious neutrality is beguilingly easy to express. As the Chief Justice wrote, speaking for the Court,

> First, the statute must have a secular legislative purpose; second, its principal or primary effect must be one that neither advances nor inhibits religion; finally, the statute must not foster "an excessive government entanglement with religion."[16]

Yet this three-pronged test has proven embarrassingly difficult for the Court to put into practice. As part of his dissent in *Wallace*, Justice Rehnquist assembled an astonishing catalogue of inconsistent judgments, some from cases that anticipated the three-pronged test, more from cases that applied it. For example,

> a State may lend to parochial school children geography textbooks that contain maps of the United States, but the State may not lend maps of the United States for use in geography class. A state may lend textbooks on American colonial history, but it may not lend a film on George Washington, or a film projector to show it in history class. A State may pay for bus transportation to religious schools but may not pay for bus transportation from the parochial school to the public zoo or natural history museum for a field trip. . . . speech and hearing "services" conducted by

the State inside the sectarian school are forbidden, but the State may conduct speech and hearing diagnostic testing inside the sectarian school.[17]

Evidently the Justices cannot even agree as to how many times the Court has *declined* to apply the three-pronged test. Justice Rehnquist, in *Wallace*, says twice (in 1982 and 1983); Justice Powell, concurring in the same case, says once.[18] Nor do they give the same estimate of their difficulties. Justice Powell says that the three-pronged criterion "is the only coherent test a majority of the Court has ever adopted." Justice Rehnquist denies not only its coherence, but the ability of the majority to agree about what it has adopted: it "has caused this Court to fracture into unworkable plurality opinions, depending on how each of the three factors applies to a certain state action."[19]

We may get a good idea how the three prongs operate by considering three cases decided in the summer of 1985: for the effect and entanglement prongs, *Grand Rapids School District v. Ball* and *Aguilar v. Felton*, both of which were school aid cases; and for the purpose prong, *Wallace v. Jaffree*, which concerned a legislative provision for a minute of silence in public schools.

Justice Brennan delivered the opinion of the Court in both *Ball* and *Aguilar*. *Ball* concerned the "Shared Time" and "Community Education" programs of the Grand Rapids School District. Under the Shared Time program, public school employees taught remedial and enrichment courses in participating private schools, most of which had sectarian affiliations. Under the Community Education program, remedial and enrichment courses were funded in a variety of locations, including among others both sectarian private and public schools. Justice Brennan held that under the second prong of the *Lemon* test, both programs were unconstitutional. Their primary effect, he said, was inescapably to advance religion, for nothing had been done to protect the secular classes from the religious taint of the surrounding environment. This seems to be true. However, it did not seem to occur to Justice Brennan that overturning the two programs was not neutral either. It allowed parents of sectarian school youngsters to be taxed for the support of public schools whose secular outlook many of them certainly disapproved, without receiving any benefit themselves.

Aguilar presented a different set of circumstances. Title I of the *Elementary and Secondary Education Act of 1965* authorized the federal government to provide funds to local educational institutions to assist poor, educationally deprived children. New York City used some of the funds received under this program to supply remedial and guidance services to children in parochial schools. The remedial teachers were public employees assigned by the City, and in marked contrast to Grand Rapids practice, they were regularly visited in their classrooms by field workers to assure that their classes were kept free of all sectarian influences. Justice Brennan held that the conscientious supervision upon which the City depended in order to dodge the second prong of the *Lemon* test impaled it on prong number three: this supervision, he said, was an "excessive entanglement" of public authorities with religious institutions. Acidly but accurately, Justice Rehnquist remarked that the Court had set up a "Catch-22."[20] New York City had been blamed for doing precisely what Grand Rapids had been blamed for not doing.

The other claims and counterclaims in *Aguilar* echoed contentions which the badly divided Court had already rehearsed in the much more explosive *Wallace*. *Wallace* was the fruit of an attempt by Alabama legislators to provoke a Constitutional test—an aim about which they had been most clear. Over a period of several years, they had passed several different versions of a moment-of-silence statute in order to see just what the Court would allow. The one this case concerned listed a number of different things the moment might be used for, one of which—not singled out in any way—was "meditation or silent prayer." Justice White thought of the list in terms of a scenario in which students asked: Are we allowed to use the moment of silence to pray? In his view, the statute was harmless because it merely answered the question "at the outset."[21] However, the Court held that the very mention of prayer was enough to invalidate the statute, because even though prayer was not required, its mention revealed a legislative purpose of "endorsing" prayer—thus failing the first prong of the *Lemon* test.

Chief Justice Burger earnestly dissented. "To suggest," he said, "that a moment-of-silence statute that includes the work 'prayer' unconstitutionally endorses religion, while one that simply provides for a moment of silence does not, manifests not neutrality but hostility to religion."[22] This was not an attack on the idea of neutrality; that would have been too much to expect, considering who had composed the

Lemon three-pronged test in the first place. And considering that the test was still in use, neither was this a lament that the cause of neutrality had been utterly abandoned. Precisely what, then, did the Chief Justice hold that the Court was doing wrong? His answer came obliquely, in a quotation from the concurring opinion Justice Goldberg had written in *Schempp*, twenty-two long years before:

> untutored devotion to the cause of neutrality can lead to invocation or approval of results which partake not simply of that noninterference and noninvolvement with the religions which the Constitution commands, but of a brooding and pervasive dedication to the secular and a passive, or even active, hostility to the religious. Such results are not only not compelled by the Constitution, but, it seems to me, are prohibited by it.

Apparently the Chief Justice thought what ailed the Court was not that it had abandoned the cause of neutrality, but simply that its devotion to the cause of neutrality was "untutored."

This is a difficult claim to evaluate, because we do not know what the difference between a tutored and an untutored devotion to the cause of neutrality might be, and the Chief Justice did nothing to make it more clear to us. Perhaps a tutored devotion to the cause of neutrality would be more sensitive to the "variability" of the line between church and state of which he spoke in *Lemon*—to the dependence of this line on "all the circumstances of a particular relationship." Perhaps a tutored devotion to the cause of neutrality would distinguish between "endorsing" and "accommodating" the religious beliefs and practices of the citizens—a notion to be discussed in the next short section. Perhaps a tutored devotion to the cause of neutrality would do something else. But in his dissent, he did not tell us. Inevitably, this raises the question whether a tutored devotion might be no better than an untutored devotion: whether the problem might lie not in the *quality*, but in the *fact* of devotion to the cause of neutrality.

Indeed that is where the problem lies: for as we have already seen, religious neutrality is simply impossible. There may be some point in illustrating this abstract thesis by closer attention to each of the three prongs of the *Lemon* test.

The purpose prong. If a law must have a secular purpose, then a law with a secular but no religious purpose is acceptable, but a law with a religious but no secular purpose is not acceptable. This clearly dis-

criminates against all uses of religious principle in arguments about
public policy—from abortion to nuclear disarmament. Of course, one
may think this a fine idea. But it isn't neutral. In fact, recalling that the
distinction between secular and religious creeds is largely conventional—
that some secular creeds even profess an ultimate concern, and that no
secular creed is without implications as to what concerns might or
might not deserve to be ceded ultimacy—we can easily see that it is
more than nonneutral. It is tendentious.

The effect prong. According to this criterion, no law is valid the
"principal or primary" effect of which is to promote, "or inhibit,"
religion. The main problem here is a variation on the one we saw a
moment ago. The effect prong permits laws which promote or inhibit
the ultimate concerns of so-called secular creeds, and it prohibits laws
which promote or inhibit the ultimate concerns of so-called religious
creeds. Yet which ultimate concerns count as "religious" is largely
conventional. In *United States v. Seegar* (1965), the Court even admitted this: in order to interpret Congressional provisions for exempt-
ing conscientious objectors from military service, it extended the coverage of the term "God" to any "sincere and meaningful belief which
occupies in the life of its possessor a place parallel" to that filled by the
personal God of the religions conventionally so designated.[23] Unfortunately, afterward the Court promptly forgot what it had admitted.
What the effect prong represents is simply hostility to those ultimate
concerns which are conventionally designated religious, as contrasted
with those ultimate concerns which are conventionally designated secular.[24]

The excessive entanglement prong. This third and last prong of the
Lemon test presents a more complicated case than either of the other
two. This is because the consequences of a ban on more than a certain
degree of entanglement of state with religion depend on the character
of the state in question. In a Lockean "night watchman" state, such a
ban would fortify the protection of sects that have no political ambitions against sects that do—a protection already afforded to some
extent even by the narrower interpretation of the establishment clause
offered in the previous section. Though this might not be a bad thing
at all, it is clearly nonneutral. It manifests a bias for sects of the former
kind, against sects of the latter kind. Now consider the welfare state.
Here, the entanglement of agencies of the government with all manner

of private institutions, serving all manner of purposes, ultimate and less-than-ultimate, is a condition of their receiving all manner of benefits. To disallow more than a certain degree of entanglement of the state with private institutions conventionally designated "religious," while continuing to allow this degree of entanglement with all others, puts institutions of the former kind at an enormous relative disadvantage. Hence it is not neutral either.

As we saw with Roger Williams, of course, some religious thinkers hold that "disadvantage" of just this sort is much to be desired. Justice Brennan, especially, was given to Williamsian warnings of the corruption of faith by government. I do not mean to imply that Williams was wrong about this; in fact, I am inclined to think he was right. But—even overlooking the very great difference between refusing benefits and being denied them—there is the simple fact that not all sects concur with him. If what it takes to relabel the denial of benefits to religious organizations a favor rather than a harm is to switch to a theology that is pro-Williams rather than anti, it certainly brings us no nearer neutrality than we were before.

Abuse of the Concept of Accommodation

The question of accommodation arises daily. Should legislatures be allowed to open their sessions with invocational prayer? May employers be required to give employees time off to observe their holy days? What about giving children time off from their daily public schooling to attend elective classes on religion at parochial schools, or granting conscientious exemption from military service to those who believe that God abhors all war? Or what about granting "old" Mormons exemption from laws forbidding polygamy, allowing Amish and Mennonite parents to remove their children from public schools before the age set forth in compulsory school attendance laws, or allowing municipalities to include nativity scenes in Christmas displays built with public funds?[25]

The Supreme Court understands that the free exercise clause encourages accommodation. "We make room," said Justice Douglas, "for as wide a variety of beliefs and creeds as the spiritual needs of man deem necessary."[26] The problem is what is to be accommodated and what is not. At first glance, the language of the free exercise clause seems to suggest that everything conceivable must be: Congress, it says, shall make *no* law prohibiting the free exercise of religion. Yet this is wholly implausible. It would render all laws unenforceable, for one might always plead reasons of religion for disobeying them. The only alternative is to define the phrase "free exercise of religion" in such a way as to make this impossible. In keeping with the suggestions made earlier, judges could say that a judicially enforceable claim to be free exercise of religion had been made when, and only when, (a) none of the creeds whose common ground is presupposed by the free exercise clause would find the practice in question abhorrent to the nature of its ultimate concern, and (b) none of these creeds would find its accommodation unduly burdensome to the less-than-ultimate concerns whose consideration its ultimate concern permitted. Issues that could not be resolved in this way—issues not located within the common ground—would be left to legislatures to quarrel over.

One can easily see why the Justices of the Supreme Court do not want to do this. They do not want to find themselves in the position of uttering oracles about ultimate concerns. What they do not realize is that they are in this position already. Until lately, the rule they have followed to resolve accommodation questions was the one given by Chief Justice Burger in *Wisconsin v. Yoder*; "only those interests of the highest order and those not otherwise served can overbalance legitimate claims to the free exercise of religion."[27] How is it possible to decide which considerations are of higher and lower order, and yet be neutral? An equally puzzling question is how, if "legitimate," a claim to the free exercise of religion can be "overbalanced" at all. These problems suggest deep confusion in the minds of the Justices as to what they are doing when they settle accommodation claims.

This confusion seems to have opened the door to two alarming phenomena, and, more recently, a change of direction. The first of the alarming phenomena is that in reasoning about accommodation, some of the Justices have betrayed a sympathy for what Rousseau called civil religion. The second is that others, in the meantime, have indulged a bias in favor of the familiar. Both the sympathy for civil religion and the bias in favor of the familiar suggest ultimate concerns which are not only outside of, but hostile to, the common ground described earlier. I will briefly consider each in turn—first the sympathy, then the bias. The change of direction will be appraised separately. It presents grave problems of its own, and no one can yet tell whether it will be permanent.

The Sympathy. Civil religionism has long struck sympathetic chords on both the Left and the Right of the Supreme Court. Among whom these chords have reverberated comes as a surprise, in particular, former Justice Brennan, than whom no other recent member of the Court has been more dedicated to a "bright line" theory of the separation of church and state, and Justice O'Connor, who has pioneered an analysis of the *Lemon* three-pronged test focusing on the idea that government must not "endorse" religion. Yet their remarks are impossible to construe in any other way than as civil religionist.

Lynch v. Donelly (1984) provides a good example. The case was about whether a municipal government could fund a nativity scene in a Christmas display. According to the Court, it could. Dissenting, Justice Brennan says

we have noted that government cannot be completely prohibited from recognizing in its public actions the religious beliefs and practices of the American people as an aspect of our national history and culture. While I remain uncertain about these questions, I would suggest that such practices as the designation of "In God We Trust" as our national motto, or the references to God contained in the Pledge of Allegiance can best be understood, in Dean Rostow's apt phrase, as a form of "ceremonial deism," protected from Establishment Clause scrutiny chiefly because they have lost through rote repetition any significant religious content. Moreover, these references are uniquely suited to serve such wholly secular purposes as solemnizing public occasions, or inspiring commitment to meet some national challenge in a manner that simply could not be fully served if government were limited to purely non-religious phrases.[28]

Compare the words of Justice O'Connor, concurring rather than dissenting in the same decision:

the government's display of the creche is no more an endorsement of religion than such governmental "acknowledgements" of religion as legislative prayers . . . , government declaration of Thanksgiving as a national holiday, printing of "In God We Trust" on coins, and opening court sessions with "God save the United States and this honorable court." Those governmental acknowledgements of religion serve, in the only ways reasonably possible in our culture, the legitimate secular purposes of solemnizing public occasions, expressing confidence in the future, and encouraging the recognition of what is worthy of appreciation in society.[29]

Notwithstanding the disagreement of Justices Brennan and O'Connor over the narrow question of the crèche itself, they agree about the general question considered here: government may—in fact, the government would be very foolish *not* to—pervert religion to its own ends. I do not suggest that sincerely asking the blessing of God on a secular enterprise is a perversion of religion. But to use God-talk that one does not regard as having any genuine meaning, in order to get citizens to do something that they would never do otherwise, is another matter altogether. Unfortunately that is what Justice Brennan means by "inspiring commitment to meet some national challenge in a manner that could not be fully served if government were limited to purely non-religious phrases."

The claim that God-talk is protected from establishment clause scrutiny because it is no longer taken seriously as referring to God is arrogant nonsense. If it really had "lost through rote repetition any significant religious content," then obviously it would be useless for "inspiring commitment." Thus when Justice Brennan stresses the merely "ceremonial" character of God-talk while Justice O'Connor emphasizes that it does not signify "endorsement" of the religious beliefs that it seems to express, what they must really mean is that the *state* does not take it seriously. But when Justice Brennan stresses how "uniquely" God-talk is suited to the furtherance of state interests while Justice O'Connor emphasizes that it furthers these interests in "the only ways reasonably possible in our culture," what they must really mean is that the citizens do take it seriously—more seriously, in fact, than they take the state. To put the matter more bluntly than Justices Brennan and O'Connor saw fit to put it themselves, they are telling us that the Constitution permits our rulers to pull all of our mythopoeic strings in order to get us to do what they want. In Plato's phrase— which under the circumstances one finds considerably more "apt" than Dean Rostow's—we have been given a recipe for the Noble Lie.

The Bias. The other tendency mentioned above was a bias in favor of the familiar. This too strikes all across the Court. *Wisconsin v. Yoder* (1972) and *Lynch* provide good examples.

Yoder arose because, in violation of the compulsory school attendance statute of the State of Wisconsin, certain parents belonging to the Old Order Amish and Conservative Amish Mennonite faiths had refused to permit their children to attend public school beyond the eighth grade. Instead, they insisted that their children be permitted to "learn by doing" within the Amish communities. They said that sending the children to the public high school would endanger both the children's salvation and their own, and argued that this made their convictions for violation of the statute invalid under the free exercise clause. Writing for the majority, Chief Justice Burger agreed with the parents, arguing that (a) compulsory public education would indeed be a serious interference with the free exercise of the Amish faiths; (b) accommodation of the Amish educational practices would not seriously threaten the interests of the state in the education of children; and therefore (c) the Amish should be exempted from the coverage of the compulsory school attendance statute.

What is interesting for our purposes is not the fact that he argued these three propositions, but the *way* he argued the first of them. The Chief Justice launched upon a long historico-cultural essay on the Amish people, featuring first their long history, and second their virtues of reliability, self-reliance, dedication to work, and respect for law.[30] The idea seems to be that a person's ultimate concern is worth taking seriously if and only if (a) it has a pedigree, and (b) he and his kind are good people, irrespective of the goodness of the practice for which he asks accommodation. Even Justice Douglas, who objected to the second criterion, approved the first: "I think the emphasis of the Court on the 'law and order' record of this Amish group of people is quite irrelevant. A religion is a religion irrespective of what the misdemeanor or felony record of its members may be. . . . the Amish, whether with a high or low criminal record, certainly qualify by all *historical* standards as a religion within the meaning of the First Amendment."[31]

Returning to *Lynch* we find the idea of pedigree again. Here, at pains to explain why inclusion of a nativity scene in a publicly funded Christmas display does not violate the establishment clause, the Chief Justice offered two arguments. The first was that this symbol of the Christmas season had lost, through long use, its specifically Christian meaning. The second was that it merely depicted "the historical origins of this traditional event long recognized as a National Holiday."[32] That someone would complain is not surprising. That the complaint comes from Justice Brennan, however, is not at all what one would expect. He says that "To suggest, as the Court does, that such a symbol is merely 'traditional' and therefore no different from Santa's house or reindeer is not only offensive to those for whom the crèche has profound significance, but insulting to those who insist for religious or personal reasons that the story of Christ is in no sense a part of 'history'. . . ."[33] This is well said; the only mystery is why Justice Brennan approved of even deeper "offenses" elsewhere in his dissent. We have already seen his remarks on the uses of God-talk.

The bias in favor of the familiar that *Yoder* and *Lynch* betray may be called "conventionalism." Though it may seem sleepy and comfortable, its Pyrrhic quality should not be overlooked. For pedigree is not a reliable indicator of truth. In the ancient Near East, conventionalism would have been dead set against accommodating the shocking novelty of Hebraic monotheism. In the Roman Empire it would have confirmed, just as staunchly, the pagan judgment that Christianity was an execrable conceit of slaves and fools. When we recognize the Amish faith as comprising "a religion within the meaning of the First Amendment" solely because of three centuries of unbroken tradition, we judge in essentially the same way. What would one have said three centuries ago?

The Change of Direction. The civil religionist and conventionalist abuses of the idea of accommodation are both driven by the urge to choose without choosing. They seek to "balance" different claims against each other while still remaining neutral—like having carnal knowledge while somehow remaining a virgin. But there is another way for a judge to choose without choosing: to let someone else make the choice. This is the basis of the Court's recent change of direction, a change which was first revealed in *Employment Division v. Smith* (1990), also known as *Smith II*.

To be sure, there are some accommodation cases in which judges *should* choose to defer to other choosers, especially to legislatures. This is not neutral; in free exercise cases, it reflects a constitutional bias in favor of just those creeds that occupy what I have called the liberal common ground. I have argued that the free exercise clause authorizes judges to enforce the accommodation of a particular practice only when *each* of these creeds can agree that the practice in question is neither abhorrent to its ultimate concern, nor unduly burdensome to the less-than-ultimate concerns its ultimate concern permits. For all other practices, the decision pro or con accommodation must be left for legislatures to fight out.

Though this is deferential, it is far from absolutely deferential. Judges must still decide, case by case, which practices really do lie within the common ground. For legislatures might still act unconstitutionally. Why might they do this? Although the free exercise clause presupposes the truth of liberalism's common ground, it cannot prevent liberals themselves from acting illiberally. Moreover, it does not exclude illiberal creeds from political rights. They too may be represented in legislatures; they too may score political victories; and among these victories, some subset may burden religious practices whose accommodation the liberal common ground would demand. The Constitution does not permit judges to undo all illiberal victories, or even, perhaps, most illiberal victories. But under the free exercise clause, it does permit them to undo the particular illiberal victories that occupy this subset.

Unfortunately, *Smith II* is far, far more deferential than this.

The case involved two employees of a private drug rehabilitation organization in Oregon, Alfred Smith and Galen Black, who were fired for sacramentally consuming peyote during a service of the Native American Church. Peyote is used by the Native American Church only in small quantities, only during religious services, and only under strict religious rules. When Smith and Black applied for unemployment compensation, the Oregon Employment Division turned them down on the grounds that their discharge had resulted from work-related misconduct. Their appeal reached the U.S. Supreme Court twice. In *Smith I* (1988), the Justices sent it back down to the Oregon Supreme Court for a decision as to whether or not the sacramental use of peyote was forbidden under Oregon's controlled substances law; this was one of the points the parties disputed. The finding in Oregon that such use was indeed against Oregon law cleared the way for a final ruling by the U.S. Supreme Court, in 1990. In its decision, the Court held that Smith's and Black's free exercise rights had not been violated by Oregon's denial of unemployment compensation.

To achieve this result, the Court resurrected the doctrine of the 1879 case *Reynolds v. United States*—so patently contrary to ordinary usage and so roundly rejected in *Yoder*—that the "exercise" of religion has everything to do with belief but almost nothing to do with conduct. What it said, in an opinion written by Justice Scalia, is that although there is a right to the free exercise of religion, this right does not excuse an individual from obeying a "valid and neutral law of general applicability" just because the law requires behavior that his sect forbids or forbids behavior that his sect requires.[34]

The quoted phrase embodies three requirements. If a law that burdens a religious practice is to survive a free exercise challenge,

1. *The law must be valid.* This means merely that it must be constitutional in other respects.
2. *The law must be neutral.* The term is a chameleon, as now we know, but here it means that the law must not be motivated by a desire to harm a particular sect.
3. *The law must be generally applicable.* This means that it is not applied to members of a particular sect alone.

In a remarkable reversal of precedent (which Justice Scalia insisted was not a reversal at all), these three are the *only* requirements the new majority on the Court found necessary. The consequences go far beyond the narrow question of whether Smith and Black should have suffered denial of benefits for sacramental peyote use. A law that is otherwise Constitutional, and that does not expressly single out a particular sect, will now be permitted to burden *any religious practice whatsoever, and to any degree*,[35] so long as the burden is "merely the incidental effect" of the law, not its "object."[36]

To know that the state may stamp out religions and religious practices only by accident, not on purpose, is not terribly comforting. Naïve, myopic, or careless legislators without a trace of malice might suppress religious schools as an incidental effect of overzealous public school attendance laws.[37] They might wipe out the Christian sacrament of Holy Communion as an incidental effect of prohibiting the serving of food or beverages in public meetings.[38] They might abolish religious counseling or pastoral care as an incidental effect of regulations for the licensing of mental health practitioners. All of these horrors could be wreaked by laws of unimpeachably general applicability; the lesser their authors' familiarity with, or the greater their indifference to, an affected sect, the greater the likelihood of their passage. No great imagination is needed to think of equal monstrosities within any category of legislation whatsoever: whether zoning laws or child welfare laws, tax codes or building codes, or regulations concerning health, safety, or morals. The potential for absent-minded repression, for a perfectly ingenuous persecution of all manner of practices that would be tolerated unanimously by the creeds that share the liberal common ground, is incalculably vast.

Justice Scalia justified the cavalier indifference of the *Smith II* majority by summoning visions of bedlam. He repeatedly quoted the *Reynolds* Court's warning in 1879 that if the individual were permitted to practice his religion even in the face of generally applicable laws to the contrary, he would "become a law unto himself,"[39] and made the threat of "anarchy" loom even over the compelling-interest doctrine of *Yoder* and related cases.[40] Unfortunately, this smoky conjuring obscured the difference between letting believers do some things and letting them do all things. It was particularly ironic in view of the fact, seen earlier, that the notions concealed in *Yoder's* bosom were more repressive than anarchistic. Indeed, the warning that even limited protection against legislative burdens on individual faith will make people "laws unto themselves" seems less an indictment of the *Yoder* doctrine—indictable as that is—than of the free exercise clause itself.

Whether by the method of *Yoder* and its cousins, or by the method of *Smith II*—whether by pretending to "balance" different claims against each other while still remaining neutral, or by choosing to let others choose and requiring *them* to keep up the pretense instead—in the oblivion of thinking that we have somehow skirted our choices, still we choose. Better to choose in vigilance of mind.

Notes

1. The degree to which they are willing to accept constitutional limits at all is of course also a function of their ultimate concerns.
2. The wording of the First Amendment offers protection only against federal laws. However, several different views of the Fourteenth Amendment, including both those favored by the Supreme Court and the one I favor (see appendix 2), imply that it offers parallel protection against state laws. The difference between the degrees of protection offered by the First and the Fourteenth Amendments is, on some of these views, important; for discussion, see chapter 9, note 13, and appendix 2, note 5, with accompanying text.
3. Should the italicized condition be taken as referring to agreement among the creeds which shared the liberal common ground *when the Constitution was writ-*

ten and ratified, or to agreement among the creeds which share the liberal common ground *now*? Abstract arguments can be offered both for taking it in the first sense and for taking it in the second. Taking it in the first sense is supported by the Reconstruction Principle, which is proposed in appendix 2 for the interpretation of clauses (in this case, the free exercise clause) too vague to be construed by the Text and Context Principles alone. Taking it in the second sense is supported by a moving legal mores test, which is proposed in the same appendix for the interpretation of clauses not merely vague, but deliberately open-ended. I think the case for regarding the free exercise clause as simply vague is stronger than the case for regarding it as deliberately open-ended. Thus far, it seems that the italicized condition should be taken in the first sense. However, besides all these abstract arguments is a hard-knocks reason for taking it in the second. *Were we to take it in the first, judges would sometimes be required to violate their own ultimate concerns.* I do not think it unreasonable to demand judicial deference to the intent of the framers and ratifiers; only a fool, however, would expect a judge to defer when it means choosing his constitutional theory over his god. We may call this the *Reality Principle.*

The label is not meant to deceive. It is not a fourth principle of constitutional interpretation, following in order after the Text, Context, and Reconstruction principles. Rather it is a formula for the inevitable limit to all constitutional interpretation.

4. The disagreement about who is a person concerns whether the unborn child is a person. The disagreement about how much moral weight personhood commands involves, among other things, a further disagreement about whether personhood itself is all-or-nothing, or a matter of degree.

5. An example of a methodological disagreement: Is *any* theory ever "proven," or is it merely the case that some have so far escaped being *dis*proven? For discussion, see Karl Popper, *The Growth of Scientific Knowledge.* An example of a disagreement about necessary substantive presuppositions: Are hypotheses (or assumptions) about supernatural agencies automatically out of bounds, or are they to be investigated (or tried) just like any others?

6. And it is based on an idea with an even more venerable history. See appendix 3.

7. Roger Williams, "Mr. Cotton's Letter Lately Printed, Examined and Answered," *Writings*, vol. 1, at 392.

8. Thomas Jefferson, *Writings*, vol. 16, at 281.

9. *Reynolds v. United States* (1879), at 164.

10. *Everson v. Board of Education* (1947), at 16.

11. *Wallace v. Jaffree* (1985), at 2509 (Justice Rehnquist, dissenting).

12. *Zorach*, at 312.

13. *Lemon v. Kurtzman* (1971), at 614.

14. *Walz v. Tax Commission* (1970), at 669.

15. *Abingdon School District v. Schempp* (1963), at 214, quoting *Minor v. Board of Education of Cincinnati* (1872). The reason for the apparent discrepancy in the date—1872 instead of 1870—is that Justice Clark took his quotation from the decision of the Ohio *Supreme* Court, reversing the decision of the Ohio Superior Court.

16. *Lemon*, at 612–13.

17. *Wallace*, at 2518–19. Some of Justice Rehnquist's examples are less convincing than others, and one is drawn from a case that clearly does not anticipate *Lemon*; hence the elision.

18. The discrepancy arises over *Larson*, in which the Court declares that application of the *Lemon* test is unnecessary under the circumstances of the case, but goes on to claim that it would have led to the same conclusion as the arguments used. The case which is counted by both Justice Rehnquist and Justice Powell is *Marsh v. Chambers* (1983). See *Wallace* at 2519 (Justice Rehnquist, dissenting), and at 2494 (Justice Powell, concurring).

19. Ibid., at the same two pages as cited before.

20. *Aguilar v. Felton* (1985), at 3443 (Justice Rehnquist, dissenting). Justice O'Connor expressed the same concern in milder fashion.

21. *Wallace*, at 2508 (Justice White, dissenting).

22. Ibid., at 2505 (Chief Justice Burger, dissenting).

23. *Seegar*, at 176.

24. Even were this distinction completely unproblematic, the effect prong could not be applied. For how is one to decide which of various qualitatively different effects is "more primary"? There is no difficulty in comparing the magnitudes of two different sounds, two different lights, or two different gravitational forces. But comparing the magnitudes of a law's effects on, say, religion and literacy, is like comparing the magnitudes of an odor and an interruption. They must be measured on scales which use qualitatively different units.

25. See, for instance, *Zorach v. Clauson* (1952), *United States v. Seegar* (1965), *Reynolds* (above), *Wisconsin v. Yoder* (1972), and *Lynch v. Donelly* (1984). *Reynolds* refused to accommodate Mormon polygamy. *Yoder* accommodated Amish and Mennonite educational practices, while *Lynch* accommodated the inclusion of a crèche in a publicly funded Christmas display. United States law accommodates objection to military service based on conscientiously held religious convictions; *Seegar* (on which more below) ruled that ethical beliefs of certain kinds are to be counted as religious even if they do not involve faith in a personal God.

26. *Zorach*, at 313. What Justice Douglas means in speaking of diverse "spiritual needs" necessitating diverse religions is not altogether clear. He may mean that the test of a creed is whether it satisfies a subjective urge, not whether it is objectively true; on the other hand he may mean that different souls must approach the one Truth by different means.

27. *Yoder*, at 215. A compelling-interest test for accommodation of religion is first stated in the narrower context of *Sherbert v. Verner* (1963), at 402–3.

28. *Lynch*, at 1381 (Justice Brennan, dissenting). The internal reference is to Eugene V. Rostow, "The Enforcement of Morals," in *The Sovereign Prerogative: The Supreme Court and the Quest for Law*. This, in turn, was written in defense of Lord Patrick Devlin, *The Enforcement of Morals*.

29. Ibid., at 1369 (Justice O'Connor, concurring).

30. *Yoder*, at 219, 223–24.

31. *Yoder*, at 246–47 (Justice Douglas, dissenting in part); emphasis mine.

32. *Lynch*, at 1363.

33. Ibid., at 1379 (Justice Brennan, dissenting).

34. *Smith II*, at 1660; the phrase is borrowed from *United States v. Lee* (1982), at 263, note 7.

35. Indeed, writes Justice Scalia, for courts to judge questions of degree does not even make sense. At 1604 he asks, "What principle of law or logic can be brought to bear to contradict a believer's assertion that a particular act is 'central' to his personal faith?" Then at 1605, note 4, rebutting objections made in the opinions of Justice O'Connor (concurring in the judgment of the Court but not its reasoning, joined in part by Justices Brennan, Marshall, and Blackmun) and Justice Blackmun (dissenting, joined by Justices Brennan and Marshall), he ridicules the attempt to distinguish asking about the "centrality of a belief" from asking about either the "constitutional significance of a burden" (O'Connor, at 1611), the "severity of an impact" (Blackmun, at 1621), or the "greatness of a harm" (his paraphrase of Blackmun). In his view, the three questions are equivalent, and equivalently undecidable.
36. *Smith II*, at 1600.
37. Compare *Yoder*.
38. The National Prohibition Act provided an exception for the sacramental use of wine. However, the categorical language of the Prohibition Amendment seemed to permit no such exception.
39. *Smith II* at 1600, 1603, citing *Reynolds* at 167.
40. At 1605: "Any society adopting [a compelling-interest test] would be courting anarchy, but that danger increases in direct proportion to the society's diversity of religious beliefs, and its determination to coerce or suppress none of them."

Epilogue
The Great Refusal

Cervantes tells a story about a dog and a madman of Cordoba. "He was in the habit of carrying on his head a marble slab or stone of considerable weight, and when he met some stray cur he would go up alongside it and drop the weight full upon it, and the dog in a rage, barking and howling, would then scurry off down three whole streets without stopping. Now it happened that among the dogs that he treated in this fashion was one belonging to a capmaker, who was very fond of the beast. Going up to it as usual, the madman let the stone fall on its head, whereupon the animal set up a great yowling, and its owner, hearing its moans and seeing what had been done to it, promptly snatched up a measuring rod and fell upon the dog's assailant, flaying him until there was not a sound bone left in the fellow's body; and with each blow that he gave him he cried, 'You dog! You thief! Treat my greyhound like that, would you? You brute, couldn't you see it was a greyhound?' And repeating the word 'greyhound' over and over, he sent the madman away beaten to a pulp.

"Profiting by the lesson that had been taught him, the fellow disappeared and was not seen in public for more than a month, at the end of which time he returned, up to his old tricks and with a heavier stone than ever on his head. He would go up to a dog and stare at it, long and hard, and without daring to drop his stone, would say, 'This is a greyhound; beware.' And so with all dogs that he encountered, whether they were mastiffs or curs, he would assert that they were greyhounds and let them go unharmed."[1]

This story may be read as a parable of what might happen if ethical neutralism were overthrown by authoritarians instead of by believers in true tolerance; by warriors who did not understand the reasons for its overthrow. That sort of thing is not unheard-of in the history of political thought. How might it happen in this case? In this way.

Ethical neutralists are like the madman before he was beaten by the capmaker. Every time they recognize an ethical motive behind a public policy, they cry, "Enforcement of morality!" and drop a heavy stone upon its head. Suppose we were to put a stop to that for the wrong reasons. We might then see a different kind of madness in its place. For authoritarians are like the madman after he was beaten by the capmaker. Every time they see the state doing something despotic, they stare at it, long and hard, and, without daring to drop their stone, say "This is an enforcement of morality; beware."

Naturally only one of these two kinds of madness can be uppermost at any given moment. However, both are dangerous. Neutralists fail to understand that it is not necessarily despotic to take an interest in the ethical well-being of the community. Authoritarians fail to understand that it *can* be despotic to take an interest in the ethical well-being of the community. The practice of true tolerance involves being able to tell the difference between the two ways of "taking an interest," and that is a hard difference to learn. The idea of true tolerance is simple; the discernment required in its practice is excruciating.

Given such a risk, why not err on the side of neutrality? Why learn true tolerance at all, if it is so difficult a discipline? That would be more than a little like getting away from a sea monster by rowing with might and main toward a whirlpool. There are at least three good reasons why this book has not rowed in that direction.

The first is an author's obligation to the truth. He should not suppress the facts about the whirlpool in order to draw attention to the monster; he should warn about both.

The second is that rowing for the whirlpool does not avoid the monster anyway. By embracing ethical neutralism, we not only invite an authoritarian backlash, but throw away the moral arguments by which this backlash might be resisted.

The third is that—as shown at length—ethical neutrality is a sheer logical impossibility.

Even so, exploding what one takes as error is not the only way to illuminate what one takes as truth. After all, to some readers it will hardly have seemed tolerant that someone has written a polemic telling how a group of others has got tolerance all wrong. Why not choose a less abrasive, a more discreet, a more "scholarly" way of illuminating the truth?

The discreet approach ignores the realities of the situation. Stances that appears to be ethically neutral never really are; they merely hide the legs they stand on. All too often they cloak moral ideas that would be spurned could they be seen more clearly. Thus ethical neutralism is not an alternative to the whirlpool; it is a form of the whirlpool. It is a sort of bad-faith authoritarianism.

The forms that bad-faith authoritarianism takes are sometimes almost too ridiculous for words. It once fell to my lot to revise a well-established high school civics textbook. Among other expository chores, I had to explain the language of the Declaration of Independence, which modern students find virtually inpenetrable. My editor, ordinarily an amiable fellow, was completely discomposed by my explanation that expressions like "the Creator" and "Divine Providence" were references to God, whom Jefferson regarded as the source of human rights. In the name of neutrality, the offending sentences were excised from my copy.

I was lucky enough to see his decision reversed on appeal; the supervising editor happened to be a self-conscious dissenter from the conventional wisdom. But I did not win all my battles, nor have colleagues who also write textbooks won all of theirs. It is not so easy to regard bad-faith authoritarianism as merely ridiculous when one loses instead of winning the right to speak; or when, wearied of having to fight over everything, one at last gives in. Apparently democracy is safe from the founding documents only if students don't know what they mean; and apparently the proper way to deal with contemporary controversy is not to present both sides fairly, but to pretend that controversy does not exist.

As I learned, what this means is that the writer is to present either *no* sides, or (in the case of certain progressive orthodoxies) *one* side.[2] This too in the name of neutrality—often with a sincerity which would be less wounding (though more guilty) were it merely pretended.

The same sort of thing goes on with writing intended for other scholars. Perhaps the pressing need to illustrate will excuse the bad taste of relating another personal anecdote. I once received a most startling review from a well-regarded university press. The reviewer extravagantly praised the manuscript, remarked that it had forced him to rethink his own positions, but then said it ought not be published. My fault was to have written that theology may have something to say about ethics. This lapse from neutrality was unforgivable, because in his view religious tolerance meant suppressing the mention of religion. Of his own lapse he was conveniently unaware. For the sin of discussing differences between Christian and secular ethics, he held me personally involved in the guilt flowing from the massacre of the Huguenots.

Although examples concerning religion are perhaps most striking, similar examples of bad-faith authoritarianism could be drawn from any sphere of tolerance. Anyone who suggests today that liberal practices and institutions depend on certain propositions about what is good and true is asking for trouble. In some mileaus and forums, even to make much of the fact that liberal practices and institutions *were once thought* to depend on certain propositions about what is good and true is asking for trouble. The offender will widely be taken as sounding the trumpet for a *retreat* from the liberal ramparts. He will not always, but he will often, find grave obstacles in the path of getting a hearing at all. He may find it impossible to publish; he may find it impossible to get tenure; all in the name of tolerance.

As in all ideological repressions, there is a way out: to join the game. In our generation, that means to disguise one's suppositions about what is good and true under the garments of neutrality. Whether this involves deceiving others only—or deceiving oneself along with them—it means, at any rate, to deceive.

Nothing can be accomplished without challenging the Great Refusal of the present vicars of liberalism: the refusal to make open commitment to particular propositions about what is good or true. What strikes me in concluding this book is that those who bequeathed our institutions to us were never tempted to the Great Refusal. Something is different in the moral climate of their heirs, and it would be worthwhile to find out what.

A good deal is heard today about the importance of individual agency—of Choice—as though that had something to do with it. I do not think that we are really much enamored of agency. I think we misunderstand it; I think, even, we fear it. For some, neutralist Choice-talk is the emblem of an effort to keep from having to exercise agency in public life at all; for some, it is the emblem merely of an effort to keep others from being able to exercise it. The fact is that we fear Choice. But why?

Well, why not? Bad choices *are* fearful. And choosing to deny all choices to others is fearful. Unconscious choices—the kind we make when we think we need not choose—these are fearful too. Such perils might seem more than enough to excuse our avoidance of choice. But they are not. For their antidote is not *not choosing*; it is choosing tolerantly, knowingly, and well.

Then again, considering on the one hand just what is this power that is placed in our hands, and on the other our stupendous liability to error, a certain holy dread ought to hang over the act of Choice. This too might seem to excuse avoiding it. But the present suggestion explains no more than the last. Cravenness and holy dread are not the same. One prevents from choosing; the other prevents from choosing lightly.

To repeat the question, then: Why do we fear Choice itself? I don't know the answer. But it takes no great wit to see that we will have to find the answer, if what merits Choice in our way of life is long to persist.

Notes

1. Cervantes, *The Ingenious Gentleman, Don Quixote de la Mancha*, 506–7.
2. Compare the experiences related by Robert Weissberg in "Political Censorship: A Different View."

Appendix One
The Counsels of Tolerance— A Subset

True tolerance is the art of knowing when and how to tolerate. To tolerate at the right time and in the right way is not a failure of moral will, or a forbearance from judgment; it is a perfection of moral will, and an exercise of judgment. For some of the ways of encouraging what is good for human beings are really bad for human beings: they take them further from the goal, not nearer. True tolerance rejects these ways, while embracing the others. It is the protection of ends, including our deepest, against ill-thought means. This is its fundamental principle.

Following is a list of some of the counsels of tolerance this book has discussed or presupposed. Few of them will seem startling. The important thing is to distinguish them from their misinterpretations. Therefore, this is only a supplement. Out of its original context, any of these counsels might seem to mean more, less, or other than it ought.

1

Evils must be tolerated in just those cases where their suppression would involve equal or greater hindrance to goods of the same order, or any hindrance at all to goods of higher order. More briefly (and less exactly): true tolerance is the protection of ends against means.

2

Although diversity is not a good in itself, the good is diverse. Virtue should be understood not as a straitjacket, but as a condition making true diversity of character possible.

3

Nothing should be tolerated that tends to destroy the very possibility of moral choice. This includes not only the obvious destroyers—

certain uses of drugs, surgery, hypnosis, sensory deprivation, and torture—but also subtler destroyers such as suffocating forms of supervision.

4

Ethically healthy traditions are not lightly to be disregarded. Nevertheless, social conventions are not facts of ethics; mores must be carefully distinguished from morality.

5

Part of true tolerance is remembering at all times that one is an object of tolerance to others. One should sometimes even deny oneself things that are innocent in themselves if others cannot bear them.

6

Individuals do not always know what is best for them. Even so, true tolerance admits that each person is in a singular position to know his own strengths, weaknesses, and circumstances.

7

While avoiding connivance at the wrongs or faults of others, one must avoid the even greater monstrosity of moral pride. If you avoid me because of what I do, do it because you are not good enough to be with a man as bad as me; not because you are too good.

8

If you say in your heart that you are too good to be around me, it were better that you sought my company. If you say in your heart that you are better than me, it were better that you connived at my wrong.

9

Avoid me if you must, but do not parade the avoidance. Warn others against me, but never do it out of malice.

10

In law, too, true tolerance permits deliberate dishonor to practices, but not to persons. At most, persons may be punished, not disgraced.

11

You may deny me optional benefits if it is your office to make the decision, but you may not deny me benefits which are my due as a human being, and especially not those that might assist the amendment of my life.

12

Whatever the law does not clearly prohibit should be treated as permitted. This counsel is only juridical; it does not mean that everything the law permits is ethically right.

13

Even when there is cause to discourage certain acts, the presumption of the legislator should always be against criminalizing them. Where possible, the acts should be discouraged in other ways.

14

No argument for making an act a crime should be entertained unless it can be framed in terms of *harms* to which the act contributes. The more trivial these harms, the greater should be the burden of justification that the state must overcome in order to make the act a crime. However, the meaning of "harm" is a reasonable object of debate; it need not be restricted to physical harms.

15

Relationships should be regulated when—but only when—the common good is intimately dependent upon their stability, their stability is intimately dependent upon very close adherence to the relevant social norms, and, because of either universal human weakness or the characteristics of one's own society, these norms are too fragile to thrive without additional support from the law.

16

The family satisfies these conditions, but even here the state should mostly confine itself to a structure of family law that allows families to get along on their own.

17

In the education and nurture of the child, unconditional love should be the rule; however, this does not imply unconditional approval of everything about the child.

18

Contempt travels easily under the mask of tolerance. To accept the unacceptable is to tell a child that nothing about him matters.

19

Children do not learn to hate themselves when they have failed to learn that they are "special," but when we have failed to love them; nor when they have not learned enough "self-esteem," but when they have not learned that the most estimable of all things are beyond Self.

20

True tolerance acts on the hope that the young will develop the qualities of character that will help them to recognize wrong and embrace right with as little external guidance as possible. This does not mean giving them all-purpose conceptual ingredients with which to whip up their own unique versions of what counts as right and what counts as wrong.

21

The young deserve the ethical reasons for our demands as soon as they reach an age at which they can understand them. This does not mean that they must be allowed to prolong the conversation indefinitely.

22

Teachers should present not only the ideals of their own tradition, but also the ideals of the significant alternatives to it—including the traditions against which their own is in part a reaction.

23

An objective teacher is not one who takes no position—which is at any rate impossible—but one who makes the young a gift of the knowledge, the ability, and the encouragement to discover and try to correct not only their errors (though those too, and with his help), but also his own.

24

Education and nurture should respect not only the differences between the gifts and callings of the students, but also the commonness of their humanity. They may learn different trades, but they must all learn the human virtues.

25

Each person is entitled to defend his understanding of the good by rational arguments, be it true or false, and to attempt to persuade others that it is, in fact, true.

26

If any person proposes a policy, he shows his tolerance for others by honoring their demand to know on what understanding of the good his proposal rests.

27

In return, they show their tolerance for him by taking his arguments seriously. They do not demean his understanding of the good by treating it as a mere subjective taste or preference, unless he refuses to offer a rational defense for it.

28

Their tolerance for him does not require them to treat his understanding as true, or even to treat it has having just as great a share of truth as other understandings. That is for him to show. However, they make this showing possible.

29

Expressive tolerance must be observed not only by individuals, but also by the state. Thus, discursive reasoning and the communication of information that republican citizens might need in order to carry out their constitutional responsibilities should be granted absolute protection.

30

Even when a form of expression falls into neither of these categories, if it has traditionally been accepted by the community the state should regulate it only with the greatest caution.

31

None of the following, by themselves, are adequate reasons to suppress expression: that it proposes greater suppression; that it counsels disobedience to law; that it attacks our way of life or form of government; that it supports beliefs that seem false or bad; or that it gives offense.

32

Individuals may not be required to act as though their religious beliefs had no valid ethical implications, or as though their ethical beliefs had no valid political implications.

33

Government should be prohibited from coercive enforcement of belief in an officially approved ultimate concern.

34

Government should be prohibited from coercive enforcement of outward acts of affirmation of such belief.

35

Government should be prohibited from coercive enforcement of outward acts for the support of an organization officially designated for promulgating these beliefs.

36

None of the last three counsels of tolerance is theologically neutral. Each involves presuppositions about the kinds of service that the ultimate concern could demand. These presuppositions are accepted by some creeds but not others. Thus, to justify religious tolerance one must be sure that the truth does not lie in any of the latter.

37

Government should accommodate outward acts in the service of various ultimate concerns wherever possible. This counsel of tolerance is no more a counsel of neutrality than the last three. Except in the light of an ultimate concern, no decision can be made as to when such accommodation is "possible."

38

One of the assumptions to be used in making such decisions is that no merely prima facie good could possibly deserve to be treated as ultimate.

39

A sincere petition by the state for the blessing of whatever God may be thought to exist is not a violation of true tolerance. However, the state may not "use" religion as a Noble Lie for its own ends.

Appendix Two
Constitutional Interpretation

The theory of true tolerance is logically independent of this book's approach to constitutional interpretation. Nevertheless, a brief account of that approach may not be out of place. This is because from time to time, I have used judicial views to illustrate lines of reasoning which violate true tolerance, and for pragmatic reasons I have also found it necessary from time to time to ask whether or not they also violate the Constitution.

My view of the relationship between constitutional interpretation and moral philosophy puts me at odds with a certain contemporary movement. The standards of the movement read, "Put moral philosophy in constitutional theory!" That sounds good; but what the standard-bearers usually have in mind is construing the Constitution so that it always "means" just what, guided by their moral philosophy, they would like it to mean. Where the Constitution means something different, they simply propose reinterpreting it.[1]

What I propose instead is that the intentions of the framers and ratifiers of a written constitution should be treated as binding whenever they can be known. The reason for this has nothing to do with the fiction of a social contract that obligates subsequent generations who did not agree to it. Still less does it express an idea that the moral philosophies that prevailed at the time our own Constitution was enacted are truer than those that prevail today. What motivates it is a conviction of the usefulness of limiting governments in ways that *do not depend* on the ideas of the people who happen to be in power at the moment—including the people who hold judicial office. If we don't like the intentions of a constitution's framers and ratifiers, that is fine; but then we should amend it, rather than pretending that it means something different than it meant at its inception. And amendment ought not be an easy thing to do.

From this follows opposition to the judicial activism of both the Left and the Right. Early in the century, when judicial activism was practiced by the Right, the Left opposed it. When, later, the Left captured the citadel of American jurisprudence and began to practice its own brand of activism, the Right decided that it preferred restraint after all. As, within the present decade, the U.S. Supreme Court shifts rightward again, we may see yet another role reversal. But both kinds of activism defeat the advantages of having a written constitution in the first place.

Originalism and Neo-Originalism

The previous remarks may seem to mark me as a partisan of the "jurisprudence of original intent," of which so much has been heard lately. Actually the label does not fit; if a label is needed at all, the position defended here should be called not originalist, but "neo-originalist." Originalism, as represented for instance by former Judge Robert Bork, has at least four deep flaws:

1. *The reasons advanced by the leading originalists for reliance on the original intentions of the framers and ratifiers are incoherent.*

For Judge Bork, confining judges within the bounds of original intent is a way to keep judges from enacting their moral views, thereby a way to liberate legislative majorities. This is true only if the original intent of the Constitution is indeed majoritarian; however, we will leave that issue aside for a moment and return to it below. The reason Judge Bork does not want judges to enact their moral views is that he is an ethical neutralist.[2] What he fails to recognize is that letting legislators enact their moral views is just as great a violation of neutrality as letting judges do so. My own reasons for confining judges within the bounds of original intent are straightforwardly nonneutral, in that they are driven by appreciation for the goods that having a constitution serves. Such confinement allows the Constitution to function as a set of limits on both legislators *and* judges, a set that does not happen to vary according to the momentary views of either group.

2. *Originalism presents the intentions of the framers and ratifiers as much less ambiguous than they really are.*

Sometimes different groups involved in the adoption of the Constitution approved the same provisions for clashing reasons. Moreover, our information about what these reasons were is incomplete. Originalists rarely go to the trouble that would be necessary to penetrate these obscurities. For instance, they sometimes allude rather vaguely to the constitutional importance of majoritarian representation (a mistake also made by their opponents), when in fact only one chamber of one branch of the government was based on majoritarian principles and a major concern of the framers was the prevention of "majority tyrannies."

3. *Originalists often construe original intentions as overriding the actual text to which the framers and ratifiers gave their endorsement.*

For instance, because the Fourteenth Amendment's equal protection clause was motivated by a desire to end discrimination against blacks, originalists often treat it as referring to that form of discrimination alone.[3] However, to construe it in this way is either to slight the fact that the framers of the Amendment could have given it narrower language but did not, or to assume that when they gave it general language they did not know what they were doing. To speak more broadly, originalists tend to ignore or at least to cramp the Constitution's open-ended provisions. This hardly qualifies as taking original intent seriously.

4. *Originalism gives no guidance for cases where the relevant intentions of the framers and ratifiers cannot be ascertained.*

Originalists often proceed as though the maxim were, "When in doubt, defer to the other two branches." In some cases that may be appropriate. However, as a general principle, it in no way follows from the axiom of relying on original intent. The framers knew in advance that their intentions would not always be clear; in fact, they were at pains to prevent some of them from being clear. After all, the constitutional

Convention met in secrecy, and its minutes were not published until years later. Therefore, it is unreasonable to suppose that they did not anticipate this situation. The originalist approach to cases where the specified intentions of the framers and ratifiers are foggy should be to ask, "How did the framers and ratifiers *intend* us to deal with such cases?" Lamentably, this is not the approach that originalists actually take.

What I have called "neo-originalism" is a way of relying on the intentions of the framers and ratifiers that avoids these four problems.[4] The procedure I suggest involves three sharply distinguished principles of interpretation, and requires that they be followed in a fixed order.

The *Text Principle* is to impute to the framers and ratifiers a *general* intention that the words that they actually wrote be taken according to their face value—as face value would have been taken in the English of the time of enactment. In other words, whatever else the framers and ratifiers may have meant, we should assume that they meant what they said. An important point is that this assumption gives priority to the general intention of having their words taken at face value over any special intentions that they might also have had. Another way to put this is to say that it does not allow special intentions to override text: so far as possible, text controls.

The reason that the Text Principle is insufficient taken by itself is that even at the time of its enactment, some of the constitutional language was ambiguous on its face. Where several meanings are possible, the *Context Principle* comes into play. This principle instructs that choice from among the possible meanings be made according to the more specific intentions of the framers and ratifiers, so far as they were in consensus and so far as this consensus can be known. As a narrowing rule, the Context Principle does not allow expansion of the original set of possible meanings. One may choose only from such meanings as remain after application of the Text Principle.

Of course, the Text and Context Principles are insufficient taken together for the same reason that the Text Principle is insufficient taken by itself. More than one possible meaning for a passage will often remain even after both are applied. Taking original intentions seriously, however, requires that ambiguous passages on a subject be treated differently than constitutional silence on a subject. Thus when confronted by an ambiguous passage, judges should not simply defer to the other two branches—although that is precisely what should be done in cases of sheer constitutional silence; confronted by an ambiguous passage they are obligated instead to attempt a rational reconstruction of the intentions behind the passage.

Of course, the different strategies that are conceivable for rational reconstruction may vary enormously in the discretion they allow these judges. However, we have already discussed the need to limit those who hold power—judges as well as members of the other branches—in ways that do not depend on the beliefs that prevail among them at the moment. Only a restrictive strategy of reconstruction can square with the recognition of this need.

Thus, the *Reconstruction Principle* does not simply instruct a judge, "Of all the possible meanings for a disputed passage, choose the one for which you can construct the argument that looks best to you." Rather, it instructs him, "Of all the possible meanings for a disputed passage, choose the one for which the best argument can be constructed *from philosophical premises that would have been broadly accepted at the time that the passage was enacted*." For instance: are wiretaps covered by the search and seizure clause of the Fourth Amendment? The question here is the meaning to be accorded the term, "search." To bring wiretaps under the search and seizure clause, one would have to show that a wiretap is *like* the "searches" possible at the time the Amendment was enacted—like it not in such respects as happen to strike the fancy of the judge, but in those respects that are *relevant to the arguments that could originally have been given* for the search and seizure clause. More generally speaking, the Reconstruction Principle might permit a judge to reason from certain Aristotelian, Lockean, Montesquieuan, Blackstonian, Federalist, or (in the case of the Bill of Rights) even Anti-Federalist premises. Any of these, as well as others, might have been employed by the framers. However, it could not permit him to reason from distinctly Spencerian, Millian, Kantian, Rawlsian, Paretian, or Heideggerian premises; these were not developed until after the framers' time. Moreover, like the Context Principle, the Reconstruction Principle is a narrowing rule. It may be used only to choose from among such meanings as remain after the Text and Context Principles have already been applied. It may not be used to expand this set of meanings.

In constitutional interpretation, reliance on original intent can take us no further than this. The Text, Context, and Reconstruction Principles will not produce a unique interpretation for each disputed passage. Arguments will still be necessary. However, not only do the three principles avoid the four pitfalls of the old, "unimproved" originalism, they also go substantially beyond it by telling us what kinds of arguments to look for.

No theory of constitutional interpretation can do more than this; therefore, it is enough. However, I do need to apply the theory to a special problem that every such theory must confront.

Difficult Cases

As remarked earlier, several clauses in the Constitution are "open-ended." That is, they refer to matters nowhere treated in the Constitution itself. Under the due process clauses of the Fifth and Fourteenth Amendments, for example, what kind of process is "due?" Likewise, in saying that the enumeration of certain rights in the Constitution shall not be construed to disparage or deny others retained by the people, to just what unenumerated, but retained, rights does the Ninth Amendment refer?[5]

The fact that the open-ended clauses make extratextual references may seem to render the Text Principle inappropriate. Although it genuinely diminishes the power of the Text Principle to narrow the set of possible meanings, to say that it renders it inappropriate would be a mistake. The reason for this is that the language of the text may provide clues as to just what extratextual matters, in any given case, the text is pointing to. Where this is so, these clues must take precedence over all other ideas that strike us.

To illustrate, let us consider the face value of the phrase "due process." First, we should recognize that the term "process" itself is much clearer than it is made out to be—certainly clear enough to tell us (as John Hart Ely puts it)[6] that "procedural due process" is redundant, while "substantive due process" is contradictory. The more difficult term is "due."

A broad way to construe this is as meaning "fair." But this is not the primary sense of the term today, nor (more important) was it at the time of the founding. When we say that a person ought to pay what is due to the grocery store, we do not construe this to mean that he need only pay what is abstractly fair. Perhaps he is a poor man, and certainly it is unfair that the poor should have to pay as much as the rich for their groceries. Nevertheless, this confers no exemption from paying his full bill. If $40 he owes, $40 he must pay.

But *why* is this what he must pay? What is it that makes exactly $40 "due?" What makes it due is that the fellow knew that in taking eight $5 items, he would be charged $40; that settles the matter. What is due, in other words, is what may be charged according to rules of transaction reasonably expected to have been understood by both parties at the time the transaction took place.

But the same idea can be applied to due process. That process of *law* is due that people at both the giving and the receiving end could reasonably have understood as being due at the time the process was supposed to take place. In other words, what is due is what was held as mandatory in the preexisting legal culture.

Now what does this mean—"preexisting legal culture"? Does it mean merely that citizens may not be deprived of the common-law, constitutional, and other[7] guarantees of procedure they enjoyed *before* the enactment of the Fifth Amendment (in the case of the national government) and the Fourteenth (in the case of the states)? But if that is what the framers of the two Amendments meant, it would have been much simpler for them to say so rather than to use the broader language that they did. The Text Principle requires us to treat them as knowing what they were doing when they chose their words. For this reason, I take the due process clause as requiring something broader than simple nonretrogression.

The "something broader" for which I think the best argument could have been made—given concerns that we know that framers and ratifiers shared—is what may be called a "moving" rather than a "stationary" legal mores test. That is, I take the due process clauses not only as prohibiting arbitrary abridgement of the common-law, constitutional, and other guarantees that citizens enjoyed before the clauses' enactment, but also as prohibiting arbitrary abridgement of such guarantees as common and Constitutional law may have evolved between the enactment of the clauses and the moment of judicial interpretation. A further point in favor of this view is that one is hard pressed to think of an argument the framers of either Amendment might have given for a stationary legal mores test that could not also be given for a moving legal mores test.

The Ninth amendment is somewhat cloudier. Clearly, it refers to unenumerated rights. Unfortunately, it does not say where these rights come from. One possibility is that they are implied by enumerated rights, in much the same fashion that unenumerated national *powers* are said to be implied by enumerated national powers. However, this is rebutted by the wording of the Ninth Amendment that describes the unenumerated rights as "retained" by the people. If they have been "retained," they must have their source outside of the Constitution.

Could the unenumerated rights be natural rights? A possible objection to this view is that historical research has not yet shown whether at the time of the founding, unwritten natural law was generally believed to survive a written constitution; some writers of the time claim that positive rights are meant to buttress natural rights, others that positive rights are meant to replace them.[8] On the other hand, the point of the Ninth Amendment seems to be precisely to ensure the survival of the rights to which it refers. Therefore, the natural law survival hypothesis cannot be ruled out. A contemporary interpreter who construed unenumerated rights in this way, of course, would have to use assumptions about the content of natural law that were accepted at the time that the Ninth Amendment was enacted, rather than such assumptions as may seem attractive to him today. The difficulty in this is that the framers and ratifiers seem to have differed widely over such assumptions, and not all of them believed in natural law at all. For this reason, I think a better case can be made for a different interpretation of the Ninth Amendment's unenumerated rights.

What other interpretation could this be? If the unenumerated rights have their source outside the Constitution but are not natural, there is only one other possibility: that like the right to due process of law, they arise from preexisting legal culture.

In one respect this is different from the hypothesis I offered about the Fifth and Fourteenth Amendment due process clauses, for rights arising under the Ninth Amendment would be substantive, not procedural. In fact, they would be precisely the substantive "liberties" that the Fifth and Fourteenth Amendments presuppose when they set forth the requirement for that procedure which is "due" before such liberties can be abridged.[9]

Despite this difference between the old and new hypotheses, the new raises the same question as the old: when we speak of preexisting legal culture, are we speaking of a "moving" or of a "stationary" legal mores test? The one we are speaking of this time is not necessarily the same as the one we were speaking of before.

Which is it, then? One argument might be that the "retained" rights arise not only outside of the Constitution, but also before it in time. If we accept this argument then we must regard the legal mores test as stationary. Another argument might be that the point in time at which the rights arise is irrelevant. Douglas Laycock, for instance, states that "in the context of a Constitution and political theory that place sovereignty in the people and limit government to delegated powers, 'retained' appears to mean 'withheld from government control'—the opposite of 'delegated' or 'surrendered' "[10] If this is true, then we must regard the legal mores tests as moving.

I side with the view that the legal mores test is moving, for reasons similar to those given earlier in connection with the due process clause. First, the framers of the Ninth Amendment could have adopted narrower language, to comport with the purpose of a stationary legal mores test, but they did not. Second, it is difficult to conceive any argument the framers might have given for a stationary legal mores test that could not also have been given for a moving legal mores test.

The difference between a moving and a stationary legal mores test is not trivial. For example, the common law has evolved a right to privacy only in our own century. While a moving legal mores test would include this under the Ninth Amendment, a stationary legal mores test would not. I am not speaking of the confection which the Supreme Court presently calls "the Constitutional right of privacy." This was derived by a different theory of interpretation, and could never have been derived by the theory that I proposed.[11] As argued in Part One of this book, it really has nothing to do with privacy. However, it has given the Court license to read its own social views into the Constitution. This miscarriage underlines the need for restraint in the use of the Ninth Amendment, and, I think, tends to vindicate the theory of interpretation proposed here.

Had judges always followed this more restrained approach to constitutional interpretation, probably the courts would have been used far less often either to block social changes, or to bring them about. Legislatures would have had weightier responsibilities in many areas, and, in order to make sure that they bore these responsibilities well, citizens would have needed to pay more attention to them than they do presently.

This, I think, is as it should be. An objection may be drawn from the fact that sometimes, extremely grave social injustices have the support of the community, and therefore cannot be remedied through legislative action at all. I do take this possibility seriously. Just what a judge should do about something against which conscience cries to heaven, but to oppose which he can find no *constitutional* reason, is a difficult matter.

I do not claim that he may never do anything. However, the rules that govern here, I suggest, are like those that govern other civil disobedience. If the judge does do something, he ought to admit, openly, that his recourse to higher law is a violation of constitutional law, and he should not resist attempts to remove him from office. Moreover he ought to bear in mind that sufficient grounds for judicial civil disobedience are unlikely to arise more than once every generation or two. If they seem to arise more often than that, either the community is insufficiently ripe for self-government—or the judge himself is insufficiently humble.

Notes

1. An early statement of this view is found in Redlich, "Are There 'Certain Rights . . . Retained by the People?'", at 787. Speaking of certain statutes of the state of Connecticut which were under legal challenge at the time, the author says, "But for one who feels that the marriage relationship should be beyond the reach of a state law forbidding the use of contraceptives, the birth control case poses a troublesome and challenging problem of constitutional interpretation. He may find himself saying, 'The law is unconstitutional—but why?' There are two possible paths to travel in finding the answer. One is to revert to a frankly flexible due process concept even on matters that do not involve specific constitutional prohibitions. The other is to attempt to evolve a new constitutional framework within which to meet this and similar problems which are likely to arise." This passage is best remembered for the sarcasm with which Justice Black quoted it in

a dissent to the majority opinion in *Griswold v. Connecticut* (1965). In that case, the Court had "evolved a new constitutional framework" similar to Redlich's in order to enact its own extraconstitutional views.

2. See his "Neutral Principles and Some First Amendment Problems." For brief discussion, see chapter 3, note 2 and accompanying text.

3. See, for instance, Justice Rehnquist's dissent in *Trimble v. Gordon* (1977), at 777–86.

4. It can also be viewed as an application of a more general approach to interpretation to the special case of constitutions. See the "Homily on Method" in my *The Nearest Coast of Darkness*.

5. The Fourteenth Amendment's privileges and immunities clause is treated also sometimes as referring to unenumerated rights; for instance, see Laycock, "Taking Constitutions Seriously: A Theory of Judicial Review." However, there seems no basis for thinking that it refers to any rights other than those already enumerated in the Constitution. Incidentally, the privileges and immunities clause provides a much more convincing warrant for an Incorporation Doctrine than the due process rationale actually used by the Supreme Court. Strictly construed, the due process clause does permit states to abridge the incorporated rights (though only after due process, naturally). By contrast, the privileges and immunities clause would make incorporated rights completely unabridgeable. I have no explanation for why the Court treats them as unabridgeable even though it neglects any clause that might support such an interpretation.

6. *Democracy and Distrust*, 18.

7. Including those originating in English royal concessions and American colonial charters.

8. For one study of the problem, see Grey, "Origins of the Unwritten Constitution: Fundamental Law in American Revolutionary Thought," 871–72, 893.

9. The contrast here is with the rights *explicitly* guaranteed by other Amendments, such as the First. These rights cannot be abridged at all; the due process clauses do not refer to them.

10. These words, along with interesting discussion, may be found in Laycock, ibid., 350–51. However, Laycock proposes that Ninth Amendment unenumerated rights are implied by enumerated rights, a view rejected above.

11. See chapter 3, note 8.

Appendix Three
Patristic Sources

Part Five examined religious tolerance and ultimate concern from the perspective of Christianity as well as five different secular creeds. The popular view is that tolerance is a secular innovation, against which Christianity held out for centuries until "converted" by secular thinkers like John Locke. I maintain that tolerance is a Christian innovation. Though Christians through the centuries have often, and notoriously, forgotten it, their own tradition was the source of the very standard by which their intolerant acts could be judged wrong. Indeed—as explained in Part Five—Locke himself was not altogether secular. He justified toleration on two grounds. One ground was Christian scripture. The other was a natural rights theory which itself depended on theological assumptions—assumptions which were offered without reference to Christianity but which would not be widely accepted outside it.

In Part Five, I also quoted from Lactantius and Hilary of Poitiers to back up my claim that not only before, but also after the outward conversion of the Roman Empire, tolerance was the doctrine of many early Church authorities. Many readers will, quite understandably, want additional support. For them I offer the following passages.

First let me expand the quotations from Lactantius. From his *Divine Institutes*, bk. 5, chap. 19:

> There is no need of force and injury, because religion cannot be forced. It is a matter that must be managed by words rather than blows, so that it may be voluntary. . . . And, therefore, no one is retained by us against his will—for he is useless to God who is without devotion and faith—and so no one departs while truth itself is compelling.[1]

Again, speaking of the pagans:

> How the poor things err, though their intention is honest! For they think there is

289

nothing in human affairs more important than religion and that it ought to be defended with the utmost strength, but as they are deceived in the very religion, so also are they in the manner of its defense. Religion ought to be defended, not by killing but by dying, not by fury but by patience, not by crime but by faith. The former action each time belongs to evil, the latter to good, and it is necessary that good be the practice of religion, not evil. If you wish, indeed, to defend religion by blood, if by torments, if by evil, then it will not be defended, but it will be polluted and violated. There is nothing so voluntary as religion, and if the mind of the one sacrificing in a religious rite is turned aside, the act is now removed; there is no act of religion.[2]

Still later:

We, however, do not ask that anyone against his will should worship our God, who is the God of all whether they wish it or not, nor are we angry if he does not worship Him. . . . Therefore, when we endure wickedness, we make opposition by not even a word, but refer vengeance to God, not as those do who wish to seem defenders of their gods and rage savagely against those who do not worship them.[3]

Next let us turn to Tertullian, whose teaching about natural right or equity offers an instructive comparison with Locke's. The following is from *To Scapula*, chap. 2:

It is the law of mankind and the natural right of each individual to worship what he thinks proper, nor does the religion of one man either harm or help another. But, it is not proper for religion to compel men to religion, which should be accepted of one's own accord, not by force, since sacrifices also are required of a willing mind. So, even if you compel us to sacrifice, you will render no service to your gods. They will not desire sacrifices from the unwilling unless they are quarrelsome— but a god is not quarrelsome.[4]

Collate what he says about "the reproach of irreligion" in *Apology*, chap. 24:

namely, for you to take away one's freedom of religion and put a ban on one's free choice of a god, with the result that it is not lawful for me to worship whom I will, but am compelled to worship contrary to my will. No one, not even a man, will be willing to receive the worship of an unwilling client.[5]

Isidore of Pelusium speaks briefly and to the point. The following is from his *Epistles*, 3.363:

Since it seems not good forcibly to draw over to the faith those who are gifted with a free will, employ at the proper time conviction and by your life enlighten those who are in darkness.[6]

Compare this epigram from his *Epistles*, 2.129:

Human salvation is procured not by force but by persuasion and gentleness.[7]

One problem is what Christians are to make of Old Testament law, which prescribes stoning as the penalty for a number of religious offenses. Evangelicals, of course, regard the Old Covenant as fulfilled in, and therefore superceded by, the New. Among early Christian authorities, Gregory of Nazianzus offers a complementary, but somewhat different view. He explains that under the New Covenant, stoning is to be understood "mystically," that is, as symbolizing a spiritual rather than a physical act—in fact, no other than the spiritual act of offering argument! The particular passage of scripture on which Gregory comments is Exodus 19:12–13, which says in part, "Whoever touches the mountain [of God] will be put to death. No one must lay a hand on him; he must be stoned or shot down by arrow, whether man or beast; he must not remain alive." Gregory's comments are found in the *Second Theological Oration—On God* (also known as *Oration 28*). I have used italics to emphasize the key sentence:

But if any is an evil and savage beast, and altogether incapable to taking in the subject matter of contemplation and theology, let him not hurtfully and malignantly lurk in his den among the woods, to catch hold of some dogma or saying by a sudden spring, and to tear sound doctrine to pieces by his misrepresentations, but let him stand yet afar off and withdraw from the Mount, or he shall be stoned and crushed, and shall perish miserably in his wickedness. *For to those who are like wild beasts true and sound discourses are stones.*[8]

The Church took much longer to realize the political implications of tolerance than to realize the importance of tolerance as such. One of the earliest to speak to these implications was John Chrystostom, in his *Discourse on Blessed Babylas and Against the Greeks*. A passage from sec. 13 provides some background:

Such is the character of our doctrine; what about yours? No one ever persecuted it, nor is it right for Christians to eradicate error by constraint and force, but to save humanity by persuasion and reason and gentleness. Hence no emperor of Christian persuasion enacted against you legislation such as was contrived against us by those who served demons.[9] Just as a body given over to a long and wasting disease perishes of its own accord, without anyone injuring it, and gradually breaks down and is destroyed, so the error of Greek superstition, though it enjoyed so much tranquillity and was never bothered by anyone, nevertheless was extinguished by itself and collapsed internally. Therefore, although this satanic farce has not been completely obliterated from the earth, what has already happened is able to convince you concerning its future.[10]

More to the point, what he says in sec. 42 implies grave doubts about alliance between the church and state:

[Pagan religion depends on force, but] Our situation is entirely different. When a Christian ascends the imperial throne, far from being shored up by human honors, Christianity deteriorates. On the other hand, when rule is held by an impious man, who persecutes us in every way and subjects us to countless evils, then our cause acquires renown and becomes more brilliant, then is the time of valor and trophies, then is the opportunity to attain crowns, praises, and every distinction.[11]

In his *History of the Arians*, Athanasius recognizes that an alliance between church and state can be used to defend heresy just as easily as to defend truth. The following is from sec. 33:

Now if it was altogether unbecoming in any of the Bishops to change their opinions merely from fear of these things, yet it was much more so, and not the part of men who have confidence in what they believe, to force and compel the unwilling. In this manner it is that the Devil, when he has no truth on his side, attacks and breaks down the doors of them that admit him with axes and hammers. But our Saviour is so gentle that he teaches thus, *If any man wills to come after Me*, and, *Whoever wills to be My disciple*; and coming to each He does not force them, but knocks at the door and says, *Open to Me, My sister, My spouse*; and if they open to Him, He enters in, but if they delay and will not, He departs from them. For the truth is not preached with swords or with darts, nor by means of soldiers; but by persuasion and counsel. But what persuasion is there when the Emperor [Constantius] prevails? or what counsel is there, when he who withstands them receives at last banishment and death? Even David, although he was a king, and had his enemy in his power, prevented not the soldiers by an exercise of authority when they wished to kill his enemy, but, as the Scripture says, David persuaded his men by arguments, and suffered them not to rise up and put Saul to death. But he, being without arguments of reason, forces all men by his power, that it may be shewn to all, that their wisdom is not according to God, but merely human, and that they who favour the Arian doctrines have indeed no king but Caesar; for by his means it is that these enemies of Christ accomplish whatsoever they wish to do.[12]

At sec. 67, he reemphasizes the point that the use of force is an argument *against* the godliness of one's doctrine:

The other heresies also, when the very Truth has refuted them on the clearest evidence, are wont to be silent, being simply confounded by their conviction. But this modern and accursed heresy, when it is overthrown by argument, when it is cast down and covered with shame by the very Truth, forthwith endeavours to reduce by violence and stripes and imprisonment those whom it has been unable to persuade by argument, thereby acknowledging itself to be any thing rather than godly. For it is the part of true godliness not to compel, but to persuade, as I said before. Thus our Lord Himself, not as employing force, but as offering to their free choice, has said to all, *If any man will follow after me*; and to His disciples, *Will you also go away?*[13]

When the Emperor, Constantius—assuming a fusion rather than a distinction of church and state—attempted to win the support of Hosius, Bishop of Cordova, for a condemnation of Athanasius, Hosius protested to Constantius in this fashion:

Cease, I implore you, from these proceedings. Remember that you are but mortal; and be fearful of the day of judgement and keep yourself pure with that day in view. Do not interfere in matters ecclesiastical, nor give us orders on such questions, but learn about them from us. For into your hands God has put the kingdom; the affairs of the Church he has committed to us. If any man stole the Empire from you, he would be resisting the ordinance of God: in the same way you on your part should be afraid lest, in taking upon yourself the government of the church, you incur the guilt of a grave offense. "Render unto Caesar the things that are Caesar's and unto God the things that are God's." We are not permitted to exercise an earthly rule; and you, Sire, are not authorized to burn incense.[14]

Hosius was unable to hold out against Constantius' violence. However, his doctrine that church and state are distinct realms, not to be confused, was eventually given the imprimatur of one of the early Popes, Gelasius I. As Gelasius writes in a letter to the Emperor Anastasius:

Two elements there are indeed, Imperator Augustus, by which this world is principally ruled: the consecrated authority of the priests and the royal power. Of these, the burden of the priests is much the weightier, because they will have to answer for even the kings of men on the day of divine judgment. For you know, most clement son, that although it is your right to take precedence over the human race in dignity, you bow your head obediently to those in charge of divine affairs, and look to them for the means of your salvation; and in partaking of the heavenly sacraments, when they are properly dispensed, you recognize that you rather must subject yourself in the realm of religion than rule in it, and, in these matters, rely on the judgment of the priests and not wish that they be bent to your will.[15]

Clearly, Gelasius' *distinction* between the respective spheres of authority of church and state does not go so far as the post-Reformation doctrine of substantial *separation* between church and state. One who embraced the distinction, but who did not carry it to the point of separation, could still justify state support for an ecclesiastic establishment—at any rate, he could do so provided the state did not deign to give this establishment theological instructions.

Nevertheless, considering Gelasius' distinction along with John Chrysostom's remarks about the deterioration Christianity suffers under the supposed protection of Christian emperors, it is not difficult to see disestablishmentarianism on the horizon. Its premises are nearly the same; between the distinction of realms and the separation of realms there is but a short interval of logic. Alas that to close this short interval, such a long bridge of years turned out to be necessary. But this shows only more clearly why the interval needed closure in the first place: the long bridge of years stands as a testimony to the all-but-insuperable temptations of temporal power.

Notes

1. Mary Francis McDonald, *Lactantius, The Divine Institutes*, 378.
2. Ibid., 379–80.
3. Ibid., 383.
4. Rudolph Arbesmann, Emily Joseph Daly, and Edwin A. Quain, trans., *Tertullian: Apologetical Works, and Municius Felix: Octavius*, 152.
5. Ibid., 76.
6. Cited in Margaret A. Schatkin and Paul W. Harkins, trans., *Saint John Chrysostom, Apologist*, 83, note 30. I have changed "seemeth" to "seems" and "thy" to "your."
7. Ibid.
8. Edward Rochie Hardy and Cyril C. Richardson, trans., *Christology of the Later Fathers*, Vol. 3 of the *Library of Christian Classics*, 137.
9. Many early Christians considered pagan gods to be real, but demonic rather than divine.
10. Ibid., 83.
11. Ibid., 99.
12. John Henry Parker, trans., *Historical Tracts of S. Athanasius, Archbishop of Alexandria*, 245–46. "Arians" were followers of the heresy of Bishop Arius.
13. Ibid., 278–79. I have replaced "ye" with "you."
14. Henry Bettenson, *Documents of the Christian Church*, 19.
15. Translated by E. Karafiol from Karl Mirbt, *Quellen zur Geschichte des Papsttums und des Romischen Katholizismus* (Questions about the History of the Papacy and Roman Catholicism), 4th ed., 1924, 85; in History Faculty, University of Chicago, eds., *History of Western Civilization*, Vol. 4, *Christianity in the Roman Empire*.

Appendix Four
Empirical Issues

This has been a book of normative theory, not empirical theory. To call true tolerance a virtue is to say that it ought to be practiced—not to say that it is practiced. Yet at many points I have made empirical claims. Sometimes these have teamed up with normative claims in arguments about the meaning of true tolerance, that is, what should be tolerated and what should not; at other times they have teamed up with normative claims in arguments about the cultivation of true tolerance, that is, how to nurture the trait and deepen it.

Research inquiring into the truth of these empirical claims would be very welcome, for much normative theory is empirically naïve. Yet I have not made much use of the empirical literature, and to those who wonder why this is so, I owe a brief answer. The plain fact is that very little of the empirical research on tolerance is helpful. What keeps it from being helpful is that it is *normatively* naïve.

Let me give an example. Suppose an empirical researcher simply wants to find out the "lay of the land"—where the population stands with respect to tolerance. Typically, he will begin by constructing a scale. Many methods of scale construction might be used, some simpler, some more complex. I will make this illustration elementary, because those who use the more complex methods tend to commit the same kinds of normative errors (though at a higher level of sophistication and dazzle) as those who use the simpler.

Suppose that on a scale of zero to ten, a researcher uses ten to represent the limit of tolerance, and zero to represent the limit of intolerance. To assign people positions on the scale, he will typically use certain controversial ideas or behaviors as litmus tests. For each idea or behavior a person is willing to put up with, he might then assign the person a certain number of points. Once this has been done with each person in a suitably large and diverse sample, the researcher can do all sorts of things. He might compare the mean tolerance scores of different population groups in order to find out whether the differences that exist are statistically significant. Or he might correlate tolerant behavior with other kinds of behavior.

From a normative point of view, such scaling has several peculiarities. Consider first the simple fact that the more a person puts up with, the higher the tolerance score he is assigned. Under only one hypothesis would the information that such a number gives be normatively interesting: if, in calling tolerance a virtue, we meant merely that *the more one puts up with, the better*. No one, of course, could seriously maintain such a thesis. To be sure, it is better to put up with unpopular opinions than to suppress them; but it is certainly not better to put up with murders than to suppress them.

To do them justice, empirical researchers often admit this. However, they miss the point in another way. They recognize that not everything should be put up with, but conclude from this that the ideal score on a scale of one to ten may be a number *other* than ten. Of course, by continuing to seek an ideal score, this continues to make the virtue of tolerance a matter of how many things one puts up with rather than which. It is as though one were to say "An ideally tolerant person puts up with any three of the following: unpopular opinions, murder, rape, and deviant sexual acts between consenting adults. Only the number is important—three, no more and no less."

Justice must be done here too. At a deeper level, researchers who construct "how many" scales do seem to know that tolerance is really a matter of "which." For this, one presumes, is why their litmus items typically *do* include unpopular opinions and deviant sexual acts between consenting adults, but do *not* include murder and rape. Which things they include probably reveals which things they think people should put up with. Well, then, what is the problem? The problem is simply that their presupposed views of what should be put up with are never explicitly defended (and may, in fact, be wrong). In a word, the scales, being based on these views, are tendentious.

If all of this is unsatisfactory, then how *should* empirical researchers study the lay of the land? First, "which" should be the empirical object of their inquiry, not the normative presupposition of their inquiry. What I mean is that instead of constructing scales with buried normative presuppositions about which things people should put up with, they should look for empirical patterns as to what people really do put up with. For instance, perhaps some people tolerate X and Y but not Z, others tolerate X and Z but not Y, and no one tolerates Y and Z without tolerating X. Imagine patterns like this involving dozens of behaviors.

Even complex patterns like these might yet be reducible to numbers by some complex multidimensional scaling technique. But why bother? For the second thing empirical researchers need to recognize is that the *reasons* for which people practice X are much more worthy of being found out (and that for normative reasons) than the correlations between people's practice of X and their other behaviors. Looking for patterns should mean, then, mostly looking for *patterns of reasons*. Perhaps some who tolerate X and Y do so for reason A, others do so for reason B, and still others tolerate X for reason A but Y for reason B. These actual reasons can be compared with the reasons normative theory suggests that they ought to have. Undertaking the comparison will help us know where to place our educational concern.

A contrast may make this more clear. Researchers looking *just* for behavioral patterns (not, as I recommend, for patterns of reasons) may find all sorts of things, for instance:

- that people who engage in given practices themselves are more likely than people who do not engage in them to tolerate their practice by others;
- that people who engage in given practices themselves are *less* likely than people who do not engage in them to tolerate their practice by others;
- that people who engage in given practices themselves are *neither more nor* less likely than people who do not engage in them to tolerate their practice by others; or
- that such differences hold for some practices, but not for others.

I merely suggest that while such discoveries might be somewhat interesting, it would give us much more useful information about the society we inhabit to find out *why* anyone might refuse to put up with the practice of something by others even though he engages in the practice himself. If people really do this, then, in the various cases in which they do, what are their reasons? Are they, for instance,

- fighting compulsions to do things they disapprove?

- making some distinction between practices, persons, or contexts which is not immediately evident?
- acting on some other rationale? Or
- simply being hypocrites?

Patterns of reasons may turn out to be very complex. People might avoid people who practice X, yet support a legal right to practicing it; but on the other hand, they might overlook the practice of X among people with whom they come in contact, yet decline to support a legal right to practice it. Neither pattern of choice is *intrinsically* either rational or irrational. Whether it were one or the other would depend solely on the reasons or non-reasons people offered for it. Another illustration is that if people do support a legal right to practice X, they may yet either support, or oppose, governmental subsidies for practicing X—again depending on their reasons for supporting the right itself. Consider the controversy over obscenity in works supported by federal art grants.

The bottom line is this. Empirical research on tolerance would never be undertaken were it not for the fact that tolerance is morally important. But if the results of such research are to inform this moral concern, researchers must be extremely well informed about the moral theory itself. Otherwise they will ask the wrong questions—worse yet, beg them.

Bibliography

Ackerman, Bruce A. *Social Justice in the Liberal State*. New Haven: Yale University, 1980. See Barry, Brian, 1983; Dworkin, Ronald, 1983; Fletcher, George P.; Galston, William, 1981; and Harman, Gilbert.

Ackerman, Bruce A. What is neutral about neutrality? In Barry, Brian, 1983 (q.v.).

Acton, John Emerich Edward Dalberg-Acton, Baron. *Selected Writings of Lord Acton*, vol. 3: *Essays in Religion, Politics, and Morality*. J. Rufus Fears, ed. Indianapolis: Liberty Classics, 1988.

Anderson, Norman. "Islamic family law." IV.11 *International Encyclopedia of Comparative Law* 55 (1983).

Arbesmann, Rudolph, Emily Joseph Daly, and Edwin A. Quain, trans. *Tertullian: Apologetical Works, and Municius Felix: Octavius*. New York: Fathers of the Church, 1950.

Aristotle. *Nicomachean Ethics*. Martin Ostwald, ed. and trans. Indianapolis: Bobbs-Merrill, 1962.

Aristotle. *On Poetry and Music*. S.H. Butcher, trans.; Milton C. Nahm, ed. Indianapolis: Bobbs-Merrill, 1956.

Aristotle. *Politics*. Ernest Barker, ed. and trans. London: Oxford University, 1946.

Arrow, Kenneth J. *Social Choice and Individual Values*, 2d ed. New Haven: Yale University, 1963.

Atkisson, R.F. Instruction and indoctrination. In R.D. Archambault, ed., *Philosophical Analysis and Education*. New York: Humanities Press, 1965.

Bailey, Charles. Rationality, democracy, and the neutral teacher. 2 *Cambridge Journal of Education* 68 (1971).

Baker, C. Edwin. Scope of the First Amendment freedom of speech. 25 *U.C.L.A. Law Review* 964 (1978).

Barber, Benjamin R. Unconstrained conversations: a play on words, neutral and otherwise. In Barry, Brian, 1983 (q.v.).

Barron, Jerome A. Access to the press—a new First Amendment right. 80 *Harvard Law Review* 1641 (1967).

Barry, Brian. *The Liberal Theory of Justice*. Oxford: Clarendon, 1973.

Barry, Brian, ed. Symposium on justice. 93 *Ethics* 328 (1983).

Bayles, Michael D. Criminal paternalism. In Pennock, J. Roland, 1974 (q.v.).

Beaney, William M. The right to privacy and American law. 31 *Law and Contemp. Probs.* 253 (1966).

Beiner, Ronald. What's the matter with liberalism? In Allan C. Hutchinson and Leslie J.M. Green, *Law and the Community: The End of Individualism?* Agincourt, Ontario: Carswell, 1989.

Bellah, Robert N. *Beyond Belief: Essays on Religion in a Post-Traditionalist Age.* New York: Harper and Row, 1970.

Bellah, Robert N. *The Broken Covenant: American Civil Religion in a Time of Trial.* New York: Seabury, 1975.

Bellah, Robert N., Richard Madsen, William M. Sullivan, Ann Swidler, and Steven M. Tipton. *Habits of the Heart: Individualism and Commitment in American Life.* Berkeley: University of California Press, 1985.

Benditt, Theodore M. Compromising interests and principles. In Pennock, J. Roland, 1979 (q.v.).

Berns, Walter. *The First Amendment and the Future of American Democracy.* New York: Basic Books, 1976.

Berns, Walter. *Freedom, Virtue, and the First Amendment.* Baton Rouge: Louisiana State Press, 1957.

Berns, Walter. Pornography v. democracy: the case for censorship. 22 *The Public Interest* 3 (1971). See Bickel, Alexander; Cohen, Marshall; Kauffman, Stanley; and McWilliams, Wilson Carey.

Bettenson, Henry. *Documents of the Christian Church,* 2d ed. London: Oxford, 1963.

BeVier, Lillian R. The First Amendment and political speech: an inquiry into the substance and limits of principle. 30 *Stan. L. Rev.* 299 (1978).

Bickel, Alexander. Response to Berns, Walter, 1971. 22 *The Public Interest* 25 (1971).

Blakely, Mary Kay. Is one's woman's sexuality another woman's pornography? The question behind a major legal battle. 21:10 *Ms.* 37 (1985).

Blasi, Vincent. The checking value in First Amendment theory. 1977 *American Bar Foundation Research Journal* 521.

Bloustein, Edward J. Privacy as an aspect of human dignity: an answer to Dean Prosser. 39 *N.Y.U. Law Review* 962 (1964). See Prossner, William L.

Bollinger, Lee C. *The Tolerant Society: Freedom of Speech and Extremist Speech in America.* New York: Oxford University, 1986.

Boorstin, Daniel J., ed. *An American Primer.* Chicago: University of Chicago, 1966.

Bork, Robert H. Neutral principles and some First Amendment problems. 47 *Indiana Law Journal* 1 (1971).

Boyle, Joseph M., Jr. A Catholic perspective on morality and the law. 1 *Journal of Law and Religion* 227 (1983).

Brandeis, Louis D. See Warren, Samuel D.

Bricker, David C. Moral education and teacher neutrality, 80 *School Review* 619 (1972).

Buchanan, James, and Gordon Tullock. *The Calculus of Consent*. Ann Arbor: University of Michigan, 1962. See Tullock, Gordon, and Rae, Douglas W.

Buckland, W.W., and Arnold D. McNair. *Roman Law and Common Law: A Comparison in Outline*. Cambridge: Cambridge University Press, 1936.

Budziszewski, J. *The Nearest Coast of Darkness: A Vindication of the Politics of Virtues*. Ithaca, N.Y.: Cornell University, 1988.

Budziszewski, J. *The Resurrection of Nature: Political Theory and the Human Character*. Ithaca, N.Y.: Cornell University, 1986.

Bunyan, John. *The Pilgrim's Progress*. A.K. Adams, ed. New York: Dodd, Mead, 1979.

Burchaell, James. The sources of conscience. 13 *Notre Dame Magazine* 20 (Winter 1984–85).

Cahill, Marion Cotter. *Shorter Hours: A Study of the Movement Since the Civil War*. New York: Columbia University, 1932.

Carnes, Patrick. *Out of the Shadows: Understanding Sexual Addiction*. Minneapolis: CompCare, 1985.

de Cervantes, Miguel. *The Ingenious Gentlemen, Don Quixote de la Mancha*. Samuel Putnam, trans. New York: The Modern Library, 1949.

Chapman, John W. See Pennock, J. Roland, 1971, 1974, and 1979.

Cicero, Marcus Tullius. *De Officiis: On Duties*. Harry G. Edinger, ed. and trans. Indianapolis: Bobbs-Merrill, 1974.

Clor, Harry M. *Obscenity and Public Morality*. Chicago: University of Chicago, 1969.

Cochran, Clarke E. *Religion in Pubic and Private Life*. New York: Routledge, 1990.

Cohen, Marshall. Response to Berns, Walter, 1971. 22 *The Public Interest* 38 (1971).

Cooley, Thomas M. *A Treatise on the Constitutional Limitations which rest upon the Legislative Power of the states of the American Union*, 6th ed. Boston: Little, Brown, 1890.

Cotta, Sergio. Law between ethics and politics: a phenomenological approach. In Pennock, J. Roland, 1974 (q.v.).

Cox, Archibald. The role of Congress in Constitutional determinations. 40 *University of Cincinnati Law Review* 199 (1971).

Culver, Charles M. See Gert, Bernard.

Danelski, David J. The limits of law. In Pennock, J. Roland, 1974 (q.v.).

Davis, Frederick. What do we mean by "right to privacy"? 4 *South Dakota Law Review* 1 (1959).

Devlin, Patrick, Lord. *The Enforcement of Morals*. London: Oxford University, 1965. See Dworkin, Ronald, in Wasserstrom, Richard A.; Hart, H.L.A., 1959, 1963, and 1967; Rostow, Eugene V.; Stephen, James Fitzjames; and Wollheim, Richard.

Downing, L.A. See Thigpen, R.B.

Durkheim, Emile. *The Elementary Forms of the Religious Life*. London: Allen and Unwin, 1954 .

Dvornik, Francis. *Early Christian and Byzantine Political Philosophy: Origins and Background*. Washington, D.C.: Dumbarton Oaks Center for Byzantine Studies and Trustees for Harvard University, 1966.

Dworkin, Gerald. Paternalism. In Wasserstrom, Richard A. (q.v.).

Dworkin, Ronald. Liberalism. In Hampshire, Stuart, 1978 (q.v.). See Hart, H.L.A., in Ryan, Alan.

Dworkin, Ronald. Lord Devlin and the enforcement of morals. In Wasserstrom, Richard A. (q.v.). See Devlin, Patrick, Lord.

Dworkin, Ronald. *Taking Rights Seriously*. Cambridge, Mass.: Harvard University Press, 1978.

Dworkin, Ronald. What liberalism isn't. Review of Ackerman, Bruce A. (q.v.). *New York Review of Books* 47 (20 January 1983).

Eisenach, Eldon J. *Two Worlds of Liberalism: Religion and Politics in Hobbes, Locke, and Mill*. Chicago: University of Chicago, 1981.

Ely, John Hart. *Democracy and Distrust: A Theory of Judicial Review*. Cambridge, Mass.: Harvard University, 1980. See Laycock, Douglas.

Ely, John Hart. The wages of crying wolf: a comment on *Roe v. Wade*. 82 *Yale Law Journal* 920 (1973).

Emerson, Thomas I. Nine justices in search of a doctrine. 64 *Michigan Law Rev.* 219 (1965).

Erasmus, Desiderius. *The Free Will*. In Ernst F. Winter, ed. and trans., *Erasmus-Luther: Discourse on Free Will*. New York: Frederick Ungar, 1961.

Falk, Ze'ev W. Jewish family law. IV.11 *International Encyclopedia of Comparative Law* 28 (1983).

Finnis, John. *Natural Law and Natural Rights*. Oxford: Clarendon, 1980.

Fishkin, James S. Can there be a neutral theory of justice? In Barry, Brian, 1983 (q.v.).

Flathman, Richard E. Egalitarian blood and skeptical turnips. In Barry, Brian, 1983 (q.v.).

Flathman, Richard E. *The Practice of Political Authority: Authority and the Authoritative*. Chicago: University of Chicago, 1980.

Fleming, James, Jr. See Harper, Fowler V.

Fletcher, George P. The watchdog of neutrality. Review of Ackerman, Bruce A., 1980 (q.v.). 83 *Columbia Law Review* 2099 (1983).

Freund, Paul A. Privacy: one concept or many. In Pennock. J. Roland, 1971 (q.v.).

Fried, Charles. Correspondence. 6 *Philosophy and Public Affairs* 288 (1977). See Reimann, Jeffrey H.

Fried, Charles. Privacy. 77 *Yale Law Journal* 475 (1968).

Frug, Gerald E. Why neutrality? 92 *Yale Law Journal* (1983). See Stewart, Richard B.

Fuller, Lon L. *The Morality of Law*. New Haven: Yale University, 1964.

Fuller, Lon L. *The Principles of Social Order*. Kenneth I. Winston, ed. Durham, N.C.: Duke University, 1981.

Galston, William. Defending liberalism. 76 *American Political Science Review* 621 (1982).

Galston, William. *Justice and the Human Good*. Chicago: University of Chicago, 1980.

Galston, William. Public morality and religion in the liberal state. 19 *PS* 807 (1986).

Galston, William. Review of Ackerman, Bruce A. (1980). 9 *Political Theory* 427 (1981).

Gatchel, Richard H. The evaluation of the concept [of indoctrination]. In I.A. Snook, ed., *Concepts of Indoctrination: Philosophical Essays*. London: Routledge and Kegan Paul, 1972.

Gavison, Ruth. Privacy and the limits of law. 89 *Yale Law Journal* 421 (1980).

Gert, Bernard, and Charles M. Culver. Paternalistic behavior. 6 *Philosophy and Public Affairs* 45 (1978).

Glendon, Mary Ann. Marriage and the state: the withering away of marriage. 62 *Virginia Law Review* 663 (1976).

Glendon, Mary Ann. *State, Law, and Family: Family Law in Transition*. New York: North-Holland, 1977.

Gray, Oscar S. See Harper, Fowler V.

Grey, Thomas C. Origins of the unwritten Constitution: fundamental law in American revolutionary thought. 30 *Stanford Law Review* 843 (1978).

Greenawalt, Kent. Some related limits of law. In Pennock, J. Roland, 1974 (q.v.).

Greenidge, A.H.J. *Infamia: Its Place in Roman Public and Private Law*. Oxford: Clarendon, 1894.

Gross, Hyman. Privacy and autonomy. In Pennock, J. Roland, 1971 (q.v.).

Gunther, Gerald. *Constitutional Law*, 11th ed. Mineola, N.Y.: Foundation, 1985.

Gunton, George. Feasibility of an eight-hour work-day. 1 *American Federalist* (1894).

van den Haag, Ernest. On privacy. In Pennock, J. Roland, 1971 (q.v.).

Habermas, Jürgen. *Communication and the Evolution of Society*. Thomas A. McCarthy, trans. Boston: Beacon, 1979.

Hamilton, Alexander, James Madison, and John Jay. *The Federalists Papers*. Clinton Rossiter, ed. New York: New American Library, 1961.

Hampshire, Stuart. Morality and pessimism. In Hampshire, Stuart, 1978 (q.v.).

Hampshire, Stuart, ed. *Public and Private Morality*. Cambridge: Cambridge University Press, 1978.

Hardy, Edward Rochie, and Cyril C. Richardson, eds. *Library of Christian Classics*, vol. 3, *Christology of the Later Fathers*. Philadelphia: Westminster Press, 1954.

Harman, Gilbert. Liberalism without foundations? Review of Ackerman, Bruce A., 1980 (q.v.). 91 *Yale Law Review* 397 (1981).

Harper, Fowler V., James Fleming, Jr., and Oscar S. Gray. *The Law of Torts*, 2d ed. Boston: Little, Brown, 1986.

Hart, H.L.A. Between utility and rights. In Ryan, Alan (q.v.). See Dworkin, Ronald, 1978.

Hart, H.L.A. *The Concept of Law*. Oxford: Oxford University, 1961.

Hart, H.L.A. *Essays in Jurisprudence and Philosophy*. Oxford: Clarendon, 1983.

Hart, H.L.A. Immorality and treason. *The Listener* 162 (30 July 1959). See Devlin, Patrick, Lord; Hart, H.L.A., 1963 and 1967; and Stephen, James Fitzjames.

Hart, H.L.A. *Law, Liberty, and Morality*. Stanford, Cal.: Stanford University, 1963. See Devlin, Patrick, Lord; Hart, H.L.A., 1959 and 1967; and Stephen, James Fitzjames.

Hart, H.L.A. Social solidarity and the enforcement of morals. 35 *University of Chicago Law Review* 1 (1967). See Devlin, Patrick, Lord; Hart, H.L.A., 1959 and 1963; and Stephen, James Fitzjames.

Henkin, Louis. Morals and the Constitution; the sin of obscenity. 63 *Columbia Law Review* 391 (1963).

Henkin, Louis. Privacy and autonomy. 74 *Columbia Law Review* 1410 (1974).

History Faculty, University of Chicago, eds. *History of Western Civilization*, vol. 4, *Christianity in the Roman Empire*. Chicago: University of Chicago Press, 1970.

Hobbes, Thomas. *Leviathan: Or, the Matter, Form, and End of a Commonwealth Ecclesiastical and Civil*. C.B. MacPherson, ed. New York: Penguin, 1968.

Hocking, William. *Freedom of the Press: A Framework of Principle*. Chicago: University of Chicago, 1947.

Holmes, Oliver Wendell. *Collected Legal Papers*. New York: Harcourt, Brace, 1921.

Horton, John. Toleration, morality, and harm. In Horton, John, 1985 (q.v.).

Horton, John, and Susan Mendus, eds. *Aspects of Toleration: Philosophical Studies*. New York: Methuen, 1985.

Howe, Mark DeWolfe. *The Garden and the Wilderness: Religion and Government in American Constitutional History*. Chicago: University of Chicago, 1965.

Husak, Douglas. Paternalism and autonomy. 10 *Philosophy and Public Affairs* 27 (1981).

Jay, John. See Hamilton, Alexander.

Jefferson, Thomas. *The Writings of Thomas Jefferson.* Albert Ellery Bergh, ed. Washington, D.C.: Thomas Jefferson Memorial Assoc., 1907.

Jones, Alexander, gen. ed. *The Jerusalem Bible.* New York: Doubleday, 1966.

Jones, Peter. Toleration, harm, and moral effect. In Horton, John, 1985 (q.v.).

Kalven, Harry. Privacy in tort law—were Warren and Brandeis wrong? 31 *Law and Contemporary Problems* 326 (1966).

Kant, Immanuel, *Groundwork of the Metaphysics of Morals.* J.J. Paton, ed. and trans. New York: Harper and Row, 1964.

Kauffman, Stanley. Response to Berns, Walter, 1971. 22 *The Public Interest* 28 (1971).

Kenyon, Cecelia M., ed. *The Antifederalists.* Boston: Northeastern University, 1985.

Kleinig, John. Principles of neutrality in education. 8 *Educ. Philosophy and Practice* 1 (1976).

König, René. Sociological introduction [to the family]. IV.1 *International Encyclopedia of Comparative Law* 20 (1974).

Konvitz, Milton R. Privacy and the law: a philosophical prelude. 31 *Law and Contemporary Problems* 272 (1966).

Kuflik, Arthur. Morality and compromise. In Pennock, J. Roland, 1979 (q.v.).

Kurland, Philip B., ed. *Religion and the Law: Of Church and State and the Supreme Court.* Chicago: University of Chicago, 1978.

Larmore, Charles. Liberal neutrality. 17 *Political Theory* 580 (1989).

Larmore, Charles E. *Patterns of Moral Complexity.* Cambridge: Cambridge University Press, 1987.

Laycock, Douglas. Taking constitutions seriously: a theory of judicial review. Review of Ely, 1980 (q.v.). 59 *Texas Law Review* 343 (1981).

Lee, Simon. *Law and Morals: Warnock, Gillick and Beyond.* London: Oxford University, 1986. See Devlin, Patrick, Lord, and Hart, H.L.A., 1959, 1963, and 1967.

Lewis, C.S. *Present Concerns.* Walter Hooper, ed. New York: Harcourt, Brace, Jovanovich, 1986.

Locke, John. *Second Treatise of Government.* Thomas Peardon, ed. Indianapolis: Bobbs-Merrill, 1952.

Locke, John. Four letters on toleration. In *Complete Works of John Locke*, vol. 4. Germany: Scientia Verlag Aalen, 1963.

Louch, A.R. Sin and crimes. In Wasserstrom, Richard A. (q.v.).

Lupu, Ira C. Untangling the strands of the Fourteenth Amendment. 77 *Michigan Law Review* 981 (1979).

Lusky, Louis, Invasion of privacy: a clarification of concepts. 72 *Columbia Law Review* 693 (1972).

Luther, Martin. *The Bondage of the Will*. In Ernst F. Winter, ed. and trans., *Erasmus-Luther: Discourse on Free Will*. New York: Frederick Ungar, 1961.

MacCallum, J.R., Jr. Negative and positive freedom. In Peter Laslett, W.G. Runciman, and Quentin Skinner, eds., *Philosophy, Politics, and Society*, 4th ser. Oxford: Blackwell, 1972.

MacIntyre, Alasdair. *After Virtue: A Study in Moral Theory*. Notre Dame, Ind.: Notre Dame University, 1981.

MacIntyre, Alasdair. *Whose Justice? Which Rationality?* Notre Dame, Ind.: Notre Dame University, 1988.

MacKinnon, Catharine A. Not a moral issue. 2 *Yale Review of Law and Politics* 321 (1984).

MacKinnon, Catharine A. Pornography, civil rights, and speech. 20 *Harvard*

McAnany, P.D. See Slough, M.C.

McBride, William Leon. The abolition of law as a standard in legal decision-making. In H. Hubien, ed., *Legal Reasoning: Proceedings of the World Congress for Social and Legal Philosophy*. Brussels: Etablissements Emile Bruylant, 1971.

McBride, William Leon. An overview of future possibilities: law unlimited? In Pennock, J. Roland, 1974 (q.v.).

McClosky, Herbert, and Alida Brill. *Dimensions of Tolerance: What Americans Believe About Civil Liberties*. New York: Russell Sage, 1983.

McDonald, Mary Francis. *Lactantius: The Divine Institutes*. Washington, D.C.: Catholic University of America Press, 1964.Civil Rights—Civil Liberties Law Review 1 (1985).

McNair, Arnold D. See Buckland, W.W.

McWilliams, Wilson Carey. Response to Berns, Walter, 1971. 22 *The Public Interest* 32 (1971).

Madison, James. Memorial and remonstrance against religious assessments. In Gaillard Hunt, ed., *The Writings of James Madison*, vol. 2. New York: G.P. Putnam's Sons, 1901.

Madison, James. See Hamilton, Alexander.

Madsen, Richard. See Bellah, Robert N., 1985.

Maine, Henry Sumner. *Ancient Law: Its Connection with the Early History of Society and its Relation to Modern Ideas*. With an introduction by C.K. Allen. London: Oxford University Press, 1946.

Mansfield, Harvey C., Jr. Thomas Jefferson. In Morton J. Frisch and Richard G. Stevens, eds. *American Political Thought: The Philosophic Dimensions of American Statesmanship*. New York: Scribner's Sons, 1971.

Marcus, George E. See Sullivan, John L.

Marcuse, Herbert. See Wolff, Robert Paul, 1965.

May, Kenneth O. A set of independent, necessary, and sufficient conditions for simple majority rule. 20 *Econometrica* 680 (1952).

Meiklejohn, Alexander. *Free Speech and Its Relation to Self-Government.* New York: Harper, 1948.

Mendus, Susan. Harm, offense, and censorship. In Horton, John, 1985 (q.v.).

Mendus, Susan. See Horton, John, 1985.

Merton, Thomas. *New Seeds of Contemplation.* New York: New Directions, 1961.

Mill, John Stuart. *John Stuart Mill: Three Essays.* Richard Wollheim, ed. London: Oxford University, 1975. See Stephen, James Fitzjames.

Miller, Perry. *Roger Williams: His Contribution to the American Tradition.* Indianapolis: Bobbs-Merrill, 1953.

Milton, John. *Areopagitica and Of Education.* George H. Sabine, ed. Northbrook, Il.: AHM Publishing, 1951.

Mitchell, Basil. *Law, Morality, and Religion in a Secular Society.* London: Oxford University, 1967. See Devlin, Patrick, Lord, and Hart, H.L.A., 1959, 1963, and 1967.

de Montesquieu, Charles Louis de Secondat, Baron. *The Spirit of the Laws.* Thomas Nugent, trans., and Franz Neumann, ed. New York: Hafner, 1949.

Moore, Barrington, Jr. See Wolff, Robert Paul, 1965.

Moore, W. Indoctrination as a normative concept. 4 *Studies in Philosophy and Education* 396 (1966).

Negley, Glenn. Philosophical views on the value of privacy. 31 *Law and Contemporary Problems* 319 (1966).

Neuhaus, Paul Heinrich. Christian family law. IV.11 *International Encyclopedia of Comparative Law* 3 (1983).

The New York Times. Beyond the (garbage) pale. Editorial, 1 April 1971.

Nicholas, Barry. *An Introduction to Roman Law.* Oxford: Clarendon, 1962.

Nicholson, Peter P. Toleration as a moral ideal. In Horton, John, 1985 (q.v.).

Niebuhr, Reinhold. The Christian Church in secular age. In *Christianity and Power Politics.* New York: Charles Scribner's Sons, 1940.

Nietzsche, Friedrich. *Beyond Good and Evil.* In Walter Kaufmann, trans., *Basic Writings of Nietzsche.* New York: Random House, 1968.

Nietzsche, Friedrich. *Thus Spoke Zarathustra.* In Walter Kaufmann, trans., *The Portable Nietzsche.* New York: Penguin, 1977.

Nozick, Robert. *Anarchy, State, and Utopia.* New York: Basic Books, 1974.

Oakeshott, Michael. *On Human Conduct.* Oxford: Clarendon, 1975.

Oakeshott, Michael. *Rationalism in Politics and Other Essays.* New York: Methuen, 1962.

O'Brien, David M. *Privacy, Law, and Public Policy.* New York: Praeger, 1979.

Pålsson, Lennart. Marriage and divorce. III.16. *International Encyclopedia of Comparative Law* 3 (1978).

Parker, John Henry, trans. *Historical Tracts of S. Athanasius, Archbishop of Alexandria.* London: Oxford, 1843.

Parsons, Talcott. *The Structure of Social Action*. Glencoe, Il.: Free Press, 1949.

Pennock, J. Roland, and John W. Chapman, eds. *Compromise in Ethics, Law, and Politics: NOMOS XXI*. New York: New York University, 1979.

Pennock, J. Roland, and John W. Chapman, eds. *The Limits of Law: NOMOS XV*. New York: Lieber-Atherton, 1974.

Pennock, J. Roland, and John W. Chapman, eds. *Privacy: NOMOS XIII*. New York: Atherton, 1971.

Perry, Michael J. Abortion, the public morals, and the police power: the ethical function of substantive due process. 23 *U.C.L.A. Law Review* 689 (1976).

Perry, Michael J. A critique of the "liberal" political-philosophical project. 28 *William and Mary Law Review* 205 (1987).

Perry, Michael J. *Morality, Politics, and Law: A Bicentennial Essay*. New York: Oxford University, 1988.

Perry, Michael J. Moral knowledge, moral reasoning, moral relativism: a "naturalist" perspective. 20 *Georgia Law Review* 995 (1986).

Perry, Michael J. Neutral Politics? 51 *Review of Politics* 479 (1989).

Piereson, James E. See Sullivan, John L.

Popper, Karl R. *The Growth of Scientific Knowledge*. New York: Harper and Row, 1968, c1965.

Prosser, William L. Privacy. 48 *California Law Review* 383 (1960). See Bloustein, Edward J.

Rachels, James. Why privacy is important. 4 *Philosophy and Public Affairs* 323 (1975). See Thomson, Judith Jarvis, and Scanlon, Thomas.

Rae, Douglas W. The limits of consensual decision. With rejoinder to comment by Tullock, Gordon (q.v.). 69 *American Political Science Review* 1270, 1298 (1975). See Buchanan, James.

Rawls, John. Kantian constructivism in moral theory: the Dewey lectures 1980. 77 *Journal of Philosophy* 515 (1980).

Rawls, John. The priority of right and ideas of the good. 17 *Philosophy and Public Affairs* 251 (1988).

Rawls, John. *A Theory of Justice*. Cambridge, Mass.: Harvard University, 1971.

Raz, Joseph. Liberalism, autonomy, and the politics of neutral concern. In Peter A. French, Theodore E. Eehling, Jr., and Howard K. Wettstein, eds., *Midwest Studies in Philosophy VII: Social and Political Philosophy*. Minneapolis: University of Minnesota, 1982.

Redlich, Norman. Are there "certain rights . . . retained by the people"? 37 *N.Y.U. Law Review* 787 (1962).

Regan, Donald H. Justifications for paternalism. In Pennock, J. Roland, 1974 (q.v.).

Reichley, A. James. Democracy and religion. 19 *PS* 801 (1986).

Reichley, A. James. *Religion in American Public Life*. Washington, D.C.: Brookings Institution, 1985.

Reiman, Jeffrey H. Privacy, intimacy, and personhood. 6 *Philosophy and Public Affairs* 26 (1976). See Fried, Charles, 1977.

Rheinstein, Max. The family and the law. IV.1 *International Encyclopedia of Comparative Law*. 3 (1974).

Richards, David A.J. Free speech and obscenity law: toward a moral theory of the First Amendment. 123 *University of Pennsylvania Law Review* 45 (1974).

Richards, David A.J. Unnatural acts and the Constitutional right to privacy: a moral theory. 45 *Fordham Law Review* 1281 (1977).

Rorty, Richard. *Consequences of Pragmatism: Essays 1972-1980*. Minneapolis: University of Minnesota, 1982.

Rorty, Richard. *Philosophy and the Mirror of Nature*. Princeton, N.J.: Princeton University, 1979.

Rostow, Eugene V. The enforcement of morals. In *The Sovereign Prerogative: The Supreme Court and the Quest for Law*. New Haven: Yale University, 1962. See Devlin, Patrick, Lord, and Hart, H.L.A., 1959.

Rousseau, Jean-Jacques. *On the Social Contract*. Judith R. Masters, trans., Roger D. Masters, ed. New York: St. Martin's, 1978.

Rousseau, Jean-Jacques. *Politics and the Arts: Letter to M. d'Alembert on the Theatre*. Allan Bloom, ed. and trans. Ithaca: Cornell University, 1968.

Ryan, Alan, ed. *The Idea of Freedom: Essays in Honour of Isaiah Berlin*. New York: Oxford University, 1979.

Sandel, Michael J. *Liberalism and the Limits of Justice*. Cambridge: Cambridge University, 1982.

Scanlon, Thomas. Thomas on privacy. 4 *Philsosophy and Public Affairs* 315 (1975). See Rachels, James, and Thomson, Judith Jarvis.

Schatkin, Margaret A., and Paul W. Harkins, trans. *Saint John Chrysostom, Apologist*. Washington, D.C.: Catholic University of America Press, 1983.

Schwartz, Joel. Freud and free speech. 80 *American Political Science Review* 1227 (1986).

Sen, Amartya K. *Collective Choice and Social Welfare*. San Francisco: Holden-Day, 1970.

Shapiro, Ian. *The Evolution of Rights in Liberal Theory*. Cambridge: Cambridge University, 1986.

Shklar, Judith. *Ordinary Vices*. Cambridge, Mass.: Harvard University, 1985.

Slough, M.C., and P.D. McAnany. Obscenity and Constitutional freedom— part II. 8 *St. Louis Law Journal* 449 (1964).

Smith, Rogers M. The Constitution and autonomy. 60 *Texas Law Review* 175 (1982).

Smith, Rogers M. *Liberalism and American Constitutional Law*. Cambridge, Mass.: Harvard University, 1985.

Stephen, James Fitzjames. *Liberty, Equality, Fraternity*. R.J. White, ed. Cambridge: Cambridge University, 1967. See Devlin, Patrick, Lord; Hart, H.L.A., 1959, 1963, and 1967; and Mill, John Stuart.

Stevenson, C.L. *Ethics and Language*. New Haven: Yale University, 1944.

Stevenson, C.L. *Facts and Values: Studies in Ethical Analysis*. New Haven: Yale University, 1963.

Stewart, Richard B. *Regulation in a liberal state: the role of non-commodity values*. 92 *Yale Law Journal* 1537 (1983). See Frug, Gerald E.

Storing, Herbert J. *What the Anti-Federalists Were For*. Murray Dry, ed. Chicago: University of Chicago, 1981.

Sullivan, John L., James E. Piereson, and George E. Marcus. *Political Tolerance and American Democracy*. Chicago: University of Chicago, 1982.

Sullivan, William M. See Bellah, Robert N., 1985.

Swidler, Ann. See Bellah, Robert N., 1985.

Tarcov, Nathan. *Locke's Education for Liberty*. Chicago: University of Chicago, 1984.

Taylor, Charles. What's wrong with negative liberty. In Ryan, Alan (q.v.).

Taylor, Monica J., ed. *Progress and Problems in Moral Education*. Slough, Eng.: NFER Publishing, 1975.

Thigpen, R.B., and L.A. Downing. Liberalism and the neutrality principle. 11 *Political Theory* 587 (1983).

Thomson, Judith Jarvis. The right to privacy. 4 *Philosophy and Public Affairs* 295 (1975). See Rachels, James, and Scanlon, Thomas.

Tiedeman, Christopher G. *A Treatise on the Limitations of the Police Power in the United States*. St. Louis: F.H. Thomas, 1886.

Tillich, Paul. *Dynamics of Faith*. New York: Harper and Row, 1957.

Tillich, Paul. *Systematic Theology*. Chicago: University of Chicago Press, 1951.

Tinder, Glenn. *Tolerance: Toward a New Civility*. Amherst: University of Massachusetts Press, 1976.

Tipton, Steven M. See Bellah, Robert N.

de Toqueville, Alexis. *Democracy in America*. Garden City, N.Y.: Doubleday, 1969.

Tolle, Gordon J. *Human Nature Under Fire: The Political Philosophy of Hannah Arendt*. Washington, D.C.: University Press of America, 1982.

Tribe, Laurence H. *Constitutional Choices*. Cambridge, Mass.: Harvard University, 1985.

Tucker, D.F.B. *Law, Liberalism, and Free Speech*. Totowa, N.J.: Rowman and Allenheld, 1985.

Tullock, Gordon. Comment on Rae, Douglas W. (q.v.). 69 *American Political Science Review* 1295 (1975). See Buchanan, James.

Turner, Frederick Jackson. The significance of the frontier in American history. In Boorstin, Daniel J. (q.v.).

Veatch, Henry B. *Human Rights: Fact or Fancy?* Baton Rouge: Louisiana State University Press, 1985.

Warnock, Mary. The neutral teacher. In Taylor, Monica (q.v.). See Wilson, John.

Warren, Samuel D., and Louis D. Brandeis. The right to privacy. 4 *Harvard Law Review* 193 (1980).

Wasserstrom, Richard A., ed. *Morality and the Law*. Belmont, Cal.: Wadsworth, 1971.

Weale, Albert. Toleration, individual differences and respect for persons. In Horton, John, 1985 (q.v.).

Weber, Max. *The Sociology of Religion*. Boston: Beacon, 1963.

Wechsler, Herbert. Toward neutral principles of Constitutional law. In *Principles, Politics, and Fundamental Law: Selected Essays*. Cambridge, Mass.: Harvard University, 1961.

Weissberg, Robert. Political censorship: a different view. 22:1 *PS: Political Science and Politics* 47 (March, 1989).

Wellington, Harry. Common law rules and Constitutional double standards: some notes on adjudication. 83 *Yale Law Journal* 221 (1973).

Williams, Bernard. Space talk: the conversation continued. In Barry, Brian, 1983 (q.v.).

Williams, Roger. *The Complete Writings of Roger Williams*. Reuben Aldridge Guild and James Hammond Trumbull, eds. New York: Russell and Russell, 1963.

Wilson, James Q. The rediscovery of character: private virtue and public policy. 81 *The Public Interest* 3 (1985).

Wilson, John. Teaching and neutrality. In Taylor, Monica (q.v.). See Warnock, Mary.

Winthrop, John. A model of Christian charity. In Boorstin, Daniel J. (q.v.).

Wolff, Robert Paul. *In Defense of Anarchism*. New York: Harper, Row, 1970.

Wolff, Robert Paul, Barrington Moore, Jr., and Herbert Marcuse. *A Critique of Pure Tolerance*. Boston: Beacon, 1965.

Wollheim, Richard. Crime, sin, and Mr. Justice Devlin. 1959:11 *Encounter* 34. See Devlin, Patrick, Lord.

Wood, Gordon S. *The Creation of the American Republic*. New York: W.W. Norton, 1969.

List of Cases

Abingdon School District v. Schempp, 373 U.S. 203 (1963).
Abrams v. United States, 250 U.S. 616 (1919).
Aguilar v. Felton, 105 S.Ct. 3232 (1985).
Alberts v. California. See *Roth v. United States.*
Atkisson v. Kern, 59 C.A.3d 89 (1976).
Baldwin v. Missouri, 281 U.S. 586 (1930).
Board of Education v. Allen, 392 U.S. 236 (1968).
A Book Named "John Cleland's Memoirs of a Woman of Pleasure" v. Attorney General of Massachusetts. See *Memoirs v. Massachusetts.*
Bowers v. Hardwick, 106 S.Ct. 2841 (1986).
Central Hudson Gas v. Public Service Commission, 447 U.S. 557 (1980).
Chaplinsky v. New Hampshire, 315 U.S. 568 (1941).
Church of the Holy Trinity v. United States, 143 U.S. 457 (1892).
Cohen v. California, 403 U.S. 15 (1971).
Eisenstadt v. Baird, 405 U.S. 438 (1972).
Employment Division v. Smith, 108 S.Ct. 1444 (1988) (*Smith I*).
Employment Division v. Smith, 110 S.Ct. 1595 (1990) (*Smith II*).
Engel v. Vitale, 370 U.S. 421 (1962).
Everson v. Board of Education, 300 U.S. 421 (1947).
Fanny Hill. See *Memoirs v. Massachusetts.*
FCC v. Pacifica Foundation, 438 U.S. 726 (1978).
Ferguson v. Skrupa, 372 U.S. 726 (1963).
Ginsberg v. New York, 390 U.S. 629 (1968).
Ginzburg v. United States, 383 U.S. 463 (1965).
Grand Rapids School District v. Ball, 105 S.Ct. 3216 (1985).
Griswold v. Connecticut, 381 U.S. 479 (1965).
Jacobellis v. Ohio, 378 U.S. 184 (1963).
Joseph Burstyn, Inc., v. Wilson, 343 U.S. 495 (1952).
Kingsley International Pictures v. Regents of the State of New York, 360 U.S. 684 (1959).

Larson v. Valente, 456 U.S. 228 (1981).

Lemon v. Kurtzman, 403 U.S. 602 (1971).

Lochner v. New York, 198 U.S. 45 (1905).

Loving v. Virginia, 388 U.S. 1 (1967).

Lynch v. Donelly, 104 S.Ct. 1355 (1984).

Marsh v. Chambers, 463 U.S. 141 (1943).

Martin v. City of Struthers, 319 U.S. 141 (1943).

Marvin v. Marvin, 18 Cal.Rptr. 815 (1976).

Maynard v. Hill, 125 U.S. 190 (1888).

Memoirs v. Massachusetts, 383 U.S. 413 (1966).

Meyer v. Nebraska, 262 U.S. 390 (1923).

Miami Herald v. Tornillo, 418 U.S. 241 (1974).

Miller v. California, 413 U.S. 15 (1973).

Minor v. Board of Education of Cincinnati, 23 Ohio St. 211 (1872).

New York v. Ferber, 458 U.S. 747 (1982).

New York Times v. Sullivan, 376 U.S. 254 (1964).

Olmstead v. United States, 277 U.S. 438 (1928).

Palko v. Connecticut, 302 U.S. 319 (1937).

Paris Adult Theatre I v. Slaton, 413 U.S. 49 (1973).

Pierce v. Society of Sisters, 268 U.S. 510 (1924).

Poe v. Ullman, 367 U.S. 497 (1960).

Prince v. Massachusetts, 321 U.S. 158 (1944).

Red Lion Broadcasting v. FCC, 395 U.S. 367 (1969).

Reynolds v. United States, 98 U.S. 145 (1879).

Roe v. Wade, 410 U.S. 113 (1972).

Roth v. United States, 354 U.S. 476 (1957).

Schad v. Borough of Mount Ephraim, 452 U.S. 61 (1981).

Sherbert v. Verner, 374 U.S. 398 (1963).

Skinner v. Oklahoma, 316 U.S. 535 (1942).

Stanley v. Georgia, 394 U.S. 557 (1968).

Trimble v. Gordon, 430 U.S. 762 (1977).

Union Pacific Railway v. Bostford, 141 U.S. 250 (1890).

United States v. Carolene Products Company, 304 U.S. 144 (1938).

United States v. Lee, 455 U.S. 252 (1982).

United States v. Reidel, 402 U.S. 351 (1971).

United States v. Seegar, 380 U.S. 163 (1965).

U.S. Dept. of Agriculture v. Moreno, 413 U.S. 528 (1973).

Valentine v. Chrestensen, 316 U.S. 52 (1942).

Village of Belle Terre v. Boraas, 416 U.S. 1 (1974).
Wallace v. Jaffree, 105 S.Ct. 2479 (1985).
Walz v. Tax Commission, 397 U.S. 664 (1970).
West Coast Hotel Company v. Parrish, 300 U.S. 379 (1937).
Winters v. New York, 333 U.S. 507 (1948).
Wisconsin v. Yoder, 406 U.S. 212 (1972).
Young v. American Mini Theatres, 427 U.S. 50 (1976).
Zorach v. Clauson, 343 U.S. 306 (1952).

Index

References in endnotes are not included unless they are to names, cases, or topics not mentioned in their accompanying text.

Topics

Names

Cases